SECRETS AND LIES

For Barbara Hager and Kurt Hager, who taught us social justice and to question the news – N.H.

For Jack and Marie Burton, with love and thanks for everything – B.B.

SECRETS AND LIES

NICKY HAGER AND BOB BURTON

First published 1999 by Craig Potton Publishing,
PO Box 555, Nelson, New Zealand.

© Nicky Hager and Bob Burton

Library of Congress Cataloging-in-Publication Data

Hager, Nicky.
   Secrets and lies: the anatomy of an anti-environmental PR campaign / Nicky
Hager and Bob Burton.
      p. cm.
Includes index.
ISBN 1-56751-183-x (cloth : alk. paper) – ISBN 1-56751-182-1 (pbk. : alk. paper)
   1. Lumber trade–New Zealand–Public Relations. 2. Industrial publicity–New
Zealand. 3. Corporations–Corrupt Practices–New Zealand. I. Burton, Bob, 1927-
II. Title.

   HD9768.N42 H33 2000
   659.2'963498'0993–dc21

                                                                  99-057398

Common Courage Press
Box 702
Monroe, ME 04951

(207) 525-0900 Fax: (207) 525-3068
orders-info@commoncouragepress.com
www.commoncouragepress.com

First Printing in the United States

CONTENTS

ACKNOWLEDGEMENTS

THE RESEARCHING and writing of this book took place over a few months and so relied greatly on the help and interest of others. I sought and received assistance from people involved in all the different parts of the story: Timberlands and the PR industry, environmental groups, West Coast communities, Parliament and the media. Unfortunately most of these people, who contributed on the understanding that they would remain anonymous, cannot be acknowledged and thanked by name. Without their help, the book would not have been possible. Special thanks to those who needed courage to be involved.

It has been a pleasure to work with my co-author Bob Burton, Robbie Burton, Craig Potton and the others at Craig Potton Publishing, editor Anna Rogers and Greg Bates and Arthur Stamoulis at Common Courage Press. I cannot imagine more positive writer-publisher relationships. Similarly, many thanks to Terence Arnold for legal advice on the project. The environment movement people who responded generously to requests for information and illustrations include: Steve Abel, Dean Baigent-Mercer, Beth Flinn, Bridget Gibb, Emma Haxton, Abie Horrocks, Peter Russell, Eugenie Sage, Michael Szabo, Alan Tennyson, Cath Wallace and Barry Weeber. I hope they, and those from other parts of the story, are happy with how their contributions were used.

Next there are the friends and family who gave me encouragement and support through the project: Mike Ennis, Kevin Hackwell, Lyn Holland, Michael Kopp, Jo Mackay, Kate McPherson, Peter Mechen, Mark Roach, Christina Wells, Fergus Wheeler, Tony Wills, Julian Young, and my sisters, Debbie Hager and Mandy Hager, and Bill Hager. Special thanks to Julia Wells for tolerance, encouragement and good ideas.

Nicky Hager

A SPECIAL THANKS to John Stauber and Sheldon Rampton at the Center for Media and Democracy in Madison, Wisconsin for their encouragement, their assistance with information and their pioneering work.

Thanks to Clare Henderson, Larry O'Loughlin, Andrew Nette and Angela Savage for their suggestions and to Emma Gunn for her support during the early years of my research on the PR industry. Thanks also to Fran Murray for her love, support and encouragement.

My work on researching corporate public relations would not have been possible without the people who have provided snippets of information and financial and moral support over the years.

Legend has it that writing a book is supposed to be a traumatic event for the authors. However, the ease with which this book came together via e-mails and only a few phone calls is testimony to a working relationship most would dream of. Thanks Nicky.

Bob Burton

FOREWORD

WE WHO ARE LUCKY ENOUGH to live in various forms of democratic societies like New Zealand, Australia, Canada, the European Union countries and the United States like to believe that we are not fooled by propaganda. We like to think that we can see through it, recognise it, and that it does not work very well in open societies like ours. The very word 'propaganda' connotes evil and dark machinations befitting the Nazi Joseph Goebbels or the oafish and grandiose efforts of Soviet Russia. We think that while propaganda might exist under vile Third World dictatorships, it cannot survive the harsh light of day in our 21st century world of mass communications, liberal governments, investigative journalists, crusading NGOs, competing political factions and well-educated citizens.

In fact, we are the most propagandised people in history. As Australian academic Alex Carey noted, police states do not need sophisticated propaganda because bullying, murder, torture and poverty are horribly crude but effective means of enforcing control. It is precisely in nations like ours that the modern propaganda industry is so invisibly pervasive and effective, and where the art and business of public relations is necessary to keep the rabble in line. That boring, innocuous term – public relations – is so much more than spin or publicity or hype. It is today the means by which the vested interests that can afford PR – governments, politicians and big businesses – maintain their power over us.

Alex Carey wrote that 'The twentieth century has been characterised by three developments of great political importance: the growth of democracy, the growth of corporate power, and the growth of corporate propaganda as a means of protecting corporate power against democracy'. In his book, *Taking the Risk Out of Democracy*, he showed that it is through public relations that propaganda is best waged.

Nicky Hager and Bob Burton's book is about this hidden force, the modern PR industry. It tells a story rarely documented so exquisitely: how powerful professional propagandists strategise to impose invisibly the will of special interests upon the public. The plot succeeded well in the case of one anti-environmental campaign until authors Nicky Hager and Bob Burton and some very courageous 'whistleblowers' came forward with what you now hold in your hands: a book that is one of the most important political exposés you will ever read.

What makes this exposé so unique and invaluable are the scores of documents upon which it is based – secret internal missives, strategies and tactics that served as the battle plan of the hidden propaganda war waged by a state-owned company, Timberlands West Coast Limited, and its mercenary PR consultants. This book delivers the goods as few have been able to do.

What *Secrets and Lies* describes is happening every day, in similar ways, on every issue of economic and political importance where public controversies rage or could erupt. The activities and events described here are not exceptions, they are the rule. What is exceptional is that they are revealed.

Outside of the world of political and industrial espionage, few industries crave and create the secrecy and confidentiality of PR. *Secrets and Lies* breaks through the secrecy and provides a unique case study, revealing, in the PR companies' own words and documents, how they operate.

When Sheldon Rampton and I wrote our 1995 book, *Toxic Sludge is Good for You*, few others had tackled the subject. Journalists, to their shame and our misfortune, are often blind to or complicit with the PR industry. Academics who investigate PR's influence report that most of what we see, hear and read as news and information on any given day is the product of PR, is massaged by spin, and in many cases is just regurgitation of press releases.

There are still only a handful of books that have examined the modern propaganda industry and they are all important. They include *Global Spin* by Australian professor Sharon Beder, *The Powerhouse* by American journalist Susan Trento, *Sultans of Sleaze* by Canadian Joyce Nelson, and *The Invisible Persuaders* by David Michie and *Green Backlash* by Andrew Rowell in Britain. I mention these books because each one is worth reading, and because it's shocking that so few critical books have been written about an industry as powerful as PR. *Secrets and Lies* is an excellent, unique and welcome addition.

Shandwick, the New Zealand subsidiary of which is exposed in this book, boasts that its 'approach is to assist clients in packaging and positioning a product, image or point of view to gain maximum advantage within the policy marketplace'. It describes its services as 'Government Relations, Media Relations, Grassroots/Grasstops Advocacy, Advocacy Advertising, Intelligence Gathering and Monitoring, Crisis Communications and Event Management'.

To the average citizen, these terms say little. But what they mean in the real world is revealed in this book: hidden manipulation, dirty tricks, influence peddling and the thwarting of democracy. We all owe thanks to the authors, and especially their sources, for *Secrets and Lies*.

John Stauber
Madison, Wisconsin
July 1999

John Stauber is founder of the non-profit Center for Media and Democracy in Madison, Wisconsin, USA, and editor of the investigative quarterly PR Watch, a journal that reports on the PR/public affairs industry from a public interest perspective. He is co-author with Sheldon Rampton of Toxic Sludge is Good for You: Lies, Damn Lies and the Public Relations Industry, an exposé of the modern propaganda business (Common Courage Press, Monroe, Maine, 1995). For information contact the Center at 1-608-233-3346 or <www.prwatch.org>.

EXPOSING PR TACTICS ACROSS THE WORLD OR ON YOUR STREET

As public relations companies export techniques for manipulating democracy around the globe, citizens in every country urgently need to share knowledge of these tactics and how to deal with them. Secrets and Lies *is a rare and detailed exposé of how modern PR companies influence politics. It is as relevant to understanding politics across the world as in your street....*

In a fifth-floor office in the nation's capital, a small group of dedicated men and women spent years writing press releases and letters to the editor about rainforest logging, lobbying the government, studying green publications, reading reports of environmental meetings and planning for the next protest. But they were not environmental activists. They had a very different role.

Their job was not to build the environmental movement but to undermine it. Meticulous plans were devised to counter and undo the efforts of environmental campaigners and, at the same time, they invisibly co-ordinated their own campaign to win government support for continued rainforest logging. Working as paid corporate activists, they were the staff of a public relations company.

The client in this case was a logging company owned by the New Zealand government, but it could have been any issue and almost any country. This book is about the tactics PR companies can use to pursue the political goals of any client able to pay their fees. It is pay-politics, where any cause, no matter whether it is unworthy or self-interested, can become a significant political campaign with the assistance of the invisible PR activists.

What follows is an insider's view of the dirty deeds of a gigantic transnational propaganda firm. The unscrupulous tactics it and other PR companies use were developed to counter US activists, but have since been exported worldwide, in this case to the island nation of New Zealand in the South Pacific. While the locations and personalities may be foreign, this should only emphasise the familiarity of the PR techniques, which influence most of the news we see and the most important political issues affecting our lives.

The PR professionals employed to manipulate politics usually succeed in operating in secrecy. The difference in this case was that some people involved in the PR campaign decided that the logging company had gone too far and that the public had a right to know. At great personal risk they broke their employee secrecy agreements so that the story could be told.

New Zealand is not a place you would expect to be a case-study of anti-environmental politics. Americans mostly see New Zealand as 'clean and green', an unspoilt country remote from the world's industrial pressures and environmental problems. But there are pressures for rainforest logging throughout the world, and the political techniques employed to support this exploitation – including anti-environmental PR tactics – naturally follow. In New Zealand the subsidiary of the public relations company Shandwick had been employed by the state logging company to "neutralise" its environmental opposition.

For decades there has been controversy over logging of New Zealand's temperate rainforests. These forests are very ancient, containing plant and animal species that have existed for over 150 million years. For 80 million years the islands of New Zealand have been cut off by ocean from the rest of the world, creating in effect a biological museum, more closely resembling forests of the dinosaur era than any others on earth.

The modern environmental movement in New Zealand grew out of a 1970s campaign that succeeded in stopping wholesale clearing of the natural beech forests on New Zealand's West Coast. The battles continued through the 1980s over logging of rimu forests, with some forests saved and others cleared and planted in pine trees. Then, when most New Zealanders would have presumed that logging of native forests was a thing of the past, proposals appeared to dramatically expand the scale of the West Coast logging.

It would not seem unreasonable to most people that the government agency doing the logging, Timberlands West Coast Ltd, would seek advice on a public relations strategy. Most members of the public, even those who opposed the logging, would probably accept a government agency putting forward its side of the story in a public policy debate. If Timberlands published a glossy annual report, wrote a few letters to the editor, addressed public meetings or took politicians and media on tours of their logging operations, most would have little objection. But much, much more was going on.

The anti-logging campaigners gradually became aware of a concerted and often aggressive counter-campaign. It seemed that anyone who supported them prominently would receive legal threats or some other response designed to deter them from advocating their views. There was a growing but ill-defined sense that there was a deliberate campaign to paint their mainstream concerns as extreme and unreasonable and that Timberlands was secretly co-ordinating a pro-logging campaign against them. But it was hard to prove and, in the absence of hard evidence, open to being dismissed. When Timberlands was accused of employing the kind of anti-environmental public relations tactics seen in other countries, the company's chief executive officer dismissed the suggestion as 'conspiracy theories'.[1]

One of the authors of this book, Nicky Hager, wondered if the tactics appearing in the forestry debate were signs of the type of anti-environmental PR he had read about from the United States. He decided to make a project of breaking through the secrecy surrounding the Timberlands campaign and began looking for insiders who would be

We were given hundreds and hundreds of pages of confidential public relations papers – probably the most detailed exposure ever of the secret tactics used in a PR campaign.

willing to talk about what was really going on. New Zealand is a good place to seek secret information like this. It is an old joke that, within minutes of meeting, two strangers will discover people they know in common. The same applies to finding insiders. Eventually determined researchers will hear about their neighbour's friend's cousin who works in the very organisation they are studying – and find that he or she may be willing to meet for a drink.

The breakthrough came in 1999 when some people offered to help – and eventually helped far beyond our expectations. They felt uncomfortable about the tactics they were involved in implementing and, once approached, decided that the public had a right to know. What began as quiet meetings ended in decisions to really spill the beans. The people concerned decided that their duty to the public outweighed their obligation to help keep what they felt were unethical activities secret.

They photocopied hundreds of pages of confidential documents, eventually handing over what may be the most comprehensive set of PR papers ever to reach the public anywhere in the world (see p. 240 for more on leaking). If you can imagine how much paper someone was able to photocopy between 10 p.m. one evening and 6.30 a.m. the next morning – non-stop – that was the size of the largest group of documents that came to make up what are now known as the Timberlands Papers.

These leaked papers gave a near-complete picture – from the inside – of an anti-environmental PR campaign. There were numerous PR strategy papers, piles of correspondence between Timberlands and its PR advisers, copies of legal advice about attacking critics and, tying the story together week by week, the minutes of the Friday morning teleconferences between Timberlands and the PR companies it employed to assist in its political campaign. This is very rare. There has probably never been such a detailed exposure of what goes on behind the glossy face of a PR campaign. The public deserves to know how ugly it looked.

The papers showed that the environmentalists' suspicions, far from being unfounded, underestimated the scale of the PR campaign against them. Here was detailed planning of how to cause trouble for the environmental groups and anyone who helped them: researching their vulnerabilities and deciding on the best tactics for countering them. Here were matter-of-fact discussions about infiltrating environmental groups to acquire information that could assist the campaign.

There were bizarre examples, such as a PR consultant sitting in that fifth-floor office writing letters in the voice of annoyed West Coasters, tired of outside interference in their lives – letters which Timberlands had arranged to get 'its' community action group to sign and post off to newspapers and to a Cabinet minister who was thought not to be 'on side'.

There was so much material in the Timberlands Papers, revealing in breathtaking detail the cynical world of public relations, that we decided to tell the story in this book. Covering all aspects of the company campaign, it serves as a textbook case of anti-environmental public relations strategies.

There is a bigger story too. The Timberlands Papers document the campaign for just one client of a couple of New Zealand PR companies. Reading through the Timberlands story, it is sobering to consider the impact the collective efforts of the whole PR industry have on every other issue, and what this means for the functioning of democratic society. The effect of these PR strategies is to undermine public participation in issues and avoid democratic decision-making if it is contrary to the interests of a client with a healthy bank account.

Politicians are accustomed to judging public concern about an issue by, for instance, the number of letters to the editor or how much the issue is in the news. But if a company or government agency can simply and invisibly spend a great deal of money to get its PR company to write dozens of letters to the editor, cultivate 'independent' supportive spokespeople and orchestrate news stories from sympathetic journalists, then the ordinary democratic processes are easily subverted.

This is precisely what Timberlands and Shandwick did. Most letters to the editor in favour of logging could be traced straight back to Timberlands and its PR firms; nearly all the voices speaking publicly in favour of logging turned out to have been orchestrated by Timberlands and nearly every news story sympathetic to Timberlands was revealed to have been arranged by the company. Almost every seemingly spontaneous sign of support for Timberlands' logging originated with the company.

The pro-logging campaign included manipulating the news media, cultivating political allies to act as spokespeople and lobbyists for its interests and attempting to buy local public support through sponsorship funding. The company set out to orchestrate a national political campaign in favour of logging where otherwise there would not have been one.

Where does this leave democracy, as politics becomes increasingly manipulated by public relations? As this book shows, the survival of democracy depends on exposing the public relations industry. It also depends on recognising the PR tactics when they are used in public debates and not being discouraged by them. We wrote this book as an example of a PR campaign but also as an example of how to counter it.

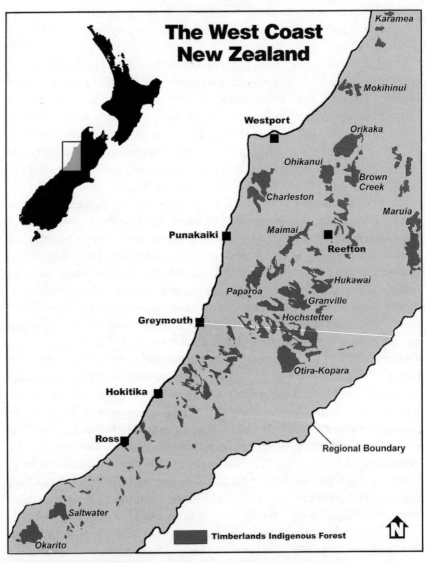

The controversial logging was occurring in the West Coast region of New Zealand, a region with 1 percent of New Zealand's population and the largest remaining areas of lowland temperate rainforest. The native forests being logged or threatened by logging are marked.

CHAPTER 1

THE PRIVATISATION OF POLITICS

Public relations ... In Mussolini's phrase, 'invention is more useful than truth'.
John Ralston Saul, *The Doubter's Companion*, 1995

There was a simple reason why the logging controversy was occurring on the West Coast of New Zealand's South Island. This region contains the largest areas of lowland temperate rainforest left in the country. It is almost the only place where publicly owned rainforests are still being logged to produce native timber, mostly rimu, which is used for finishing and joinery in the building industry and for furniture making. The beech timber is largely exported. In most of New Zealand – the kauri forests in the north, the tall podocarp forests of the Central North Island and remnants of forest elsewhere – logging of public native forests ended in the 1970s and 1980s, if not earlier. In many regions of New Zealand, you can drive all day through farmland, towns and plantation forests without encountering a single stand of the native forest that once covered more than three-quarters of the country.

The issues in the debate over Timberlands logging are easily summed up. The company could argue that its logging was much less destructive than in the past: after selective logging a forest cover still remained, in contrast to the clearfelling it had done until 1994. The company had also started using helicopters to lift felled trees to nearby collection areas, reducing the amount of roading and damage to the forest. The logging produced a valuable commodity and some local employment. All this was true.

On the other side, the environmentalists argued that the ancient rimu and beech forests targeted for logging were so valuable as remnants of natural New Zealand, and as habitat for endangered native wildlife, that they should not be logged at all. They could point to how little rich lowland native forest was left anywhere in New Zealand, with most forests having been cleared for farming, settlement and pine plantations. They said that the timber industry had already had more than its share, that the country's timber needs could be met from plantation forests and that the remnants of native forest left were needed for conservation. All this was true too.

At this basic level, both sides of the argument were correct. In the end, the public and government would have to choose. The trouble for Timberlands was that history was not on the side of continued logging of rainforests. While many New Zealanders still used rimu timber and bought rimu furniture, few connected it to the felling of trees that had been standing since the now-extinct moa birds walked in the forests. If asked whether logging should continue in public native forests, a large majority said no.

Environmental groups believed that if they could bring the issues to the attention of the public then, sooner or later, public pressure would reach a point where the logging would be ended. So too, of course, would be the lucrative native forest logging business that the Timberlands managers had worked to maintain. Timberlands did not want to stand back and leave it to the public and government to decide, and knew that simply restating its version of the truth was not going to be enough. The battle was on.

The weekly public relations teleconference on 9 April 1998 began as usual at 9.30 a.m., with the senior staff of the small state-owned company gathered around a speaker phone in the boardroom of their Greymouth headquarters. On the line were consultants from their Wellington and Christchurch-based public relations companies, chewing over political news from Wellington and planning the next week's activities in the company's campaign to win government approval for its new beech forest logging plans and defend its existing logging of rimu forests.

In the 'political' section of the agenda, Rob McGregor of the Wellington PR company Shandwick New Zealand reported on discussions he had had with two staff in the office of Prime Minister Jenny Shipley, Timberlands' chief political ally. He suggested Timberlands start sending its beech PR packs and promotional videos to 'our friends in Parliament'. Kit Richards of Timberlands reported that Ken Shirley of the ACT Party was backing the company's rimu logging in the Buller region. Shandwick was given the task of drafting a letter to ministers in response to public comments by Minister of Forestry Lockwood Smith suggesting that this logging, which had been the focus of environmental protests for over a year, should end.

Moving on to 'media' issues, Shandwick reported on the success of Timberlands' legal threat against a guest on the *Kim Hill* show, which had forced the guest to retract comments critical of the company's logging. They undertook to send a copy of the retraction to the minister's office. Legal threats had worked on an Auckland magazine too: the editor of *Spirit* magazine had withdrawn an article about the anti-logging campaign just before publication. Kit Richards reported that he had made a complaint to the editor of *New Zealand Geographic* about a journalist who wanted to enter Charleston Forest to be shown the impact of logging by environmental protesters. They then discussed trying to get a 'reputable' journalist to 'sell' Timberlands' story about its beech forest logging plans.

The next item, as usual, was environmental groups. They discussed a new branch of the environment group Native Forest Action established in Auckland, and set themselves the task of finding out who was in charge of it. The following week Shandwick would take on the job of getting itself onto the new branch's mailing list to monitor what the group was doing.

And so it went on. New PR publications were planned. Possible upcoming protests were discussed. Shandwick was assigned the job of replying to the latest pro-forest conservation letters to the editor. The 55-minute meeting was typical of the weekly conferences, illustrating a small part of the enormous effort that was going into political campaigning by the government-owned logging company.

This is the kind of meeting that the public usually never gets to hear of and about which few, if any, Cabinet ministers and MPs would ever be told, let alone being permitted to see the records of what was decided there. The public relations campaign was costing the public (through Timberlands) up to a million dollars a year, yet it was being conducted almost invisibly.

Timberlands West Coast Ltd was set up to manage the state's pine plantations and native forests on the West Coast for timber production after the New Zealand Forest Service was closed down in the late 1980s. As a state-owned enterprise, it was supposed to get on with making money from the state forests while the government looked after policy issues. It had much of the same autonomy as a private company. Based in Greymouth, it employed 40-50 staff and about 100 contractors in 1998, most of them working in the pine plantations. On the other side of the issue, the main environment organisation campaigning for protection of the West Coast native forests over many years had been the Royal Forest and Bird Protection Society, working together with ECO, Greenpeace and the West Coast-based Buller Conservation Group. The logging issue was brought to a head by a new environment group called Native Forest Action (NFA), formed in 1996 and made up of energetic young environmentalists, which set out to bring the West Coast logging to national prominence.

The Timberlands Papers span the entire period of the company's existence, since it was formed in 1990. Staffed by former Forest Service staff, Timberlands was not content with leaving policy to the government and set out to do what it could to ensure it maintained native forest logging access indefinitely. The managers of the state company had control of the company finances and were able to spend large sums on public relations. The first set of PR strategy plans date from 1991, only a few months after Timberlands began operating, devising goals and strategies that were the basis of PR activities through the decade.

The second large set of documents in the Timberlands Papers date from 1994, when Forest and Bird organised high-profile protests at Timberlands' continued clearfelling of the South Westland forests. In response new, more aggressive PR strategies were produced. In 1996 Native Forest Action began a concerted public campaign to finally end all logging of

CHARLESTON FOREST CAMPAIGN

E tū, e Tāne

Stand up for the forests

Native Forest Action's tree-sitting protest brought the logging issue to national prominence in 1997-99. PR strategies and plans to counter this campaign make up the largest part of the leaked Timberlands Papers.

public native forests. Timberlands' efforts to counter this campaign from 1997 to 1999 make up the third and by far the largest part of the Timberlands Papers.

What is public relations? In the minds of most people, PR practitioners write media releases, produce glossy brochures and always smile. The most powerful tool used by PR companies, however, is strategic thinking: Which information should be emphasised and which downplayed or hidden? Who are the potential allies and how can they be brought on side? Who are the opponents and how can they be won over or undermined? Careful planning goes into anticipating problems or crises that might arise and devising strategies to deal with them. This emphasis on strategy provides an immediate advantage over many politicians, journalists and other participants in political issues who play their individual roles, whether as queens or pawns, without studying the overall chess game.

PR, of the type revealed in the Timberlands story, is frequently dishonest, which gives rise to the reputation many PR people have earned of being insincere at best and paid liars at worst. Commentators often refer to them disdainfully as 'spin-doctors' or 'flacks'. The unpopularity of the PR profession is so widespread that most in the industry call themselves something else like 'public affairs manager' or 'external relations officer' – in Timberlands' case, 'corporate communications spokesperson'. But unpopularity does not stop them being hired or being effective. In all the important work they do, the PR consultants remain invisible.

Indeed, invisibility is a central part of the effectiveness of the PR industry. Why? In the case of Timberlands, there are issues about the legitimacy of a government company playing a political role at all. More generally, PR companies prefer to arrange 'third parties' to front for their clients' interests, pulling strings rather than acting openly. As a representative of the world's biggest PR firm, Burson Marsteller, told an advertising conference: 'for the media and for the public, the corporation will be one of the least credible sources of information on its own product [and] environmental and safety risks.... Developing third party support and validation for the basic risk messages of the corporation is essential. This support should ideally come from ... political leaders, union officials, relevant academics, fire and police officials, environmentalists, regulators'.[1] Invisibility is the goal; secrecy is the means.

The calculated way that PR people approach their work is seen in Timberlands' original 1991 PR strategy document, which outlined the priority components for the Timberlands campaign: '1. Identify and target messages to each target audience: MPs, especially Cabinet, shadow spokespeople, Heads of Departments, Local community leaders, Key national movers'; '2. Attract and mobilise key third party support', and '3. Neutralise likely opposition. Identify key figures. Monitor their programme. Counter misconceptions'.[2] Misconceptions, in practice, turned out to mean any arguments and facts that were unhelpful to the PR campaign.

The 'likely opposition', the environment movement, has wide public support and considerable credibility in New Zealand. At the same time, many New Zealanders were inclined to be sceptical of promotion of logging by a logging company. The goal of the PR strategy, according to a 1997 'communications programme' written by Shandwick, was addressing 'all key audiences, and issues, and providing Timberlands West Coast with a strong, seamless and cohesive communications strategy which will swing the communications "pendulum" back in Timberlands' favour'.[3]

The Timberlands' strategy focused on four central elements: neutralising opponents, creating public and political credibility for Timberlands, building the impression of an independent public campaign supporting Timberlands and organising lobbying at the political level.

Timberlands' main PR firm, Shandwick New Zealand, is part of the global Shandwick public relations company with headquarters in London. It boasts more than 92 wholly owned and 38 affiliate offices around the world. The bible on the PR industry, *O'Dwyers PR Directory*, listed Shandwick in 1996 as the second largest PR firm with $171 million in turnover worldwide, making the global top 10 in 'environmental PR'.

John Stauber and Sheldon Rampton, editors of the United States-based investigative magazine on the PR industry, *PR Watch*, put it slightly differently, describing Shandwick as 'a leading anti-environmental greenwasher'.[4] They quoted Shandwick in 1994 claiming that 'we're helping companies... maximise green market opportunities, mitigate environmental risks and protect the bottom line, with access to the corridors of power at the federal level and every state capital, local business community and newsroom'. A look at some of Shandwick's activities around the world is a useful introduction to anti-environmental public relations.

In 1994, for instance, the Malaysian Timber Council, reeling from an environmental campaign against tropical timber consumption, called in Shandwick to convince consumers in Germany that buying teak, meranti and other tropical timbers was environmentally sustainable. In 1996, for the Malaysian Timber Council, Shandwick produced a film aimed at German school children which claimed that Malaysian timber is sustainable. The film was soundly criticised by Rettet den Regenwald e.V. Rainforest Rescue, a German environmental group that worked to have the film kept out of German classrooms.

In their book *Toxic Sludge is Good for You*, Stauber and Rampton detailed Shandwick's work for one of the oldest, most notorious anti-environmental front groups, called the Council for Agricultural Science and Technology (CAST).

CAST, formed in 1972, survives on corporate funding from 'hundreds of companies invested in genetically engineered foods, agricultural chemicals, food additives and corporate factory farming, including Dow, General Mills, Land O'Lakes, Ciba-Geigy, Acher Daniels Midland, Monsanto, Philip Morris, and Uniroyal'.

The role of CAST is to position itself as 'the source for public policy-makers and news media on environmental issues'.[5] As Stauber and Rampton wrote, 'CAST is a classic industry front group claiming "to provide current, unbiased scientific information concerning food and agriculture". In fact, for over two decades CAST has vigorously and publicly defended and promoted pesticide-contaminated foods, irradiated fruits and vegetables, and the use of hormones and drugs on farm animals.'

People listening to interviews with the industry researchers and scientists involved with CAST may well think the researchers are presenting an independent view and that CAST is an independent community group. According to Stauber and Rampton, the CAST researchers 'are often on the receiving end of large grants and other payments from the same agribusiness corporations that subsidise CAST'.

In 1997, Shandwick secured the contract for a project to attempt to defeat global warming measures being promoted by the Clinton administration, in a nation that is a world leader in energy consumption and greenhouse emissions. The main tool used by Shandwick was the creation of a new group called the Global Climate Information Project (GCIP), backed by trade associations representing the companies with most to lose from trying to control global warming: leading oil, coal and automobile producers, including some of the most notorious polluters in the United States.

A GCIP news release, sent from Shandwick Public Affairs' Washington office, gave the impression the group had a benign and wide constituency. It stated that GCIP was 'supported by organisations representing small business, industry, agriculture, labor and citizen groups'.[6] The central target of the campaign was to prevent the signing of a global warming treaty which, under the United States Constitution, would have to be ratified by the Senate. To mobilise politicians and the public, GCIP launched a blitz of newspaper, TV and radio ads that made alarming predictions about the impact of the treaty on the American economy.

The message repeated in the advertisements was 'the UN Global Climate Treaty isn't global. Americans will pay the price. 50 Cents More for Every Gallon of Gasoline. Most Countries are Exempt. It's not Global and it Won't Work.' The TV ads contained dire warnings, for instance, that 'Gasoline and home heating oil could increase by as much as 50 cents a gallon.... And higher energy costs mean higher costs for food, clothing – most things we need.'[7] The organisation's claims about itself were misleading and the messages were alarmist and inaccurate, but neither Shandwick nor its clients were publicly called to account. The use of front groups and the 'spinning' of messages is standard stuff in modern PR.

The TV advertisements were run heavily in Washington DC, targeting members of Congress, decision-makers and reporters, and in New York, where many of the most influential reporters and editors are based, as well as in key congressional districts around the country. At first the Clinton administration buckled in the face of the onslaught, announcing a relatively weak position of seeking only a stabilisation of greenhouse gases on the 1990 levels. But the lobbying effort of real community groups saw Clinton's position toughen to a 5 percent reduction. At the Kyoto greenhouse negotiations in late 1997 the United States encountered strong opposition from the European Union, which was arguing for a 15 percent reduction. Eventually the Kyoto negotiations agreed to a 7 percent reduction. According to National Environment Trust greenhouse campaigner, Kalee Kreider, 'maybe for their 30 million the [GCIP-Shandwick campaign] got a couple of percent difference'.

A final example, found among the Timberlands Papers, is a fax from an overseas Shandwick office taking credit for helping Shell to manage bad publicity over its role in Nigeria. Shell's oilfield operations had created major environmental and social problems in oil-rich Ogoniland. Major spills from poorly maintained oil pipes damaged scarce agricultural land and fisheries, while the flaring of excess gas caused major pollution problems. When the Ogoni author Ken Saro-Wiwa launched a campaign against Shell, it responded by monitoring his movements.

In November 1995, Ken Saro-Wiwa and eight others were executed after being convicted by a military court. The executions were widely condemned by human rights, environmental and writers' organisations and Shell faced a major international backlash. Following the execution,

Shell confirmed that it had bought guns for the Nigerian police.[8] Shandwick helped Shell to deal with the international backlash.

Shandwick New Zealand had been enquiring overseas for advice on how to handle the Body Shop, which had provided support for Native Forest Action's campaign against Timberlands, and was told about a PR consultant in Shandwick's New York office who helped on the Shell contract and might have ideas to help in New Zealand. His colleague Daphne Luchtenberg noted that they had had 'dealings and similar wranglings' with the Body Shop over Shell and Nigeria – 'Ken Sarawiwo [*sic*] – do you remember?' – as Timberlands was experiencing. 'Colin Byrne advised them on that and he would be good to include in the [Timberlands weekly] conference call,' she wrote. 'Colin B also has a free-lance consultant who is very hot on European environment issues and if the timing is right he might be involved.'[9]

Shandwick established itself in New Zealand in 1988, buying a long-standing PR firm called International Public Relations Ltd. The company's original 1991 pitch offering its PR services to Timberlands, found among the Timberlands Papers, emphasised its international standing: 'The world's largest public relations consultancy, Shandwick has 2,400 staff operating from nearly 100 offices in 21 countries. As the New Zealand component of Shandwick, IPR employs 17 full-time as well as 60 part-time staff.'

The proposal boasted that 'some of our more recent achievements would include intensive campaigning that led to the deferral and we believe

REMEMBER KEN SARO-WIWA

BOYCOTT SHELL OIL

Shandwick's New York office helped Shell to 'manage' bad publicity over its controversial role in Nigeria. Other recent clients include genetic engineering firms Ciba-Geigy and Monsanto.

ultimate demise of capital gains tax'. IPR also proudly pointed to its success in campaigning for the 'repeal of land tax' and 'promulgation and promotion of an environmental policy for a major SOE'. It offered to provide '24 hour availability of staff members in event of attack from environmental pressure groups'.[10] Timberlands hired the company.

In 1999 Shandwick New Zealand was listed as having only five consultants, including chief executive, Klaus Sorensen,[11] the director of government and corporate relations, Rob McGregor,[12] and Chris Mason.[13] It had a small client base, including the Professional Firefighters Union and its touted gain of Southern Cross Healthcare as a client in 1998. Sorensen and McGregor feature as the chief advisers in the Timberlands campaign.

Commonly, more than one PR firm will work on the one client's campaign, with a senior firm being assigned overall responsibility for strategy development while others work on more specific roles or implementation. For the Timberlands campaign, Shandwick had the lead role while Christchurch-based Head Consultants primarily supervised the production and dispatch of publications, briefings to ministers and MPs and press releases[14]. Warren Head, the principal of the firm, was assisted by Shelley Grell in the Timberlands campaign. A third company, Morris Communications Group in Wellington, also provided some services.

In December 1998 Native Forest Action (NFA) complained publicly about the tactics it believed were being used against it. Spokesperson, Dean Baigent-Mercer, said that ever since Timberlands had brought in Shandwick, the campaign over West Coast logging had turned dirty.[15] The Timberlands Papers confirm that Shandwick began to play a much more active role in the campaign in mid-1997, following a major PR strategy meeting on 1 July 1997 between senior Timberlands staff and Klaus Sorensen at which a raft of new campaign plans had been agreed.

The NFA statement hit a raw nerve with Shandwick's chief executive, Klaus Sorensen. Used to operating away from public gaze, Sorensen decided to defend his company's activities publicly. Shandwick, he said, was disappointed at the 'tiresome antics' of NFA, whose allegations concerning his company were 'incorrect'. 'I resent NFA's conduct. The only dirty tricks I am aware of is their continued misinformation.'[16]

Particularly galling for Sorensen was Baigent-Mercer's claim that Shandwick was 'an American company that specialises in anti-environmental campaigning'. 'We are a locally owned and operated, all New Zealand company,' Sorensen protested. While Shandwick New Zealand is legally registered in New Zealand and employs New Zealand staff, it is part of the global Shandwick network, as a simple click on the Shandwick website reveals. The records of the Wellington Companies Office show that it is in fact 100 percent foreign owned, with 1,011,999 shares owned by Shandwick Investment Ltd and one share owned by Briefcope Ltd, both located at 61 Grosvenor Street, London. By far its largest area of operations is the United States, with offices in 19 cities.[17]

'I have not had any discussion with overseas affiliates concerning Timberlands. I doubt if they would know it existed,' Sorensen claimed. The Timberlands Papers, however, include various communications to and from overseas Shandwick offices, such as the Shell example, in which Sorensen and his colleagues sought help with the Timberlands campaign. Shandwick New Zealand also boasted to the London Shandwick office about the success of the Timberlands public relations strategy as part of a company pitch for a contract.[18]

So sensitive was Sorensen to criticism of Shandwick that he went public again in May 1999 in response to a small letter to the editor in the *Wanganui Chronicle* by Darrell Grace that had questioned the role of 'Shandlewick International' in Timberlands' campaign. Sorensen wrote to the paper a month later saying that 'this sort of hysterical assertion is consistent with the regular misinformation propounded by Native Forest Action', and noting as an aside that he 'would be interested to know Mr Grace's connections'.

Sorensen then repeated his claim that 'at no time have we sought any assistance or input from our international affiliates in respect of the

Directors

Name	
Lawrence Ronald Valpy BRYANT	**Date Appointed:** 28-FEB-1995
Klaus SORENSEN	**Date Appointed:** 01-FEB-1999

Shareholders (as at incorporation or last annual return if any.)
Number of shares 1,012,000

Name	No. of Shares
BRIEFCOPE LIMITED	1
61 Grosvenor Street, London W 1, United Kingdom	
SHANDWICK INVESTMENT LIMITED	1,011,999
61 Grosvenor Street, London W 1, United Kingdom	

Klaus Sorensen, chief executive of Shandwick New Zealand, in the Press: *'We are a locally owned and operated, all New Zealand company'.*

work we carry out to assist Timberlands'.[19] Timberlands CEO Dave Hilliard followed up with a letter to the *Wanganui Chronicle* two weeks later sticking up for Shandwick. 'Shandwick NZ Ltd is a company of fine repute, professional integrity and expertise. I fully support Klaus Sorensen's response to Darrell Grace's outburst against Shandwick,' he wrote.[20]

Leaving aside Sorensen's misleading comments over foreign ownership and support, there is also an important truth in what he was saying. Shandwick New Zealand and Head Consultants are small companies made up of New Zealanders, as is generally the case in the New Zealand PR 'industry'. They are not giant firms controlled by hotshot foreign PR specialists. But this is not at all reassuring. What the Timberlands Papers show is that these small companies, staffed by average people, could still have considerable impact on national politics in pursuit of their client's interests. No matter how unworthy the cause, there is little to stop PR people using tactics imported from overseas companies like American Shandwick to manufacture political advantage. The 'communications' people become political activists for their clients and whether they restrict themselves to tools that are ethical is largely voluntary.

There are about 150 main PR companies in New Zealand (including 40 larger ones), each with a range of clients, plus many more in-house PR people in companies, government departments and Parliament. The director of communications in the Prime Minister's Department has a list of about 150 government PR people.[21] Obviously, some of the private and government PR people are doing politically innocuous work and some will be ineffectual. But you can still multiply the impact that the Timberlands-Shandwick campaign was able to have on national politics by 100 times or more, for all the other companies and clients. This shows the scale of the impact that PR continuously has on all the news we hear and on the processes of government.

The comments by the chief PR people, revealed in their own letters and notes, suggests they enjoyed undermining the environmentalists' campaign. But their main defining feature is being apolitical and willing to work for whoever will pay. In the morning Shandwick might be working on the Timberlands issue, then in the afternoon applying strategic thinking to a totally different client, such as the popular Professional Firefighters Union's campaign against government restructuring and cost cutting in the fire service. The political implications of PR must therefore be considered in overview, for they stem from which political and corporate interests in society can more often afford the PR consultants' high fees and what tactics these interests are willing to have used on their behalf.

The Public Relations Institute of New Zealand (PRINZ) estimates that there are 1500 PR people working in New Zealand. The Engineers Union (which represents them) estimates that there are 2000 journalists. But these figures give no sense of the inequality. If, for instance, there could be three full-time journalists probing Timberlands and the native forest issue, with support staff and resources matching the full-time PR staff working for Timberlands, the public and politicians would have a good chance of getting a balanced picture of the issue.

But in reality the focused and well-resourced PR staff are matched by many scattered journalists doing occasional one-off stories on the issue or simply reporting the press releases that land on their desks, amidst all the other stories and issues they must also cover in a week. The specialisation and strategy are all on one side. It is an unequal fight. The public is left rightfully suspicious that much of the news reaching it could be traced back to PR plans devised in the Beehive and by companies like Shandwick.

As award-winning Australian journalist David McKnight wrote, 'Good PR depends on bad journalism ... public relations firms systematically factor in the laziness and pressures of work of journalists.... One of my most fundamental objections to PR is that it reinforces existing inequality in society. Because PR is paid service and because the already existing wealth and power in society is able to pay handsomely for the services of PR firms, PR tends to be a force for social conservatism and entrenching privilege and power.'[22]

PR people may be apolitical, but the picture that emerges of those who gathered each week for the Timberlands teleconferences is far from flattering. Fortunately, in the case of West Coast rainforests, there were other forces at work too. The Timberlands Papers reveal a company campaign that was failing. In the later documents even Timberlands could see that its strategies were not working. Voluntary, poorly resourced and part-time, the environmentalists were winning.

CHAPTER 2

'NEUTRALISING' THE OPPOSITION

The most pressing hurdles to Timberlands' ability to achieve its objective are: The extent to which opposition from the environment movement may create widespread public support and pressure at the political level to curtail or end Timberlands' activities.... The environmental movement is important only in so far as it can create public and political support for its goals. Timberlands' primary objective therefore must be to limit the movement's ability to influence public and policies....

Timberlands West Coast Corporate Communications Strategy, 1994

In September 1998, responding to a question from a parliamentary select committee, Timberlands chief executive Dave Hilliard gave details of the company's public relations plans for the year. Hilliard was a long-term campaigner in favour of native forest logging. He had gone straight into the New Zealand Forest Service (NZFS) as a 17-year-old school-leaver in the late 1960s, gaining a reputation for aggressively opposing environmental campaigns. In the early 1980s, as NZFS second-in-command at Whirinaki in the central North Island, he mobilised locals and blocked buses of conservationists as he tried, unsuccessfully, to maintain logging of that area's remarkable tall and dense rainforests. Later as an NZFS forester, he battled environmentalists over logging of various West Coast forests.

Hilliard's written answer to the committee, describing what he referred to as Timberlands' 'communications' plan, consisted of an innocuous-sounding list of items such as producing publicity materials and brochures, education and sponsorship and media releases. But this careful reply left out much more than it included. Hilliard could scarcely have mentioned that a central part of Timberlands' PR strategy was attacking and attempting to undermine critics of the company's native forest logging.

As CEO, Hilliard must have known that, sitting in a Timberlands filing cabinet, were secret PR strategy documents that spelt out detailed tactics for what the documents described as 'neutralising' the opposition. One document explicitly directed that at the core of Timberlands' PR strategy was countering its opponents. 'The main thrust of the Communications Strategy,' it stated, 'is to limit public support for environmentally based campaigns against Timberlands, thereby limiting public pressure on the political process.'[1] Timberlands' PR staff had systematically devised plans to attempt to 'neutralise' all the various critics of its logging: environmental groups, scientists, members of Parliament.

The public approach – the PR 'spin' – involved attempting to discredit the opposition as being small, extreme and embarked on a campaign of misinformation. Behind the scenes more aggressive tactics were being employed. To gain advance warning of the plans of conservation groups, Timberlands organised monitoring of groups and key individuals. Critics of the company were on the receiving end of a string of legal threats; for conservation groups dependent on public donations and small grants, Timberlands investigated their finances and targeted organisations giving them money. Tactics were devised to counter each individual or group who supported the conservation campaign and any journalists who covered their activities.

PR managers and companies challenged by community groups hate surprises. 'Crisis management' is reactive, stressful and amounts to damage control at best. In the lexicon of the PR industry, it is far better to undertake 'crisis preparedness' training, with an early warning system based on monitoring your opponents and other potential crises in order to give you time to take 'pro-active' measures to 'manage' an issue.

Shandwick recommended that Timberlands establish a process 'to manage issues and prepare for any crises that could beset the company'.

In Shandwick's view, the most worrying potential crises were 'Govt curtailing of unsustainable logging, limitation of native forest logging, privatisation, sabotage of equipment,

Timberlands CEO Dave Hilliard, pictured here in the company's 1998 annual report, joined the Forest Service in the late 1960s, later gaining a reputation for aggressively opposing environmental campaigns.

occupation of forest, timber end-users targeted'. It recommended that Timberlands establish a 'monitoring system' to ensure it was 'effectively capturing necessary information on the issue'.[2] Monitoring is a sufficiently bland term that could mean uncontroversial activities such as monitoring media coverage of its critics. But although useful information can be gleaned perfectly legitimately in this way, it is of little use in a 'proactive' strategy intended to pre-empt moves by the opposition rather than simply react to them.

In the case of Timberlands, monitoring was considerably more devious and intrusive. When the various Timberlands PR strategy documents refer to 'monitoring', this in practice included collecting information on individuals, sending PR staff and others to conservation meetings incognito and arranging for fake approaches to environment groups to gather information. Timberlands and its PR firms in effect ran an intelligence operation: infiltrating, monitoring the actions of opponents and building up information to assist their strategies of attacking and countering the groups and individuals.

In several known instances, 'moles' attended conservation group meetings to collect information. When NFA began a tree-sitting occupation of Timberlands' Charleston Forest in 1997, Timberlands was caught by surprise. With many of the original members of NFA coming from the Victoria University Environment Group (VEG), Timberlands decided that that group could be an important source of information about the West Coast protests.

Shandwick arranged monitoring of VEG by finding a student on the Victoria University campus prepared to attend its meetings for payment and report back to the PR company on what was said. The son of a senior Shandwick staff member agreed to do the job, becoming a member of VEG and attending its meetings to glean information. He was paid $50 per hour for these services. VEG organisers, asked about his presence during the researching of this book, recall him regularly attending meetings, never offering to help or showing interest in conservation but asking frequent questions about planned protests and other activities in the West Coast native logging campaign.

Another case involved a one-off meeting in Christchurch at which Shandwick staff thought NFA might be speaking. Shandwick alerted Timberlands PR staff to a press release advertising a meeting in Christchurch, which would involve the presentation, by community groups, of the Roger Award for the most anti-social foreign company. Shandwick's Rob McGregor joked that 'fortunately they are targeting Transnational Corporations, we used to call them Multinationals, so Timberlands is ineligible for an award!' Jokes aside, however, McGregor considered the meeting worth monitoring. 'Despite the fact that NFA for once isn't among the esteemed list of speakers,' McGregor wrote, 'there could be value in monitoring what is going on there.'

The Wellington-based McGregor thought that since 'this is all happening in Shelley's patch' – that is, Head Consultants in Christchurch, Timberlands' other PR firm – 'you may like to consider asking her if she would be able to go along incognito'.[3]

Another mole, Barry Nicolle, later declared that he had acted on his own initiative; however, he had still reported throughout to Timberlands, for which he worked as a contractor. For three months in 1998 he travelled from Hokitika on the West Coast to Christchurch several times to attend evening meetings of the newly formed Christchurch branch of NFA. He recorded what went on at the meetings in diaries and on tape. In December that year he approached the *Press* and other news outlets with a story about the supposed inner workings of NFA. In the subsequent *Press* article, headed 'Forest group manipulative for own ends – Coaster', he described himself as someone who had 'become interested in NFA's activities this year' but later 'didn't like what he saw so decided to go public about it'.

Until NFA pointed out Nicolle's link to Timberlands, the *Press* had been content to describe him merely as a 'former supporter' of Native Forest Action. Asked by the *Press* two days after the first publicity if he had ever worked for Timberlands, Nicolle was quoted as saying he had 'in the past worked for the company'.[4] Timberlands chief executive, Dave Hilliard, leapt to Nicolle's defence, stating 'This company categorically denies the allegations set by NFA. It seems, like so many other Coasters working to save their futures, this person has taken action on his own behalf.'[5] Nicolle may have acted on his own behalf, but he had liaised with Timberlands' staff throughout the whole exercise. Two months later his name was being publicly displayed as co-ordinator of Timberlands' possum control in one of its forests.[6]

On the same day as Nicolle's publicity, the minister responsible for forestry, David Carter, put out a press release saying that Nicolle's revelations proved NFA was distributing 'political propaganda from the Labour and Green Parties'. Carter went on to warn 'genuine people' not to be 'politically tainted by getting involved with Native Forest Action'. Within days Nicolle was appearing as the main speaker at public meetings around the Coast supporting Timberlands and attacking conservationists. On 12 February 1999, when the pro-Timberlands group Coast Action Network was 'officially launched', he was spokesperson. A few months later he was cheerfully telling journalists that 'I made out I was a greenie and went to NFA meetings'.[7]

Timberlands' PR companies have also attempted to monitor communications between NFA and its members. In September 1997 and again in March 1998 Native Forest Action received letters from a Wellington woman called Maree Procter expressing interest in the forest campaign and asking for her home address to be put on the mailing list. She was, in fact, an employee of Shandwick. The signature on her letter is the same as that on Shandwick letters she had written overseas, likewise collecting information but in those cases seeking negative stories about Timberlands' environmental critics.[8]

Included in the Timberlands Papers is a letter sent from NFA to all its members in March 1997, the second month of the Charleston treesitting. The fax stamp at the head of the faxed page clearly shows that it had been sent to Timberlands from Shandwick in Wellington.

When NFA established a branch in New Zealand's most populous city, Auckland, Shandwick covertly arranged to receive the NFA Auckland branch's mailings to members. The Timberlands Papers reveal Shandwick was keen to get the lowdown on who was involved and what NFA were doing. 'NFA has set up a branch in Auckland. Need to find out who is in charge,' the minutes of the weekly PR teleconference stated.[9] The next week it was reported to the PR teleconference 'NFA Auckland branch – Baigent-Mercer are [*sic*] in charge'.[10]

Shandwick's Rob McGregor was responsible for ensuring that the monitoring system was put in place: 'Rob McGregor [Shandwick] to talk

An employee of Shandwick New Zealand was instructed to write to Native Forest Action posing as an interested member of the public seeking information about the campaign.

Maree Procter
47 Turville Cres
Newlands 6004

27 March 1997.

Dear Sir/Madam,

Approximately August/September last year I sent a donation into yourselves on the understanding that you would keep me up-to-date on what you were doing.

I had a newsletter immediately afterwards but have not had anything since. Can you please ensure I am on your mailing lists. I enclose a donation to contribute to costs.

Many thanks

Maree

34

to Anne Grey'.[11] The following week little had changed. The minutes of the teleconference item on 'NFA Auckland' noted 'Shandwick to get on mailing list [via] Anne Grey', with McGregor assigned to follow through once more.[12]

The following week the minutes recorded with satisfaction under the topic 'Shandwick to get on mailing list of NFA Auckland' that it was 'in hand', courtesy of Rob McGregor.[13] A few months later the weekly teleconference minutes record that 'Project: NFA Monitoring' was continuing and would be 'ongoing' with responsibility allocated to Lee Harris Royal at Shandwick.[14]

Acting like a police intelligence unit, Timberlands arranged for participants in anti-logging protests to be photographed or videoed, with this information forwarded to the two PR companies. Timberlands staff took numerous photographs of individuals protesting outside an international forestry conference in Rotorua in February 1998 and circulated copies to

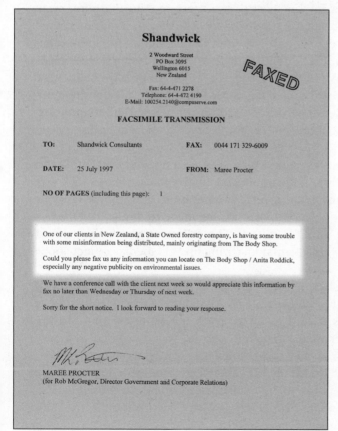

Shandwick

2 Woodward Street
PO Box 3095
Wellington 6015
New Zealand

Fax: 64-4-471 2278
Telephone: 64-4-472 4190
E-Mail: 100254.2140@compuserve.com

FAXED

FACSIMILE TRANSMISSION

TO: Shandwick Consultants   FAX: 0044 171 329-6009

DATE: 25 July 1997   FROM: Maree Procter

NO OF PAGES (including this page):   1

One of our clients in New Zealand, a State Owned forestry company, is having some trouble with some misinformation being distributed, mainly originating from The Body Shop.

Could you please fax us any information you can locate on The Body Shop / Anita Roddick, especially any negative publicity on environmental issues.

We have a conference call with the client next week so would appreciate this information by fax no later than Wednesday or Thursday of next week.

Sorry for the short notice. I look forward to reading your response.

MAREE PROCTER
(for Rob McGregor, Director Government and Corporate Relations)

Shandwick requested information to use in attacking the Body Shop, which had been supporting the forest conservation campaign. Note the letter is signed by the same person as the letter to NFA opposite.

Shandwick and Head 'to show them what we're up against'. When there was a public demonstration, including members of Parliament, in Christchurch's Cathedral Square, Timberlands' Christchurch PR firm, Head Consultants, was there with a video camera. Minutes of the weekly PR teleconference recorded that Shelley Grell from Head Consultants was tasked with 'Video on ChCh protest to be sent to Timberlands'.[15]

The following year Timberlands were at it again. 'NFA: Sent photos of protest outside [Timberlands] office to Shandwick and HCL,' the minutes of one week's teleconference recorded.[16] Monitoring also extended to keeping track of protesters in the Charleston forest. 'Have been several people at Charleston but only on fine days with no great activity, however the helicopter is back today,' the teleconference minutes recorded.[17] Timberlands staff also monitored NFA radio communications during protest actions and on two occasions radio-schedule lists were stolen from protest bases by Timberlands contractors.

Less controversial, but part of the same monitoring effort, was monitoring of all information produced by critical conservation groups: publications, press releases and websites. The Timberlands Papers regularly feature reports attempting to track all the activity of NFA. 'NFA: A new series of posters is appearing in Wellington. To be sent once received from Minister's office – action Klaus Sorensen,' the teleconference minutes recorded.[18] The following week Timberlands and Shandwick were discussing NFA again. 'Latest NFA brochure discussed,' said the minutes.[19]

When NFA and Forest and Bird released a booklet presenting the case for preserving various of Timberlands' native forests, Shandwick was on the trail of the unseen booklet. 'Attempting to get original copy of NFA/F&B 12 page booklet. Approach to be made to Minister's Office – Rob McGregor,' the minutes noted. The following week they noted 'Shelley Grell [Head Consultants] following up Akld media contact about this'.[20]

Material published on the Internet was scrutinised as well, to check if it contained useful intelligence: 'NFA: All quiet at present. Lobbying in Wellington. Websites re NFA to be assessed and reported on – Shelley Grell.'[21] A week later monitoring the website was described as 'ongoing'. The following week they noted 'some information has been received, no need to continue searching'.[22] Timberlands also needed to track the website of Forest and Bird. 'RF&B website needs to be monitored in case of new information about [Timberlands West Coast] put on it,' the minutes of one teleconference recorded.[23]

One of the main agenda items for each week's PR telephone conference was a discussion of news about NFA, noting all activities, news of individual members and planned activities. No detail was too small for Timberlands. 'NFA: Acknowledged poster put up around Wellington during last few days,' one set of minutes recorded.[24]

Whether NFA media events gained coverage was a particular obsession of Timberlands. The following month they were tracking whether an NFA protest received any media coverage. 'NFA protest in Wellington, no mention in Wn papers only in *Greymouth Evening Star*. Article to be faxed to HCL and Shandwick – Anne Pearson.'[25] The following week they were worrying about an NFA stunt at Parliament in Wellington: 'NFA publicity stunt to dump chainsaws on steps of Parliament has not erupted into a media frenzy as they would have hoped. We believe they are stepping up their campaign.'[26]

Even NFA activists being dealt with by the courts appeared on Timberlands' radar screen: 'A Cotter being processed for trespass – 25 September'.[27] On other occasions an NFA strategy meeting caught their attention: 'NFA: Gathering at Charleston over long weekend noted'.[28] Sometimes no news was good news for Timberlands: 'NFA: No issues. No interest in helicopter accident.'[29]

Even the absence of posters rated a mention in their weekly phone conferences: 'NFA: No posters around Wellington'. What protesters were wearing and where they were living was also worthy of investigation. 'NFA attempted to block road on Monday morning. All seemed to be wearing "rainbird" brand. Beanies were found named with "Rainbow Skifield". Follow up with J Pearson [Timberlands' lawyer]. Few now living around Nile River area,' Kit Richards reported.[30]

Timberlands knew it was up against strong public support for the protection of native forests and environmental groups with wide credibility. Aware of this, and of its own lack of broad support, Timberlands' next strategy was, in the language of the PR trade, to 'position' its opponents as being 'extreme'. In the hope of making the accusation stick, Timberlands repeatedly used the words 'extreme' or 'extremists' to describe opposing organisations and individuals. 'Timberlands is accused of environmental vandalism,' Dave Hilliard wrote in 1997, 'by a group of extreme activists who are self-appointed, misinformed, and politically motivated.'[31] Comments like this became the norm.

As the second strand of this strategy, Timberlands' statements and spokespeople routinely referred to the company's opposition as being small. Timberlands was up against almost all the large environment groups such as Forest and Bird, ECO, Greenpeace, Federated Mountain Clubs and Native Forest Action, not to mention a majority of the public, but the company aimed to marginalise them and create the impression that they were insignificant, irrational outsiders.

In a 1997 communications strategy Shandwick explained the line: 'Current environmental opposition is based on a small but determined group of relatively extreme environmentalists who do not support the sustainable management philosophy, enshrined in legislation and supported by the more responsible environmental groups.'[32] Timberlands sought to portray its opposition as fringe, and its few environmental supporters – the controversial Maruia Society and, for a short time, the World Wide Fund for Nature – as 'mainstream'.

This message was repeated over and over. In a letter to its SOE minister, Jenny Shipley, Timberlands CEO Dave Hilliard, explained, 'As you will be aware Timberlands is the target of an ongoing campaign by a small group of extremely dedicated environmental activists….We have found these activists to be persistent, obstructive, time consuming and, this is perhaps the most worrisome aspect,' he warned, 'to have a blatant disregard for the facts and perpetuate misinformation.'[33] A year later, with the campaign against Timberlands continuing to grow, Hilliard told the Minister of Forestry's office that the company was operating 'in the face of determined opposition from a very small yet vocal and committed [group of] protesters'.[34]

The third strand of Timberlands' lobbying and public statements strategy was to 'position' itself as providing accurate information, while claiming that its opponents were engaged in a campaign of spreading misinformation. Timberlands sought to justify its ballooning PR budget as necessary to correct the 'misinformation campaign' of the opposition. Publications and statements from those against the logging were consistently dismissed in this way, again in the hope that the slur would come to be believed.

Often Timberlands blended several of its core attack points into one letter, such as this one drafted by Shandwick for the *Otago Daily Times*: 'The extremists reject the concept of sustainable management, the cause of the mainstream conservation movement, for which Timberlands has received accolades from organisations including WWF [and] the Maruia Society'.[35]

When companies make statements attacking their opponents, these can backfire. It is much better when groups that appear to be at arm's length take up the same key messages. Various spokespeople for the company's front group, Coast Action Network,[36] were happy to oblige. Barry Nicolle, for instance, the Timberlands contractor who had monitored Christchurch NFA meetings, told local media that he was 'one of a majority of West Coasters who have had a gutsful of propaganda aired by extreme conservation groups'. He said, 'A small group of motivated radicals are prepared to go to extremes in their efforts to sabotage the West Coast forestry industry.'[37] His predecessor as CAN spokesperson, Cotrina Reynolds, had told journalists that the region's employment was under threat from people with 'extreme environmental views', who were spreading 'propaganda' that West Coasters 'want to clear fell everything and there'll be no forests left'.[38]

In 1994 Timberlands had finally stopped the practice of clearfelling, where all standing trees were cut down. Environmentalists had long campaigned to end clearfelling and all knew about and welcomed the change as less damaging for the forests. Yet in communications with ministers in subsequent years, Timberlands repeatedly claimed that environment groups were erroneously and mischievously accusing it of clearfelling forests when, in fact, the conservation case was based on the damage to the forest that even selection logging regimes cause.

It was a clever PR tactic. Constantly defending itself against claims its opponents had not made helped Timberlands to define its opposition as engaged in 'misinformation'. Without having to cite evidence, Timberlands turned defence into attack, forcing its opponents to disprove a negative.

It was a tactic Shandwick employed when it drafted a set of model letters to the editor for Timberlands' letter-writing campaign. In a document identifying the 'key messages for pro-active responses to letters to the editor,' Shandwick wrote: 'While logging at Charleston is not carried out on a sustainable basis, in practice only selective logging is undertaken in Charleston forest. There is no clear-felling as environmentalists claim...'.[39] Many of the subsequent letters contained such phrases as 'a repetition of the NFA group's usual mish mash of factual inaccuracies and misinformation'.[40]

The 'misinformation' charge was taken up and repeated often in statements by government ministers and other pro-Timberlands MPs. It had another use: keeping news out of the media. The charge of 'misinformation' was used to try to convince journalists not to use press statements from and cover protests by environmental groups. On one occasion, in the first weeks of NFA's tree-sitting occupation in 1997, a PR consultant phoned journalists who were hundreds of kilometres from the protest claiming that they were being conned because there were not actually any protesters in the forest. Journalists are of necessity cautious about getting news right and so are susceptible to being put off stories if doubts are created. The result is that information or stories about which the public has a right to be informed are quietly spiked.

Efforts to cast doubt on the integrity of opposing groups are spelt out specifically in the Timberlands Papers. For instance, notes from a meeting between Timberlands and Shandwick recorded that a 'Strategy Overview Discussion identified a number of opportunities where public relations can be applied to further the interest of Timberlands'. One of these opportunities was 'Environmental Front: Anti-NFA letter writing campaign (stock letters)...Dominion/Press letter re. NFA lies'.[41] This is a government body planning a letter-writing campaign attacking a conservation group, plans that were to be carried out for it by Shandwick. Another PR strategy paper contained the story angle that Paula de Roeper of Timberlands was planning to propose to a national magazine, focusing on the 'Lack of integrity of Forest & Bird.... forfeiting jobs and social structure of community through the population's innocent misunderstanding – orchestrated by F&B/NFA'.[42]

Sometimes Timberlands' attacks on Native Forest Action went to absurd lengths. The company's monitoring of the Internet revealed that the Australian-based Rainforest Information Centre website featured information from NFA criticising Timberlands' beech forest logging plans. In November 1998 the Rainforest Information Centre received an e-mail letter encouraging it to remove the criticisms from the website. 'Native Forest Action are selfish, greedy, righteous, ignorant and downright liars,' the writer fulminated. 'They have proven to be guilty of deliberately misleading the New Zealand public.'

In a more conciliatory tone, the writer suggested that the Rainforest Information Centre 'carefully screen any information given out by such extreme preservationists – check out the real story at the Timberlands website.... Don't let these liars get any credibility.' Like the writers of various of the anti-NFA letters to the editor of West Coast newspapers, the author turned out to be an employee of Timberlands, working in its strategic planning section.[43]

Imagine heading down to the post office to collect an unexpected registered letter. Inside is a missive from a legal firm you have never heard of threatening to sue you and your environmental colleagues up to $100,000 because you have been protesting against native forest logging. It would be enough to scare many people off.

In the United States legal threats against community groups have become common. Most cases never proceed to court or, if they do, rarely succeed. Their purpose is not redress for actual harm, but to discourage opponents of the corporations making the threats. Two leading American academics, George Pring and Penelope Canaan, who have studied the phenomenon, labelled legal threats against community activists 'strategic lawsuits against public participation'. They are now regularly referred to by the acronym SLAPPs.

Pring and Canaan's decade-long study found that 'SLAPPs are filed by one side of a public political dispute to punish or prevent opposing points of view. They are an attempt to "privatise" public debate – a unilateral effort by one side to transform a public political dispute into a private legal adjudication shifting both forum and issues to the disadvantage of the other side.'[44]

Although the vast majority of SLAPPs are dismissed, as a New York judge observed, they frequently succeed in discouraging both the politically outspoken and observers and stifle important public discussion and dispute. 'Short of a gun to the head, a greater threat to First Amendment expression can scarcely be imagined,' he said.[45]

Timberlands eagerly embraced this tactic. It made numerous threats via its lawyers, Pitt & Moore, against environmental critics and others who supported them. None of them ended up in court; the main aim appears to have been intimidation.

The principal targets, not surprisingly, were the environment groups protesting against the company. The Timberlands Papers include much correspondence between Timberlands and Pitt & Moore about ways in which the company might have protesters arrested for criminal offences or make a civil claim, 'for example a civil injunction or proceedings for deliberate interference by unlawful means with TWC's contractual relations'.[46]

One Pitt & Moore letter of 18 April 1997, following up on a telephone discussion that day, listed 25 'possibilities of criminal action against one or more of the protesters'.[47] The list contained everything from disorderly assembly to excreting in a public place, in each case with details of whether the police have the right to arrest without warrant and the penalty. Dozens of environmentalists were arrested and taken to court on a range of offences in the 1997-99 period, for actions that, in

New Zealand, are usually viewed as peaceful protest and kept out of court. Timberlands even succeeded in enlisting the full support of the local police in using the flimsy pretext of 'finding lost property' to break up a protest camp and take all the equipment, food and personal belongings to the police station.

Pitt & Moore authored a 'How to deal with protesters' sheet advising Timberlands contractors how to make trespass warnings and a trespass warning poster to put on logging roads and offering advice on delivering legal letters to protesters. The lawyers understood that Timberlands might not want to be directly associated with heavy-handed legal threats. A letter from Pitt & Moore partner Jane Pearson noted that 'If Timberlands wishes to distance itself somewhat [from the trespass warning letters], I am more than happy to send the letter on your behalf on Pitt & Moore letterhead, although we may need to use your staff to identify the protesters and deliver the letters to them'.[48]

During the Charleston forest tree-sitting protest in early 1997, Timberlands' managers quickly lost patience with the protesters. The general manager of planning, Kit Richards, said, 'We will either get the logs or cover the costs from named parties. We know who they are.... They have made their point ... To continue is a waste of time.'[49]

A week later a registered letter was sent from Pitt & Moore to NFA's Wellington post office box addressed, sweepingly, to 'Native Forest Action, its members, anyone acting or protesting on its behalf or anyone else protesting about the felling of native trees'. It warned its readers that 'If Timberlands is unable to continue with its logging operations due to protest action, Timberlands will suffer civil loss'. Nor did the company feel constrained by the normal legal protocol of individually naming who it was warning. 'You are put on notice that Timberlands will hold Native Forest Action, its members, anyone acting or protesting on its behalf or anyone else protesting about the felling of native trees in its forests personally responsible for damages for all economic loss suffered by Timberlands due to breach of its supply obligations.'

If that was not enough to deter protest, it kept its best line until last. 'These damages are likely to be in excess of $100,000,' Pitt & Moore wrote, without detailing how it arrived at this figure.[50] On the day the letter was posted Timberlands issued a media release to contain any criticism of its tactics. Downplaying the legal threat, Timberlands CEO Dave Hilliard described the letters 'as basic housekeeping' and 'confirmed' that it had started to 'issue notices of warning to Charleston protesters'.

PITT & MOORE

BARRISTERS, SOLICITORS AND NOTARIES PUBLIC	Partners	Directory

Partners
John Michael Hollyer LL.B.
Graham Wallace Allan LL.B.(Hons)
David William Farnsworth LL.B. Notary Public
Dennis Edward Creed LL.B.
William Barton Rainey LL.B.
Robert Alan Lane LL.B. Dip Acc
Consultant
Richard Barton Rainey O.B.E. Notary Public
Associate
Jane Margaret Pearson LL.B.(Hons)

Directory
78 Selwyn Place, Nelson
PO Box 42, Nelson, New Zealand
Telephone 03-548 8349
Fax 03-546 9153
email pittmoore.co.nz

Writer's direct dial
no. 545 6717

18 March 1997

Our Ref:

JMP:he:c4:178

BY REGISTERED POST

Native Forest Action, its members,
  anyone acting or protesting on its
  behalf or anyone else protesting
  about the felling of native trees
c/ Native Forest Action
P O Box 11 964
WELLINGTON

TIMBERLANDS WEST COAST LIMITED ("TWC")

We act for TWC.

You should be aware that the protest action in TWC's forest is an unlawful activity by obstructing TWC's log recovery operations.

TWC views any involvement in the protest as deliberate interference by unlawful means with its contractual relations with third parties, and/or its trade and business.

If TWC is unable to continue with its logging operations due to the protest action, TWC will suffer civil loss. You are put on notice that TWC will hold Native Forest Action, its members, anyone acting or protesting on its behalf or anyone else protesting about the felling of native trees in its forests personally responsible for damages for all economic loss suffered by TWC due to breach of its supply obligations. These damages are likely to be in excess of $100,000.

PITT & MOORE
per:

Jane Pearson
ASSOCIATE

Pitt & Moore threat to NFA, 18 March 1997. Inside was a letter from a legal firm they had never heard of, threatening to sue them and anyone else protesting against native forest logging for up to $100,000.

Hilliard's media release was carefully crafted to suggest that the threatening letter had been sent out of concern for the welfare of individuals. Acknowledging that Timberlands had already indicated protesters might be sued for damages, Hilliard said that 'in fairness it was now important that the protesters fully understood the implications of their actions'. Contradicting Timberlands' internal PR strategy documents, Hilliard wrote 'the protest has achieved nothing and will not advance the conservation debate at all'. The legal threat, however, was designed to deter further protest. 'It is time to weigh up the potential personal cost and long-term impact of court convictions and debt to individuals,' Hilliard warned, 'as will surely occur if the protest continues.'[51]

The forest protesters were initially shocked by the letter but, after getting legal advice, and learning the new term SLAPP, they were more annoyed than intimidated by the tactic. As is best in such cases, they simply ignored the threats and no legal action eventuated.

Another Pitt & Moore letter to Native Forest Action claimed that a poster and press release had been 'defamatory and libellous and likely to cause Timberlands pecuniary loss'. It said that the poster implied that Timberlands 'operates most improperly and not in due accordance with corporate ethics or laws'. The press release, which was issued following the sale of a closed Westport sawmill, 'clearly intended to expose Timberlands to public hatred and contempt'. The Westport sawmill had taken logs from the disputed Charleston Forest until 1994 when, amid protests by the local sawmillers, Timberlands gave priority to a mill 140 kilometres away. The mill had subsequently gone bust and most of the jobs reliant on native logging in the Buller region had been lost.

The letter requested apologies, retraction of the press release and removal of all the posters by 5 p.m. on 20 May 1997. Their letter went on to warn that if 'you do not agree to our requests, we will advise Timberlands to seek a declaration from the Court that Native Forest Action Incorporated is liable to it in defamation, and/or an order requiring you to publish a correcting statement'. That was not all: 'In such an instance punitive damages may be sought against you'.[52]

Again NFA simply ignored the letter. Timberlands was persistent, sending another letter after the deadline had passed. This, too, was ignored. Despite the dire warnings about the heavy damage Timberlands had sustained as a result of the press release and the posters, nothing more was heard. SLAPPs usually rely on scaring the target. When this did not work, Timberlands quietly backed down. Forest and Bird also received, and ignored, various defamation threats from Timberlands.

During the tree-sitting protest the Alliance Party deputy leader, Jeanette Fitzsimons, wrote to the logging helicopter contractors, Heli Harvest Ltd. She pointed out that, under Civil Aviation Act regulations that came into effect on 1 April 1997, there was a duty on pilots to avoid unnecessary danger operating in areas where people were present. The legislation, she said, could open the way for the prosecution of pilots if protesters were in the flight paths. 'I would urge you to postpone your operations in the area occupied by the protesters until they have left,' she wrote. 'If you do in fact fly in these conditions I would regard it as a serious breach of the safety regulations and would consider what other actions should be taken.' [53]

Heli Harvest was co-operating closely with Timberlands in its political campaign. On the day it received the Fitzsimons letter, the manager, John Funnell, forwarded it to Minister of State Owned Enterprises, Jenny Shipley, 'to see if Jeanette Fitzsimons can not be encouraged to go about her job in a more positive manner in the interests of the country in total. Not acting for a select group who fail to understand or do not want to understand that Timberlands are making significant progress in working towards harvesting timber in a totally sustainable way.' [54]

Heli Harvest also took the extraordinary step of threatening to sue Jeanette Fitzsimons:

> *As you were the person who officially advised us that we would be in breach of the Civil Aviation rules and regulations if we operated in the forest, and because we have no means of contacting the organisation you apparently represent, we have no option other than to serve notice on you.... We wish to advise you that should we be prevented from undertaking our contractual obligations as a result of the illegal occupation of the land by protesters, we would seek compensation appropriate to our losses from those responsible. This unfortunately may include yourself if you refuse to pass this information to the group in question.* [55]

Jeanette Fitzsimons was unimpressed, describing Heli Harvest's letter as a 'pathetic attempt at intimidation'. She told journalists that she did not claim to represent the forest protesters. Further, she noted that the protesters were camping legally on public land until such time as they were personally served with a trespass notice, which most had not been. [56]

In November 1998, when the government was moving towards a decision to phase out the logging in the forests where NFA had been protesting, Timberlands threatened legal action again. CEO Dave Hilliard went on National Radio saying that if the logging ended, the company would seek several million dollars in compensation from its own controlling shareholder, the government. While trying to avoid talk of suing during an interview, he attempted to argue for the principle that any constraint on corporate behaviour required compensation. 'We could be any company. We have a contract with another party who happens to be the Crown and Timberlands wouldn't be suing the Crown,' Hilliard claimed. 'We would be just simply looking to our rights under our contract. If, in those rights, it requires compensation to be paid for any changes to the contract, well then obviously we'll be looking to ... how we can best benefit our shareholders, ultimately the people of New Zealand, by doing so.'

To leading political figures, this was a government-owned agency out of control, using threats of legal action to lobby those to whom it was answerable. Opposition leader Helen Clark was astonished. Timberlands, she said, 'keeps saying that it operates only according to government policy and direction. If it then wants to turn around and bite the government by suing because it doesn't like the government policy and direction.... I think that the government should give serious consideration to disbanding the board and looking at whether it wants to continue with the state company at all.'[57]

Not sensing that it was overplaying its hand, Timberlands continued with the legal threats. In 1999, the company emulated the actions of anti-environmental groups in Australia and sent a bill to protesters seeking compensation for time lost from logging operations because of protest actions. Following anti-logging protests in January and February 1999, Native Forest Action received a formal tax invoice for $1,562.62, itemising the supposed costs of staff time and vehicle mileage spent dealing with the protests. A month later the group got a reminder invoice for these uninvited services. In June 1999 Timberlands advanced to threats in a letter from corporate services manager Jacqui Low: 'Dear Sir, Overdue Account: According to our records $1,562.62 remains unpaid on your debtors account.... Previous requests for payment have been ignored and we therefore insist on settlement within seven days otherwise the debt will be passed on to our legal department.'[58] NFA was advised to inform Timberlands that it did not accept liability and as before, to take no notice of the threats.

On many more occasions, legal threats were considered but Timberlands did not pursue them. One set of teleconference minutes noted 'NFA: Booklet [of forest reserve proposals] to go to Shandwick. We need to obtain copies of the original.' The first thoughts in reviewing the document were not for its policy proposals but its potential for legal action. 'We will review its content for libellous action,' the minutes noted, before going on to suggest 'perhaps we need to consider personalising some of our media releases'.[59]

Timberlands had become obsessed with finding any opportunity to make legal threats against its opponents. Minutes of another teleconference recorded 'To discuss with Pitt & Moore the NFA pamphlet from Rotorua [a forest industries conference]. Could be libellous?' Shandwick's Rob McGregor was charged with following through.[60]

Politicians and environmentalists were not the only ones on the receiving end of legal threats from Timberlands. A series of such moves were made against journalists who had incurred Timberlands' displeasure; some of them proved effective in silencing coverage critical of the company.[61] Despite all the threats and the tens of thousands of dollars spent on legal advice, not one action was initiated by Timberlands, let alone proceeded to hearing.

The rise of SLAPPs in the United States has created a number of responses by environmentalists and civil libertarians. Environmental law groups have developed materials and run training courses for citizens on what their rights are and how to deal with legal threats. Some individuals who have been 'SLAPPed' have successfully counter-sued. In New Zealand and Australia, too, legal threats against community groups have been increasing but, without the constitutional right to free speech that exists in the United States, community groups are in a weaker legal position. Some even argue that simply referring to a legal threat against a community group which has not gone to court as a SLAPP may be defamatory because it implies an inaccurate motive for the action.

The proliferation of legal threats against community advocates in the Unites States has prompted the passing of legislation in about a dozen states seeking to protect the public right to free speech. In California the legislature found 'there has been a disturbing increase in lawsuits brought primarily to chill the valid exercise of the constitutional rights of freedom of speech and petition for the redress of grievances'. The California legislature, in what has become model anti-SLAPP legislation, made provision for those being sued to apply for the action to be struck out within 60 days. In this way members of the community can obtain

an early determination on whether the action has any probability of suc-
ceeding and if their strike-out motion is successful can be awarded costs
for their legal expenses.

In the wake of the 'McLibel' trial in Britain, in which McDonalds
sued some of its critics and created a PR disaster for itself, many PR practitioners warn companies against taking legal action. There is a further
risk for companies. In initiating a legal action, they risk opening themselves up for the legal process of 'discovery', where the court can direct
that relevant documents be made available to the opposite parties. For
companies that thrive on secrecy, the risk of documents becoming public, and doing far more damage than the statements or actions that caused
the initial offence, is significant. That may help to explain why, although
Timberlands made plenty of legal threats, none were ever taken further.

FACSIMILE TRANSMISSION

Att::	Paula de Roeper	**Fax:**	Auto
At:	TWC	**From:**	Lee Harris Royal
Date:	29 September, 1998		
Pages:	10	**CC:**	
Re:			

☐ **Urgent**   ☐ **Confidential**   ☐ **Please Comment**   ☐ **F.Y.I.**

Dear Paula

Attached is a profile document outline from Klaus plus the Bodyshop material you asked for.
The economic status for F&B is in process....I hope to have that to you this afternoon.

The key issue in the Bodyshop material is the connection between the New Zealand Bodyshop
franchise owners and Art for Art's Sake, who (at the time this material was gathered) used
Rimu in their framing. The 'path' for this is Charleston Forest ⇒ Westco Lagan ⇒ Avonhead
Sawmilling ⇒ Art for Art's Sake.

I hope this is of assistance

Kind regards,

Lee Harris Royal

---

*Shandwick investigated the finances of Forest and Bird and dug out
information to attack the Body Shop.*

48

The Royal Forest and Bird Protection Society, New Zealand's oldest and largest conservation organisation, has been Timberlands' most consistent critic over the last decade. This position has earned it repeated public criticism from the company for its 'extreme' views. Privately, using the well-established PR tactic of researching any vulnerabilities or problems that can be exploited to attack the opposition, Timberlands employed Shandwick to investigate the society's finances.

The Timberlands Papers reveal precisely how this work was undertaken. In October 1997 Klaus Sorensen was delegated to check the annual returns of Forest and Bird: 'F&B balance sheet analysis to be done'. Meanwhile Timberlands staff were also involved: 'Full report to be accessed – Anne Pearson [Timberlands]'.[62] The following week Timberlands was still digging, with a detailed report due any time: 'F&B balance sheet analysis due at Timberlands shortly – Klaus Sorensen, Access to full report continues – Anne Pearson'.[63]

Late in October 1997 the report, entitled 'An analysis of the recent financial performance of Forest and Bird Society', prepared by Klaus Sorensen, chief executive of Shandwick, was finally completed and sent to Timberlands. The paper presented income and expenditure trends and a detailed financial breakdown and sought to identify weaknesses in the society's finances.

Despite the amount of time it had taken, Shandwick found little to warrant any recommendations. 'The treasurer,' Sorensen wrote, 'refers to the fact that too much time was spent on "management and organisational matters" and not enough on fundraising. To which one might add, too much time on activism and not enough time on forests and birds and conservation projects.'

In the absence of any hard material, Sorensen resorted to speculation: 'It would not be unrealistic to conclude that the reason for the expenditure falls in the areas of subscriptions, donations and grants reflects a growing unhappiness amongst traditional Forest and Bird members over what they see as the changing priorities, away from conservation projects and towards politicised actions'.[64]

Subsequent teleconference minutes mention work to find out the timing of Forest and Bird's annual general meeting, when members would raise issues about the society's activities and finances. In early 1998 Rob McGregor from Shandwick was delegated to 'Follow up the scheduled date for AGM of RF&B'.[65] The papers give no indication of what happened then.

This 1997-98 interest in Forest and Bird's finances is reminiscent of an earlier PR strategy devised to attack the society. An October 1995 public relations strategy paper entitled 'Forest and Bird: An endangered species?' analysed the society's finances, constitution, structure and vulnerabilities and proposed a 'concerted, long-term campaign aimed at discrediting Forest and Bird and dismantling its support base'. The authors of the paper, which was sent to selected natural resource users to seek financial support for the anti-Forest and Bird campaign, clearly did not want their identity to be widely known. The paper had no letterhead, no author names and no contact details. It merely stated 'Prepared by B.I.F.S. Consultants', which is not listed in any directories of public relations companies.

It is not surprising that the writers did not want their names on a document intended for (even limited) circulation. It contained a variety of dirty tactics, 'punitive action', including infiltrating Forest and Bird, and 'investigating the personalities'. The report recommended that 'a background on personalities within Forest and Bird will be undertaken to assess whether there is scope for pursuing avenues that may diminish the public credibility of these individuals. It is recognised that there is potential for this option to create unfavourable publicity unless managed carefully.'[66]

The paper, part of which is reproduced in Appendix D, appears to have been written for a timber company, which was at that time milling Timberlands rimu trees but subsequently stopped when the supplies were exhausted. The introduction to the paper explains that a response was needed to a 'disturbing trend' in which Forest and Bird had used minority shareholders to raise questions at a shareholders' meeting of the company about its West Coast native forest logging. The report said that, in conjunction with the timber company, 'we propose to develop a concerted campaign to counter Forest and Bird's activities'.

The paper had been leaked to environmentalists by a concerned official in a central government agency, to which it had been sent with a compliments slip attached from a major New Zealand fishing company well known for its anti-environmental views. Other people in the fishing industry later confirmed that it was being circulated. It is not known who the anonymous writers were or whether they had any connection with Timberlands or its PR companies, but the paper illustrates the tactics possible.

During the 1997-98 period Timberlands also attempted to cut off one of Native Forest Action's sources of campaign funding. This effort centred on the Body Shop, which Timberlands believed (incorrectly) was a major funder of the NFA campaign. The plan, devised and executed by Shandwick staff, was to find embarrassing information about the Body Shop's environmental record and use this to put pressure on the company to stop supporting the anti-native forest logging campaign.

The 'Body Shop initiative', described in detail in the Timberlands Papers, began in mid-1997 when the Body Shop displayed a Native Forest Action petition calling for an end to West Coast native forest logging and helped advertise a rally at Parliament.

The 'initiative' began with Rob McGregor of Shandwick writing to Anne Pearson at Timberlands: 'when we were walking past the Body Shop we saw a petition, you'll note the date of the rally is the day before the Ministers meet to consider the Officials report on options for Timberlands West Coast – no coincidence we think'. For the Shandwick staff, the Body Shop's support for rainforest protection was unwelcome and could not go unchallenged. McGregor explained to Timberlands that 'Klaus and I have yet to give this our full consideration – we wanted to get copies of the material to you without delay. However we have some tentative ideas. We should put this on the agenda for our telephone conference on Friday.'[67]

The following week the Body Shop's support for NFA was listed on the PR telephone conference agenda. 'Franchise owners of Body Shop are pro-active in green movement. Need to develop a campaign targeting them,' the minutes said.[68] Shandwick's Klaus Sorensen was charged with developing the campaign.

Shandwick then sent requests to consultants in overseas Shandwick offices looking for dirt on the Body Shop. They wrote to the international offices complaining that 'one of our clients in New Zealand, a State Owned forestry company, is having some trouble with misinformation being distributed, mainly originating from the Body Shop'. Shandwick did not waste any time getting to the point. 'Could you please fax us any information you can locate on Body Shop / Anita Roddick, especially any negative publicity on environmental issues', Maree Procter wrote on behalf of McGregor, who wanted the material quickly. 'We have a conference call with the client next Friday so we would appreciate this information by fax no later than Wednesday or Thursday.'[69] This was the same Maree Procter who had written twice to NFA as an interested member of the public seeking information on campaign plans.

The London office sent two reports on the Body Shop's international financial performance. In a cover note Neil Huband wrote: 'There is one thing I should mention, Anita Roddick has never had a particularly good relationship with the City partly because she is prone to campaigning against companies she considers not as ethical as the Body Shop claims to be'. Roddick, he added 'almost always receives coverage but this sort of impromptu environmental campaigning does nothing to improve the city's views of the company'.[70]

Daphne Luchtenberg of Shandwick's New York office replied that 'As far as we know we do not work for the Body Shop anywhere', but she mentioned that Shandwick had been part of the 'dealings and similar wranglings with The Body Shop over their campaign against Shell and Nigeria'. She offered help for Timberlands from American Shandwick staff who had assisted in that contract.[71]

Meanwhile Shandwick had been researching the financial affairs of Ashleigh Ogilvie-Lee, the owner of the Body Shop in New Zealand, and her husband Michael, and came up with what it thought was the information it wanted. In October 1997 Shandwick reported: 'NFA: Body Shop question has been addressed and action expected over the next week'. Sorensen was pleased with their progress.[72]

Shandwick had found that Michael Ogilvie-Lee owned part of a chain of shops called Art For Art's Sake which, in a small proportion of its picture frames, used rimu sourced from Timberlands. Sorensen had first offered the story to journalists from his old stamping ground, the *National Business Review*, in August 1997. They did not bite. Next he had phoned Maria Slade, a journalist on the *Independent* newspaper, proposing she do a story showing up the Body Shop's supposed hypocrisy. Later that day he sent her the information his firm had assembled.

He reported to Timberlands: 'Body Shop ongoing – publication of article anticipated. Suggestion that once published then an invitation to view sustainability be extended to Body Shop.'[73] The following week Shandwick was eagerly awaiting the dirt hitting the fan: 'Publication of article re Body Shop in Independent today'.[74]

It was an attack that backfired. The day before the *Independent* deadline Michael Ogilvie-Lee, now alerted to the use of Timberlands rimu, changed his company's policy to ensure that this wood was not used. The *Independent*'s front-page story was changed just before deadline. The final story, headlined 'Body Shop backs tree huggers', reported that Ogilvie-Lee 'had now persuaded the Art For Art's Sake chain to boycott Timberlands rimu, and [was] urging fellow traders to do the same'.[75]

A year later, when, along with other businesses, the Body Shop helped fund more advertisements in favour of stopping the logging, Timberlands and Shandwick went back on the offensive. Shandwick's

Lee Harris Royal wrote to Timberlands' Paula de Roeper: 'Attached is a profile document from Klaus plus the Body Shop material you asked for. The economic status of F&B is in process.... I hope to have that to you this afternoon. The key issue in the Bodyshop material is the connection between the New Zealand Body Shop franchise owners and Art for Art's Sake, who (at the time this material was gathered) used rimu in their framing. The "path" for this is Charleston Forest → Westco Lagan → Avonhead Sawmilling → Art for Art's Sake. I hope this is of assistance, Lee Harris Royal.'[76]

The report included printouts of Ashleigh and Michael Ogilvie-Lee's personal shareholdings, clippings received from Shandwick in Australia, and the reports from Shandwick in New York and London. (When Dave Hilliard was asked in 1999 if Timberlands had ever received information or advice from overseas Shandwick offices, he replied: 'No, no, it's rubbish. These conspiracy theories are rife, it's how they try and justify their position really. But it's rubbish as far as we're concerned.')[77]

Parliamentary journalists tell stories of other efforts to discredit the Body Shop. They mention Klaus Sorensen wandering around the press gallery spreading a story about a house owned previously by Ashleigh and Michael Ogilvie-Lee in Roseneath, Wellington. He claimed that the couple had used rimu timber in renovations several years before.

In December 1998 Timberlands was still talking about taking legal action against the Body Shop. In reply to a question from a parliamentary select committee about its expenditure on public relations, Timberlands grumpily attempted to justify its PR spending. 'This is particularly important where private companies and others, such as the Body Shop, have been funding and assisting with campaigns of misinformation about Timberlands' activities to boost their own sales and apparent conservation status. Recourse through the courts has been considered and not discounted to recover the pecuniary loss from commercially hostile activities.'[78]

When a journalist contacted Ashleigh Ogilvie-Lee about Hilliard's comments to the select committee, she was incensed at being threatened. She immediately phoned Native Forest Action to offer the group a five-figure donation for the following year – far more than she had ever given before. Timberlands' tactics had again backfired.

CHAPTER 3

GOLIATH STRIKES BACK

People in New Zealand don't actually appreciate hearing, seeing or reading of people sitting up trees to stop logging. I think that those that take that more radical view, they're wrong, quite simply, and when they try to press their cause by misinforming people or distorting the facts or telling out and out lies, well that to me is criminal, because if they were to succeed in doing what they aim to do and it's based on misinformation and lies, then future generations of New Zealand are going to have to pay for it, aren't they?

Dave Hilliard, 1999[1]

In February 1997, high above the floor of the Charleston rainforest, where Timberlands loggers were working their way along one side of a forested valley, a small group of Native Forest Action supporters established a tree-top protest, erecting tiny platforms made from wooden planks and rope. Timberlands immediately pulled its loggers out of the area, leaving a stark 'front': on one side tall rainforest, on the other a broken landscape where every saleable rimu tree had been felled, an area the protesters grimly named the 'Valley of Death and Destruction'. Timberlands hoped that, if it avoided direct confrontation, the protest would quietly run out of steam.

At first there were only about 20 protesters, from retired people to students. A few came from nearby West Coast towns but most were from faraway cities. The longer the protest went on, the more media coverage it gained. Newspaper articles featured photos of the treetop protest; radio stories sympathetically profiled the personalities of the protesters and the issues behind it. For many New Zealanders, the protesters were ordinary people, bravely trying to stop a corporation's logging of majestic native trees. It was David versus Goliath in New Zealand's rainforests.

In the first weeks Timberlands used legal threats, sent a series of self-justifying backgrounders to politicians and made some petty attacks on the protesters. On one occasion Kit Richards of Timberlands sent a letter and photographs to various ministers and Opposition MPs complaining that Timberlands' supervisors had 'found items of protesters' rubbish including Wellington flight tags' near the protest site in Charleston Forest. Richards attached photographs as 'evidence', showing a plastic drink bottle, a Kettles chips package and a few other items placed together on the stump of a recently felled tree. NFA replied that they, too, had seen the rubbish – it had been left by the loggers.

Despite Timberlands' actions, the protest continued into the autumn months. Support grew not only for the protest but also for the protection of the forests. International biologist David Bellamy offered his support to the protest and the campaign.[2] Even the West Coast mayors, historically noted for hostility to environmentalists, went to visit the protest camp as part of a tour looking for support for a compensation request to the government in exchange for ending the logging. Although the group did not make any public statements to the media, the fact that they visited was reported.

In response to the mounting public pressure the government announced it was looking at options to resolve

In February 1997 Native Forest Action established a treetop protest in Charleston Forest. The logging issue began to gain national prominence.
Photo: Alan Tennyson

the controversy. Timberlands was rapidly losing control of the debate. Rather than tolerate the protest, it went on the attack.

Early on 16 April 1997, the day after the visit from the mayors, a large group of Timberlands staff arrived in Charleston Forest with police, dogs and helicopters and began removing rimu logs. Two months earlier the protest had halted the logging, with many logs left where they had been felled. Now Timberlands wanted to remove these from the midst of the protest area.

But the purpose of the day was not only to collect logs. After nine weeks of the protest Timberlands had had enough. In official company papers, the day was described, in pseudo-military fashion, as 'Operation Alien'.[3] (Internal Timberlands reports consistently refer to the protesters as 'aliens'.) It was the company's chance to try to regain control of 'its' forest. Although only five 'aliens' were arrested that day, it marked the beginning of a much more aggressive attitude to policing the forest.

Timberlands described the operation as just being 'business as usual' – recovering 600 tonnes of rimu logs – but Operation Alien had vindictive motives as well. During the morning the Timberlands manager in charge of the operation instructed the helicopter pilot to try to wreck one of the main tree sitters' platforms, which had appeared in several newspaper photos.

Log-lifting helicopter over Charleston Forest. 'The logging helicopter... hovered over the tree for a few seconds before swinging the hanging log into the top of the tree. I scrambled, terrified for my life with debris and sticks raining down on me and the five-tonne log swinging above me' – Jenny Coleman, 18 April 1997.
Photo: Ben McDonald

The helicopter lifted a 5-tonne log from the skid site where the logs were stacked. It then diverted from its normal flight path and flew across the valley to the platform tree, which was in unlogged forest. With the log slung under the helicopter like an aerial battering ram, the pilot attempted to smash up the platform.

This would have been dangerous at the best of times, but what Timberlands did not know and had not checked was that an NFA member, Jenny Coleman, was just preparing to climb the tree when the helicopter began smashing into it. She was a zoology graduate who had studied marine sciences before joining the Native Forest Action campaign and becoming one of its most experienced climbers.

In a statement made afterwards, she said she had seen the logging helicopter divert from its usual route to hover briefly by her climbing tree shortly before she reached it. She had unpacked her climbing gear and was preparing to 'rig' the tree when the helicopter suddenly returned.

The logging helicopter… hovered over the tree for a few seconds before swinging the hanging log into the top of the tree. I scrambled, terrified for my life with debris and sticks raining down on me and the five-tonne log swinging above me… [I] turned to see the hanging log smashing branches from the tree above the platform and the tree swaying and creaking towards where I was.

I was completely freaked out and terrified for my life, and scrambled on my hands and knees, slipping on the muddy ground up the bank and down the ridge towards the river, away from the chopper. I leapt into a hollow under a rotten tree stump below the edge of the ridge and vomited with fear as I crouched in the wet ferns.[4]

Interviewed by a film-maker a few days later, Timberlands general manager Kit Richards confirmed that 'what [the helicopter pilot] was doing was removing the platform. He actually used that log to break the platform because the protesters were obviously making an effort [pause] it would remain a point of interest to try and climb.' When asked about the risk to Jenny Coleman, he said 'Oh, we've heard that claim, and we had staff on the ground standing next to that tree….The protesters had made a move to try to get to the tree [but] they moved away again as our staff approached.'[5]

The subsequent Civil Aviation investigation found that this was not true. The report by investigating officer Damian Paine concluded 'it is evident that no ground search of the area directly adjacent to the base of the platform tree was undertaken prior to the helicopter manoeuvring overhead the platform tree'. Timberlands had relied on advice from contractors in two helicopters who could not see anyone below.[6]

Timberlands' handwritten diary of the operation gives an idea what it was like that day. A large group of Timberlands staff and contractors and eight police watched the operation from the far side of the river where the logs were being piled, relying on helicopters to try to spot protesters in the heavy bush. For the environmentalists attempting to avoid arrest in the forest it was a distressing day; for the long-thwarted Timberlands staff, Operation Alien was the protesters' comeuppance.

Charleston staff and contractors arrive 5.45am. Weather crap and clears.
1. *Debrief of staff.*
2. *Set up HQ – flitch site.*
3. *Police arrive.*
4. *Heli Harvest [log-lifting helicopter] arrives from Nelson.*
5. *Bush men and RH etc into logging area. Daylight.*
6. *J Cowan and Police do heli-inspection of the area – No contact.*
7. *J Funnell, W Pratt and C Cowan [helicopter contractors] Heli-inspection. No contact – area declared clear.*
8. *Lift commences 9.06am.... Funnell spots tree platform.*
9. *First lift complete – No contact. Second run commences...*
10. *Funnell and LM decide area clear – W Pratt to destroy platform. RH states make sure no aliens are in it. Pratt and crew and Cowan and [his crew] cannot see any aliens – proceed to break platform and ropes (visibility good).*
11. *Pratt sights protester in bush heading towards river. RH, CH and Mat hear woman screaming on ridge 30 metres from platform....'*[7]

That was not the end of it. Shortly after the diary records: 'Pratt [pilot] moves to another area. 2nd platform found – near stream.' But they realised this one should not be interfered with. 'Leave, is in Riparian Zone.'

Later that day, Timberlands contractors were sent to the 500-year-old rimu tree that hosted Jenny Coleman's tree platform. In an area that was not otherwise being logged, they set to work and felled the tree: 'Fly in Olsen – cut down tree and fly out,' the diary recorded. Not content with their handiwork, they scrawled obscene messages about two of the leading tree sitters: 'Annette Cotter you dyke bitch' and 'Richard you're a fuckwit too'. It was to be the only tree they felled that day, prompting NFA to describe it to the media as 'spite felling'.

When, the following week, MP Rod Donald asked SOE minister Jenny Shipley in Parliament about the police and Timberlands' actions, she replied her advice was that 'nobody was put at risk'. She claimed that 'everybody was warned at the entrance to the forest if they went on to the forest floor illegally they would be putting themselves and others at risk. I am advised that in every instance where there was any risk logging was stopped and people were told to move.'[8] The forest entrance was in fact several kilometres from where the logging operations and the protest camp were located. The main people kept out at the entrance were journalists.

Timberlands' attempt to deal with the platform problem created another obstacle. The tree sitters, upset about the near accident, decided to complain to the Civil Aviation Authority (CAA). Three days after Operation Alien, a formal complaint was laid about 'serious and unnecessary danger to people engaged in a peaceful protest'. The CAA agreed to investigate, but Timberlands was not prepared to allow the statutory investigation to proceed along its own neutral track.

Behind the scenes, a Shandwick staff member, Rob McGregor, undertook the task of lobbying an acquaintance within the CAA on behalf of Timberlands and its helicopter contractor. In a fax stamped CONFIDENTIAL to Timberlands' general manager operations, John Birchfield, McGregor later reported on his efforts: 'I spoke with Martyn Gosling from Civil Aviation.... After much reminiscing, he said they are "still tying a few loose ends together" but the message for Timberlands is "Don't panic"'. Gosling is the CAA public relations person.

In an attempt to discredit the complaint, McGregor told Gosling that it was politically motivated. 'I explained Timberlands' concerns – a significant part of your operation is reliant upon the helicopter and that without the helicopter you would not be able to continue with the sustainable logging of the exotic forest. I also pointed out that this point was not lost on the complainants and had presumably motivated their complaint to CAA. They are fully aware of the political considerations behind this complaint and seem to appreciate your perspective.'

McGregor was pleased with his lobbying work, reporting to Timberlands, 'I got the strong feeling that there are not going to be any problems for you from this inquiry. I was also told that we have to re-main silent on this for the time being.'[9]

The CAA files, obtained under the Official Information Act, contain a report on the case written by the authority's Aviation Enforcement Unit controller, Peter McNeill, a week before this private lobbying and the comments McGregor took as reassurance from Martyn Gosling. McNeill's report stated that the investigating officer had 'raised the question of whether what was done, namely the operation of the helicopter with a sling load to demolish a tree platform, amounted to operating an aircraft in a careless manner in terms of section 43A'.

McNeill referred that judgement to a specialist. While Shandwick's McGregor was reassuring Timberlands, the matter had only just reached the desk of the helicopter operations specialist, Ted Hawker. McNeill himself did not reach his conclusion on the case for another month. Shandwick's pleading on behalf of Timberlands that a conviction would disturb operations and the suggestion that the CAA appreciated their 'perspective' raises serious questions about the investigation into a life-threatening incident.

This was not the only involvement of Martyn Gosling. On the day of the alleged offence, Gosling was quoted in the news as saying that Timberlands had conducted the helicopter operation in a safe manner – even though no CAA staff had been present and no investigation had occurred.[10] The following day, after NFA had announced that it intended to lay a complaint with the authority, Gosling was lobbied by Heli Harvest. The helicopter contractor John Funnell (who refused to be interviewed in the formal CAA investigation) faxed Gosling a long justification of its actions that the company had prepared for SOE minister Jenny Shipley's private secretary.

In the end the CAA concluded that no offence had been committed, in a large part because of a technicality. New civil aviation regulations that had come into force two weeks before Operation Alien might have led to a conviction for Heli Harvest Ltd, but an administrative anomaly meant that the necessary punishment provisions did not come into force until a month later. Still open, however, was the question of whether the platform smashing constituted careless operation of a helicopter.

Doubts remain about the investigation. Its final stage appears highly inadequate. The issue of careless operation was referred to the CAA helicopter specialist, Ted Hawker, who made contact with John Funnell, the owner of the logging helicopter who had previously refused to co-operate in the investigation. Despite all the signed statements and other evidence already collected by the CAA investigating officer, their telephone conversation (of which no record was made) seems to have determined the outcome of the three month investigation.

Hawker's report quotes Funnell saying that his observations from the helicopter 'indicated that the area surrounding the platform tree was clear of persons'. But, much stranger than this, the report shows that Hawker's decision is based on a version of events which contradicts everything else in the investigation: 'The helicopter was then used to deny persons access to the platform by removing the rope ladder leading to the platform with a log slung underneath the helicopter. I have spoken to John Funnell about this and was told that all they tried to do was pull the rope up and away from the tree, thereby denying people access to the tree.'[11]

There was no rope ladder and the investigation had already proved without doubt that the objective was to destroy the platform. Hawker's report concluded that 'reasonable steps were taken to ensure that the area was clear of persons prior to and during the operation' and, most important for whether there would be a conviction, 'I do not consider the use of a helicopter, using the underslung log to lift the rope away from the tree, as careless or dangerous'. The fact that these strikingly inaccurate findings relied on a casual phone call with the owner of the company in risk of conviction, gives little confidence in the CAA process. When Shandwick was actively working to influence the investigation, it must be asked whether Timberlands' PR concerns interfered with the requirement for impartiality in an official investigation.

Timberlands was sufficiently reassured by Shandwick's informal contacts with the CAA to deny publicly that the incident had even occurred. In a letter to the editor of Victoria University's *Salient* complaining about a story the magazine had published, Timberlands' Dave Hilliard said that a report of the event in the magazine had been 'to say the least, a flight of fancy.' He wrote: 'At the time of the alleged incident there were several Timberlands staff, an independent inspector from Occupational Safety & Health (OSH) and a police observer. All were within sight of where this incident was reputed to have occurred. All these persons have sworn that no such incident occurred and that at no time was any individual in danger.' These 'observers' were actually half a kilometre away across the river, but Hilliard was feeling confident. 'The whole incident is now the subject of a formal CAA investigation,' he continued, 'the outcome of which Timberlands staff eagerly await.'[12]

Operation Alien began a series of more aggressive statements and tactics by Timberlands against the forest protesters.

Two days later NFA members protesting in another logging area in the nearby Buller Gorge provided an excuse to turn criticism back onto the environmentalists. The destruction of the treetop platform had shaken the protesters. Clearly, there were no guarantees that the helicopter crew could see people on the ground or that ground checks would be done. To prevent a further risk to ground-based protesters, a number of distress flares were obtained for use in any future potentially dangerous situations.

The logging helicopter had moved to the nearby Buller Gorge area after temporarily completing its work in Charleston Forest. One of the NFA members camped in logged forest in this second area became worried about the helicopter operating too close to where he was hiding. Fearing a repetition of the recent near-miss, he waited until the helicopter moved about half a kilometre away and then let off a distress flare to mark his position.

Smarting from the bad publicity it had received over the destruction of the treetop platform, Timberlands seized the opportunity to discredit the protesters. Dave Hilliard described the flare incident as 'reprehensible' and 'disgusting' behaviour. 'They're not protesters,' he told the media, 'they're trespassers and criminals.'

The police, who had taken no interest in the platform-smashing incident, used a private helicopter to search for the person who had let off the flare. Greymouth Senior Sergeant Phil Deazley said it 'bordered on a criminal act' and said a flare was 'capable of bringing down a helicopter'. Jenny Shipley stated that the protesters 'must not put lives at risk with irresponsible or illegal behaviour'. It mattered little that the flare was not aimed at or near the helicopter.

Less than a fortnight after the platform-smashing incident, things turned even nastier. While thousands of veterans across New Zealand were remembering distant wars at Anzac Day dawn memorial services, a crew member of Heli Harvest's twin-engine Mil-8 Russian ex-military helicopter made a startling discovery: a single 140-gram stick of gelignite taped to the wheel of the machine.

The heavy-lift helicopter, owned by the Taupo-based company, was the one contracted by Timberlands to lift rimu trees from the logged forests. At the time of the incident, the helicopter was parked on private land at Karamea, 100 kilometres to the north of Charleston Forest.

When police went to the site and 'disarmed' what would later be referred to by media as a 'bomb', they were informed that the helicopter had been watched by a security guard until 3 o'clock that Friday morning. When the helicopter crew were conducting a pre-flight check at 7 a.m. they found the gelignite taped to the machine.[13] The gelignite, a stick of Powergel, had been manufactured in Auckland and, although the purchase and sale of explosives required permits, serial numbers were attached only to each package not to individual sticks.

Over the long weekend few knew of the incident. On the following Monday news of the gelignite was confirmed by police after a local radio station had received an anonymous tip-off. It became big news, quickly being picked up by media outlets around the country.

Greymouth police acting regional commander, Senior Sergeant Phil Deazley, considered the motivation obvious, pronouncing that the 'bomb'

When news of gelignite on a logging helicopter reached the forest protesters, they could see how damaging it might be to their non-violent campaign.

63

was an act of 'eco-terrorism',[14] even though no suspects or anyone involved with Native Forest Action had been interviewed. Sergeant John
Canning from the Westport police said 'it goes past protesting as we
know it in New Zealand – it borders on terrorism'.[15] Timberlands chief
executive, Dave Hilliard, told television journalists that the explosive
device was 'eco-terrorism at its worst'.[16] Police undertook fingerprint
tests and forwarded the gelignite to the head of explosives at the Department of Labour in Christchurch for examination.

Jenny Shipley contradicted earlier reports and insisted that a fuse
had been found with the gelignite.[17] Senior Sergeant Deazley sought to
reassure journalists that 'it is not a fake bomb. It is the real thing.'[18] All
this was taking place on the first day after news of the explosive appeared. Late that afternoon the head of Heli Harvest, John Funnell, said
on radio that, given the absence of a timing device, he did not think the
explosive was intended to go off in the air, but on the ground. 'All those
people are married with children, and I just think that's grossly unfair,
and we view that as an act bordering on terrorism,' he said.[19] Funnell
conceded he had no evidence that protesters had planted the Powergel,
but claimed he had no information that 'it was anything other than a
group such as this'.[20] He declined to name the pilots, in order to protect
the men involved.[21]

In Parliament that afternoon Jenny Shipley rose in question time
to respond to a question from Greens MP, Jeanette Fitzsimons, on
whether she had any evidence to support the 'eco-terrorism' claim.
Shipley was forced to concede that 'she had no evidence who had
planted the bomb'.[22] She did say, however, that police 'had forensic evidence available to them and have utilised all of the resources available
to try to identify the person or persons who have been involved'.

Across the Tasman there have been many unproven claims of 'eco-
terrorism' by sections of the Australian timber industry.[23]

If the Anzac Day 'bomb' was intended to discredit the protest, it
failed. When news of the allegations first reached environmentalists they
could see how damaging they were to a campaign that relied on public
support. An accusation of 'eco-terrorism', especially when made by authority figures such as the police, put them in the almost impossible
position of proving their innocence by media deadlines.

The environmental groups involved in the logging issue knew they
were not responsible for the explosive. If anyone had known anything,
it would eventually have surfaced. It was also highly unlikely to be an
individual environmentalist working alone as the chances were small of

one person locating the helicopter during its brief and irregular visit to the isolated Karamea location.

Native Forest Action reacted quickly. Its spokespeople, aware of dirty tricks in Australia, pointed to overseas examples of false bomb accusations used to discredit environmentalists. Lance Armstrong, a Tasmanian Green MP, happened to be in New Zealand and spoke out. NFA even offered a reward of $3,000 for information on the real culprits. Supporters of the anti-logging campaign, including MPs, did not believe the accusations and publicly supported the group.

Furious at the partisan statements of West Coast police officers, NFA contacted police headquarters.[24] Subsequently, the South Island regional commander, Paul Fitzharris, assured Kevin Hackwell from NFA that the police had an open mind on the investigation. He noted that they had interviewed none of the people associated with the protest.

By Thursday, Senior Sergeant Phil Deazley, who on Monday had proclaimed the 'bomb' an act of 'eco-terrorism', was claiming that 'we have always had an open mind' on the investigation. The term 'eco-terrorism' was not meant to imply that any particular group, and particularly Native Forest Action Group, was involved in this offence'.[25]

Timberlands was feeling the heat too. The day after portraying the incident as an act of 'eco-terrorism', a company spokesperson denied that Hilliard had blamed anyone: 'Timberlands is not pointing the finger at anybody'.[26]

By the time the news interest blew over a few days later, the general public, even on the West Coast, did not believe that Native Forest Action was responsible. The mayor of Buller, Pat O'Dea, said 'because of the politics of these type of things it could have come from anywhere'.[27] He stated that 'A lot of people are quite happy to have the protesters there. They believe Timberlands has cheated on the Accord and the trees should stay there … because there is no benefit [to Buller from milling them]'.[28] West Coast MP Damien O'Connor also rejected Timberlands' finger pointing and suggested that many on the Coast bore a grudge against the company.[29]

The enthusiasm by both the police and the Department of Labour for releasing details of the 'bomb' was shortlived. Both government departments have refused to release any material in response to Official Information Act requests made in the course of writing this book, claiming that doing so 'could be prejudicial to the law'.[30] This means that there is no way of independently checking how seriously the police searched for a culprit after the possibility of a hoax was raised.

Whatever the motive for the 'bomb', it was exploited immediately by Timberlands. Fears of the 'bomb' being used to justify a crackdown on the protests proved justified. Shipley told Parliament that 'no matter how strongly people feel about this issue there is never any justification for putting human life at risk'. 'Given recent events,' she warned, 'which clearly threaten everyone's safety, Timberlands is now considering anew what action it should take if any unauthorised persons are found in the forests.'[31]

It had not taken Timberlands long to consider what action to take. The day after news of the explosive first appeared, the company said it would not tolerate any further disruption of its logging plans. 'Attitudes have hardened significantly. They're not welcome in our forests any longer,' Hilliard told the media.[32] He dismissed any possibility that the 'bomb' was a dirty trick aimed at discrediting protesters: 'It is ridiculous and insulting, to say the least, that anyone can try to pin the accusations on the people that work for Timberlands on the West Coast, or West Coast people in general.'[33]

Hilliard ridiculed the suggestion that NFA was being set up: 'I think the protesters have a bit of inflated feeling of the importance of their protest and themselves given that it's basically ineffectual.' Hilliard expressed a lack of interest in the NFA campaign: 'I mean, Timberlands is not really interested in anything to do with the lobbying they're trying to do'. For Hilliard there was a simple conciliatory solution to the controversy: the protesters should withdraw. 'The only way to resolve the issue now,' he suggested, 'is for the protesters to remove themselves and lower the heat in the argument.'

To the environmental protesters it all felt too convenient. They were never interviewed by the police about the extremely serious crime of which they had been accused, but the incident became an excuse for Timberlands to stamp down on their long-running protest. In the following weeks the police co-operated with Timberlands arresting protesters in Charleston Forest.

Subsequently, Timberlands supporters have used the term 'eco-terrorist' to discredit environmentalists; this attack included the Greymouth newspaper printing a series of letters accusing Sean Weaver and other NFA members of supporting 'eco-terrorism'. A leading private investigator in the United States, Sheila O'Donnell, who has investigated many instances of harassment of activists, explained her concerns about accusations of 'eco-terrorism'. 'I see that calling an environmentalist a terrorist sets up a fear dynamic,' she told journalist David Helvarg. 'It makes the police and private security firms begin to worry. It sets the stage for a counter-reaction and makes anti-environmental violence seem like an acceptable response.'[34]

In the week after the 'bomb' was found, a group of men hired by Timberlands found the main protest camp. They clearfelled an area nearby for a helicopter landing and seized all of the protesters' tents, food and personal belongings. For the next three days police held the protesters' personal possessions under the pretext that they were 'lost property', until an increasingly insistent series of orders from the South Island regional commander in Christchurch forced their return. The environmentalists had to stay in the forest without tents, sleeping bags or food until more equipment could be tramped in to rebuild the camp. For weeks afterwards, hired guards stayed in the forest all the time, with trip-wires across main tracks (which caused a noise if walked into) so they could try to catch protesters who came and went at night.

There was an interesting sequel. In early 1999, when 'NFA eco-terrorist' letters to the editor were still appearing in the West Coast papers, Timberlands contractors discovered that one of their road-making machines had been vandalised on a logging road in Charleston Forest. Although this occurred at the same time as ongoing non-violent but controversial NFA protests, including blockading a nearby logging road and two members locking themselves onto the logging helicopter, the loggers let it be known within the local community that they did not suspect NFA. 'It's not their style,' they said.[35]

At the same time as Timberlands began arresting the forest protesters and was refusing to allow journalists into the forest, unless escorted by Timberlands staff, Shandwick came up with a new theme to push in the company media statements and publications: corporate openness and an Open Forests policy.

Operation Alien had been the beginning of more heavy-handed tactics by Timberlands. In response, in June 1997, Native Forest Action planned a new kind of protest action. The group invited its supporters from nearby West Coast towns and elsewhere in the country to be part of a Mass Walk into Charleston Forest to see the logging for themselves. The organisers hoped that involving large numbers of people – too many to stop and arrest – they would reassert the public's right to be in a publicly owned forest and avoid the kind of aggressive confrontation with Timberlands that had been occurring.

Timberlands turned to Shandwick for help in developing a strategy to minimise the political impact of the protest. The week before the mid-June protest was to occur, Shandwick completed its report on how Timberlands should deal with the potential crisis.

Shandwick recommended that although the police should be notified as soon as possible, 'at the same time, we strongly recommend a non-confrontational approach to any trespass this weekend when the organisers want maximum television coverage. This will deny them the footage they want of demonstrators being arrested in State Forest.'

Arresting peaceful protesters, Shandwick felt, was best kept for when the TV cameras were not there. 'Come Monday, when you will want to recommence forestry operations the number of occupiers will have lessened and the story will be old news,' Shandwick wrote. 'At that point the Police can be asked to arrest/remove any remaining protesters.' Anticipating that there would be media coverage of arrests, Shandwick recommended that a 'Reserve press release should be prepared to support the removal of any remaining occupants on Monday'.

Shandwick advised that TVNZ journalists in Christchurch would probably already know about the imminent protest and be planning to

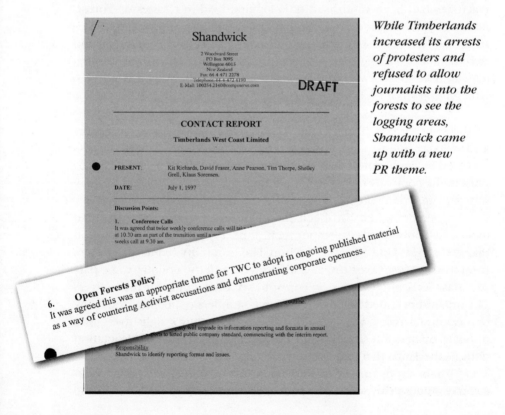

While Timberlands increased its arrests of protesters and refused to allow journalists into the forests to see the logging areas, Shandwick came up with a new PR theme.

send a crew. Instead of waiting for the protesters to show the forest to the cameras, Shandwick recommended that 'you pre-empt the planned action by contacting Television and offering them the opportunity to film the forest from one of the company's helicopters on the Friday afternoon when forestry operations are taking place'.

Filmed from the air, Shandwick hoped that the logging of the ancient rimu forests would not look so bad. Nothing should be left to chance. 'Any obvious area, such as the site where the Charleston Forest logs are dressed, should be tidied to ensure that the camera crew and occupants are denied any opportunity for "incriminating" pictures,' Shandwick advised. It recommended that 'a draft release should also be prepared explaining the company position on helicopter extraction and your commitment to the environment'.[36]

In the end Timberlands decided on an even more 'proactive' approach. In the week before the planned protest, advertisements appeared in the local papers announcing a Timberlands Open Day in Charleston Forest on 15 June, the day of the protest. Throughout the day the company ran free buses into the forest, where visitors were given sausages and watched helicopter displays. The location chosen for the event was none other than the 'site where the Charleston Forest logs are dressed', which had indeed been tidied up to ensure no destruction was visible. Visitors were kept well away from the main logging, which was occurring in an entirely different catchment.

In terms of openness, the open day was a sham. But as a public relations tactic it was a success, upstaging the planned protest action. Timberlands was so pleased with the day that, at a meeting with Shandwick staff two weeks later, it agreed to make corporate openness a theme in future PR activities. The minutes of the meeting noted: 'Open Forests Policy. It was agreed this was an appropriate theme to adopt in ongoing published material as a way of countering Activist accusations and displaying corporate openness.'[37]

Meanwhile Timberlands continued to arrest protesters in the forest, refuse permission for journalists to enter the forests with environmentalists and even, in one case, threatened a Labour MP with arrest if he went into the forest with Native Forest Action. A good example of the open forests policy came in March 1998, when a journalist spent part of a day in Charleston Forest with Timberlands' loggers getting their side of the story and was then complained about to his editor for attempting to enter the forest with NFA to be shown the impact of the logging. The weekly teleconference minutes recorded: 'Journalist from

New Zealand Geographic wanted to enter Charleston forest with the protesters. Kit Richards rang the editor to lay a complaint.'[38]

From then on, whenever Timberlands' monitoring gave them notice of a planned protest, preparations were made. When Timberlands got wind of a possible environmental protest to be held in its Maruia Forest in August 1998, it made sure it got into town first to limit the possibility of adverse coverage. The minutes of the weekly telephone conference with Shandwick noted that 'J Birchfield [Timberlands general manager operations] has visited the local school as a PR visit and contacted the local farmer who owns access to the forest'.[39]

Within days of the bomb accusations, Timberlands had sent loggers back into Charleston. Every day they were flown by helicopter into inaccessible locations, more than a day's long tramp into the forest, where the protesters would have trouble obstructing them. The loggers resumed their gradual undoing of the forest, working their way along fine valleys and up gullies that had previously been too rugged or inaccessible. Every month the helicopter would be back, lifting the felled trees from the forest. Each time it would leave tall piles of several hundred felled trees in nearby log dumps. But although the protest had not yet stopped the felling, it had become a national political controversy. Both Timberlands and the protesters knew that it was now in the cities that the campaign to protect the rainforests would be won or lost.

CHAPTER 4

COUNTERING FREEDOM OF SPEECH

We don't have a think-tank with a strategy session to conspire against people who say things. We don't bother with that sort of stuff. I mean, we live in a democracy, everyone's allowed to express their view.

Dave Hilliard, 1999[1]

Students in New Zealand schools are taught that democracy is based on encouraging citizens to express their opinions freely on issues of concern. Textbooks give details of dictators on distant continents or in bygone eras who deprived their people of freedom of speech and suppressed dissidents. Pupils from two Wellington schools came close to having a practical lesson in the threat to free speech, courtesy of Shandwick and Timberlands.

In May 1997 about 100 school children attended a conservation rally at Parliament calling for an end to West Coast logging. In the weeks before the rally, their teachers and principals had made a class project of forest conservation, with visiting speakers on ecology and most of the children individually making and painting large cut-out birds and

Shandwick tracked down the principals of two schools they believed had allowed students to join this conservation rally and sent letters to discourage them from doing so in future.
Photo: Alan Tennyson

other native animals. At Parliament they were met by the Minister of Conservation in a friendly and low-key event.

Timberlands was incensed by the small protest. Shandwick set to and, after investigation, traced two schools they thought students had come from. Rob McGregor drafted a letter for Timberlands to send to the principals, which began 'We understand that children from your school may have recently taken part in a presentation outside Parliament opposing our company's operations'. After stating Timberlands' usual arguments in defence of its logging, the letter warned that:'we consider our reputation besmirched by what would appear to be an ill-considered action that disregarded the facts of the matter and co-opted children for political gain. We must advise that, in the event of any further action of this nature, we will seek legal redress.'[2]

The final version of the letter sent two days later omitted the legal threat, but Timberlands still challenged the principals about their pupils being 'involved in an action based on misinformation, designed to advance a "political" agenda'. The principals were surprised and annoyed that the company would track them down and criticise them over such a minor event. They had received signed permission from parents for each child wanting to take part and had talked the issue through with the pupils to check they understood what they were doing. One of the principals described the letter as 'over the top' and said he suspected it was intended to discourage them from being involved in the issue.

A fax to Timberlands from McGregor accompanying the revised letter showed the company's own political agenda:'could you please send me copies of the letters when you have sent them and I'll fax a copy to Cath Ingram in the Minister's [Jenny Shipley's] office'.[3] The company wanted to show its minister that it had dealt with the criticism.

When the respected Professor Alan Mark of Otago University wrote a careful letter to Timberlands explaining his concerns about the logging, the letter was referred to the PR company Shandwick for reply. One of the two main consultants contemptuously wrote in a memo to the other:'Klaus, Take a look at this smart bastard – what a pity he doesn't live on the West Coast! R McG.'[4]

Shandwick was keen to make sure that copies of Timberlands' response to Alan Mark's letter were distributed to a number of ministers. In a memo to Timberlands, McGregor from Shandwick wrote:'A F Mark Letter: Here's the latest letter with the new revisions included. Could you please check it and gain the necessary approvals for dispatch. On second thoughts, I don't think we should send it off from here because the copies to the Ministers should have a Compliments Slip signed by Dave [Hilliard]. Do you agree? ... I'll e-mail it to you so you can print it out onto your letterhead and dispatch.'[5]

Shandwick's approach to dealing with the concerns of critics was always flexible. When a wide range of well-known New Zealanders, including artists, writers, actors and sportspeople, put their names to a statement in 1997 calling for an end to logging of West Coast publicly owned forests, they got the kid gloves treatment.

The celebrities' statement was discussed at Timberlands' weekly PR telephone conference. They decided that Shandwick's Klaus Sorensen should organise 'an information package to be sent to all celebrities who signed NFA petition'.[6] Rather than attack them directly, Timberlands paid Shandwick to write to every one of them replying to what, they told the celebrities, was the 'mischievous disinformation' of 'activists with extreme and uncompromising ideologies'.

Sorensen's letter was a masterpiece of spin-doctoring. Where blunt threats were appropriate for dealing with some critics, celebrities warranted a calm measured statement of 'facts'. 'More than 500 West Coast families rely on the West Coast forestry industry for a living,' Sorensen wrote, failing to mention that the vast majority of these families rely on plantation forestry; only about two dozen jobs are in native logging.

'Did you know 80% of the total West Coast region was assigned to the Department of Conservation at the time the West Coast Accord was signed 11 years ago?' Sorensen's letter continued. To drive the point home he emphasised that 'only about 5% of the West Coast native forest was set aside for production purposes while the rest was formally protected'. The text was carefully crafted to appeal to the notion of 'balance', but Sorensen's 'facts' vary from the real history and context. Only 10 percent of the total area of the West Coast was actually allocated either to reserves or logging under the 1986 West Coast Accord, with roughly half of the remaining lowland native forests going to reserves and the rest being left open to logging. The other 75 percent of Sorensen's total was allocated to the Department of Conservation (DOC) a year later, making up the claimed 80 percent. It consisted of mountains and glaciers that were unloggable and had long been protected by DOC's predecessor, the Department of Lands and Survey.

Rather than trying to justify logging New Zealand's rainforests, Sorensen appealed to the celebrities' sense of global responsibility: 'Did you know the West Coast Rimu supply saves in the order of 1,000 hectares of tropical rainforests in South Asia and Pacific Islands from destruction each year?' While Shandwick had been busy defending the logging of tropical rainforests for the Malaysian Timber Board against the efforts of German environmentalists, Shandwick was simultaneously writing that New Zealand had a responsibility to log its rainforests to save rainforests elsewhere. According to conservationists, logging the rimu rainforests in New Zealand would simply add to the total amount of rainforests being logged rather than substitute for logging elsewhere.

The following week Shandwick was busy organising to get Dave Hilliard's signature sent to Shandwick for inclusion on the celebrity letters.[7]

A particular point of vulnerability for Timberlands was any challenge to the economics of its logging operation. Where earlier governments had ruthlessly axed government financial support for industries, Timberlands relied on a special sweetheart deal with the government to underwrite its ongoing operations.

When Auckland accountant Tony Sage wrote a detailed critique of Timberlands' economics, he came in for special attention. The con-

Borneo rainforest. Letters sent to pro-conservation celebrities argued that logging New Zealand rainforests would save tropical rainforests in South Asia/Pacific Islands from destruction. Shandwick was simultaneously defending tropical rainforest logging for its client the Malaysian Timber Board. Photo: Trace Hodgson

servative accountant had become interested in Timberlands because his daughter was a field officer for Forest and Bird and he had visited the company with her during a trip to the South Island. Writing in the *New Zealand Herald*, Sage had described Timberlands' logging of native forests as a 'disguised government welfare programme' with an anti-conservation agenda, which had been allowed to continue when similar government-controlled enterprises had either been dispensed with or privatised. He drew attention to Timberlands' low royalty payments to the state for the native trees it logs – only $5 per cubic metre, which would amount to between $10 and $25 for each ancient rimu tree and a tiny fraction of what private native forest owners demand. Sage described such low prices as a 'huge concealed subsidy' to the company.[8]

Shandwick's McGregor prepared a feature-length article attacking Sage's argument and sent it to Dave Hilliard, who replied that he was not happy with the first draft. 'My thought was to hit hard in the first 200 words (all most readers will bother with) then go into countering Sage with further opinion and more information,' he wrote in a memo to McGregor.[9] Hilliard, however, was happy to allow Shandwick to make the decisions. 'It may seem like I do not like your draft. That is not the case. It got my mind going. If you do not like my ideas I will not be offended at all. Perhaps you can make use of some of this stuff anyway.'

A year later Tony Sage wrote a critical letter to the editor of the *Independent*, questioning expenditure on Timberlands' PR campaign. This time he got an aggressive response directly from Klaus Sorensen of Shandwick. 'Your correspondent Tony Sage seems eager to disclose other people's involvements,' Sorensen wrote, 'but strangely reluctant to disclose his longstanding involvement in those organisations opposing sustainable forestry and the West Coast Accord.

'This is, of course, not surprising', he continued, 'since Mr Sage and his daughter Eugenie, one of the main organisers of Native Forest Action, are part of the orchestrated letter-writing programme by that organisation, but would prefer not to tell newspaper editors of their organisational memberships and philosophical agendas. Shandwick New Zealand, by contrast, has acted for Timberlands on a completely transparent basis for some years.... Unlike Mr Sage, we deal only in the facts.'[10] Eugenie Sage had never been a main organiser or even a member of Native Forest Action, but had many times openly been a spokesperson for the organisation for which she worked, Forest and Bird. Her father had a right to comment on the issue without this sort of attack.

Criticism from religious leaders required yet another approach. In mid-1997 a group of Anglican church leaders, co-ordinated by Canon Ted Abraham, sent an open letter to the government questioning West Coast native forest logging. News of the open letter appeared in newspapers in early September. At the next weekly telephone conference call it was agreed that Shandwick would handle the 'troublesome clerics'.

The teleconference minutes noted that Klaus Sorensen from Shandwick would 'write to canon, Ted Abraham, re their support of NFA – draft to CEO'.[11] The next Tuesday, Timberlands received a draft letter from Shandwick to be sent to each of the Anglican leaders. The letter attacked the 'incorrect assertions' and 'fallacious claims' in the church letter.

The matter was not left there. The minutes of the following Friday's telephone conference cryptically agreed that the 'letter to Anglican Ministers to be followed up,'[12] with the job going to Jacqui Low, the corporate services manager in Timberlands' Greymouth headquarters. Early the next week the *Greymouth Evening Star*, Timberlands' local and sympathetic newspaper, ran a story 'Civic Leaders Angry at "Green" Religious Letter'.[13]

After the letter had been given to the newspaper, it sought comment from local mayors about what they thought of the church leaders commenting on the logging issue. 'The churches should get on with their own business and stop meddling in things that do not concern them,' the Grey District mayor, Ron Hibbs, was quoted as saying. 'He was absolutely appalled by the letter.' Two days later a couple of local Anglican priests had a letter in the *Greymouth Evening Star* distancing themselves from the church leaders' statement.[14]

In December 1997 Cath Wallace, a senior lecturer in public policy at Victoria University and prominent commentator on conservation issues, attended a conservation conference in Taupo organised by Auckland University's School of Environmental and Marine Sciences. She arrived to find Timberlands' logo featuring prominently and a large display promoting its beech forest logging plans, in return for the $4,000 Timberlands had given to the conference organisers from its sponsorship budget. Offended to see the company using a conservation conference to 'greenwash' itself, she light-heartedly added a note under a Timberlands logo: 'logs old growth forests'. Timberlands, it turned out, did not have much of a sense of humour.

Although Wallace has been acclaimed globally as one of the world's leading advocates for the environment, receiving the international

Goldman Prize in 1991, she would not get the kid gloves treatment re-served for the celebrities who opposed logging.

Shortly after, Timberlands asked Shandwick to investigate what could be done to get back at her. Shandwick drafted a letter of com-plaint to the vice-chancellor of Wallace's university, Professor Les Holborow. To Timberlands' general manager, Kit Richards, Shandwick wrote 'attached is an official letter of complaint to the Vice Chancellor of Victoria for your consideration. Having spoken with a friend of Rob's [McGregor, Shandwick], who is involved with Victoria, we are now in a position to share with you some background information on Ms Wallace.... We hope that this is of some interest to you, if only in terms of providing more of a profile on Ms Wallace, and look forward to your comments on the letter.' [15]

Shandwick went on to describe her job, her successes and the sup-posed jealousy some fellow academics felt towards her because of her success. Attached to this, Shandwick provided Timberlands with a draft letter to the vice-chancellor attacking Cath Wallace as lacking objectivity, promoting an extreme environmental viewpoint and doing 'little to en-hance the reputation of the university'. The Shandwick-drafted letter to Professor Holborow stated that 'The purpose of this letter is to draw your attention to a recent contact our company had with a member of the university'. Although it was abundantly obvious that the purpose was to get at Cath Wallace, Timberlands stressed that 'In doing so, I would ask you to accept that our concern stems from our extensive commitment to education'.[16] The PR telephone conference minutes plot the rest of the planning:'Letter re C Wallace being reviewed' [17] and then, later,'Letter to Prof. Holborow sent before Christmas'. [18]

Cath Wallace replied to the vice-chancellor saying that Kit Richards' letter seemed disingenuous. She said that she had publicly opposed Timberlands' logging of old growth forests and that 'the incident of which he writes is simply a convenient opportunity to put pressure on me'. 'What we have here', she wrote, 'is an issue that has been under debate for a long time and Timberlands is looking for ways to put pressure on those who disagree with it.'[19] The university replied to Timberlands and that was the last she heard of it.

A few months later Timberlands' PR machine considered pursu-ing another critical academic, David Round, a law lecturer at Canterbury University. In an article published in the *Marlborough Express*, he criti-cised the ecological impact, economic viability and legal basis of Timberlands' native logging. 'The organised logging of native forests by

Crown agencies belongs only in the past,' he argued.[20]

For some reason Timberlands' media monitoring service missed the article, so the company only became aware of it several weeks later. In a fax to Timberlands, Shandwick wrote 'unfortunately that [David Round] article is rather dated now, it appeared on 9 July. Could we please discuss this at our Friday Conference. My feeling is that the Round article, although it is clearly labelled as "Opinion", is so unbalanced we need to request a right of reply. What say you?'[21] The minutes from the following week's teleconference revealed that Timberlands and Shandwick had settled for a letter to the editor and had 'decided not to actively pursue through university'.[22]

Individually these actions seem variously petty or heavy-handed, but the overall strategy is very deliberate: to wear down Timberlands' opponents, discourage others from joining a broadly based coalition against native logging and, where it is considered appropriate, directly attack the critics.

Letters to the editor are one of the most read sections of newspapers, representing the views of a cross-section of society. As with talkback radio, letters are influential not only in providing public space for discussion of issues but also for setting an agenda. Issues that might be ignored on the editorial floor often make it into the letters columns. It is a space that Timberlands' PR machine sought to colonise.

Timberlands' problem in early 1997 was that, although a stream of letters was being sent to papers all around the country attacking native forest logging, very few letters were appearing spontaneously in defence of the company's operations. The obvious message to politicians and other observers was that many more people opposed the logging than supported it.

Where public support is lacking, a public relations budget can still get a client a long way. Shandwick hired an extra employee to draft pro-Timberlands letters to editors and established an 'automatic' letters to the editor system, so that no criticism of Timberlands went without response. A draft communications strategy prepared by Shandwick stated: 'As part of this strategy Timberlands should ensure that it takes issue, by letter, with every criticism of the company and its activities.... Key Recommendation: Establish "automatic reply" for any letters to editor.' Running the campaign was to be the responsibility of Shandwick.[23]

The system was simple. Shandwick was to 'receive all letters, draft three or four standard "template" letters and use these with adaptations to provide Kit Richards with drafts for final modification and approval'.[24] Most of the letters were 'signed' by Timberlands CEO Dave Hilliard, after copies of Timberlands' letterhead and a copy of Hilliard's signature were sent to Shandwick so that the letters could be sent directly from their office.

Shandwick determined that letters would be classed into a standard number of categories and 'proactive' responses drafted to deal with the likely issues to be answered: 'Letter 1. Charleston Forest.... Letter 2. Pinus Radiata vs Indigenous Decorative Timbers.... Letter 3. Accord Issues.... Letter 4. Sustainable Beech Management Project.'[25] Having the letters ready meant that Shandwick could quickly get a response submitted while the original letter was fresh in the minds of readers.

Thereafter the Timberlands Papers are full of messages like this one from Shandwick: 'I have forwarded a draft response to Ann Graeme's letter in the Greymouth Evening Star. I note that the current clippings included letters in The Press, 22 and 23 June, from Mike Smetham, Matt Oliver and Dr Dave Kelly (again) that I consider warrant a response....'[26] In Shandwick's fifth-floor offices in central Wellington a veritable cottage industry was established to produce letters to the editor.

In Shandwick's fifth-floor offices in central Wellington a veritable cottage industry was established to produce letters to the editor. An extra employee was hired primarily to draft pro-Timberlands letters and thereafter every pro-forest conservation letter or article anywhere in the country was replied to.
Photo: Beth Flinn

In a 'strategy overview' discussion the following year Timberlands and Shandwick 'identified a number of opportunities where public relations can be applied to further the interest of Timberlands'. Specifically, on the 'environmental front', Timberlands planned to ensure that letters attacking NFA and praising Timberlands would appear. In an internal report of the discussion, which was held at Shandwick's offices, they noted the need for 'Anti-NFA letter writing campaign (stock letters) ... Dominion/The Press letter re. NFA lies, ...Thank you TWC for supplying my son's football team, etc'.[27] These are hardly letters that the chief executive of a government company can write to the paper, but subsequently a stream of letters to the editor from local Timberlands supporters appeared attacking prominent NFA members as being 'eco-terrorists' and pointing out the value of Timberlands' sports sponsorship budget.[28]

Keeping track of the letters to the editor was important for Timberlands; the PR conference minutes noted that 'Monitoring of letters to editor continues'.[29] This took the strain off Timberlands' head office and allowed the letters to be carefully crafted to emphasise the issues the company wanted to advance. Whenever the conservation campaign was gaining, the letters to the editor would be cranked up again. In May 1998, for instance, when the government announced it would cut short the Timberlands logging in the Buller region that had been the target of the Charleston tree-sitting protest the year before, Shandwick was directed to 'increase proactive activity... in attempt to pre-empt NFA, e.g. reply to editorial letters'.[30]

Sometimes Shandwick got letters ready for specific media outlets, even if there had been no coverage of the issue. McGregor wrote a memo to Timberlands' Paula de Roeper about a reserve letter for the *Otago Daily Times*: 'here's the letter all ready prepared for when the ODT runs anything from or on NFA'.[31] They were, he wrote, 'ready to attack any publicity after they hear NFA has set up a Dunedin branch'. The draft letter to the editor, written far away in Wellington, ends: 'sentiment on the Coast suggests NFA might instead concentrate on a sustainable Dunedin and forget about our largely forested and protected area'.[32]

When the Dunedin University student magazine *Critic* ran an article criticising Timberlands' beech scheme plans, Shandwick was asked what should be done. Shandwick's reply to Timberlands PR manager Anne Pearson is illuminating about the PR company's whole approach to criticism. Rob McGregor said he had first seen the article that morning and had been thinking about it as well. The first concern he raised was not about correcting facts and informing the public, but about keeping the logging plans secret. 'I think it does need a reply,' he said, 'but, as I understand the situation, we don't want to confirm any of the details about the sustainable beech proposal – is this correct?'

They did, however, need to have their say. Summing up their strategy, he said 'I am of this view because we need to underline the fact that whenever they pop up we: 1. Let them know we've seen what they're saying about Timberlands; and 2. Rebut their arguments and undermine their case'.[33]

While Timberlands spent hundreds of thousands of dollars of public money promoting its viewpoint on rainforest logging, those supporting the protection of the rainforests mounted a campaign on a shoestring budget. With donated funds amounting only to thousands of dollars a year, their campaign relied on volunteers, word-of-mouth advertising and low-cost publicity such as posters. Others supporting the campaign used graffiti. Goliath's swords versus David's slingshots. But Timberlands did not want the conservation side of the debate to be heard at all. It spent tens of thousands of dollars more, with the help of Shandwick and paid contractors, to try to silence its critics.

In June 1997 Rob McGregor registered his concern that anti-Timberlands graffiti was flourishing in Wellington. Large walls displayed such messages as 'Every 15 minutes another giant old rimu tree falls – Mr Bolger, stop the butchers'; others had succinct messages like 'Timberlands – Rainforest Vandals' and 'Timberlands – bad fellers'. Spinning to control the news agenda was familiar territory for Shandwick but controlling graffiti was taking them into uncharted territory.

Dealing with graffiti was not in the PR plan developed for Timberlands by Shandwick, so McGregor sought instructions. In a memo to the company he noted 'there are at least two prominent anti-Timberlands statements scrawled on Motorway overpasses here in Wellington. What is your policy regarding this type of graffiti?' Then he suggested: 'we could arrange to have them removed by waterblasting if necessary'.[34]

Soon Timberlands and Shandwick were making it their business to have all graffiti concerning Timberlands or native logging removed by contractors, sometimes repeatedly on the same sites. Shandwick staff photographed each piece of graffiti they spotted around the city and sent copies to Timberlands in Greymouth. The Wellington City Council responded to some Timberlands complaints and had graffiti removed, but mostly Shandwick and its contractors handled the task.

Then in September 1997, presumably emboldened by months of graffiti removal, Shandwick extended its 'public relations' work to trying to eliminate poster messages too. Native Forest Action members found that their posters, stuck to lamp-posts around the city, were being painted over with thick khaki-coloured paint – exactly the same paint being used at that time to cover graffiti messages. In areas that routinely featured all manner of posters about concerts, exhibitions and political concerns, only the posters concerning native forest conservation were being blotted out. For the company that insisted on having its say in every news story and replying to every letter to the editor, freedom of speech was a one-way street.

At a weekly teleconference the following month the graffiti campaign was discussed. Shandwick's Klaus Sorensen stressed the need for a 'strategy for dealing with media if an arrest should be made over the graffiti in Wellington'.[35] Shandwick produced a paper called 'Timberlands West Coast Issues Analysis, Wellington Graffiti Campaign', which looked at options for a more active campaign to counter the graffiti. 'Timberlands proposes taking a more active role in curtailing the NFA Graffiti campaign in Wellington. This analysis considers the options available to the company and provides a recommendation.' Shandwick acknowledged that the public was not against the graffiti – 'the population is generally tolerant and

Shandwick paid contractors to remove all graffiti messages about forest conservation in the capital city. 'The current erasure response by the company is discreet and effective,' Shandwick wrote.
Photo: Alan Tennyson

accepting' – but its presence was adversely affecting one of Timberlands' target audiences, senior politicians. 'Annoyance with the campaign,' Shandwick wrote, 'is largely confined to some Ministers/the Prime Minister and reportedly some parts of the Wellington City Council.'

Because the public did not object to graffiti, Shandwick considered it important that the campaign be invisible. 'The current erasure response by the company is discreet and effective,' Shandwick wrote, pleased that 'there is no obvious company involvement'. But every time graffiti was removed it reappeared. 'NFA are persistent.... This has resulted in the company's annoyance growing as the cost of removal grows.' As Timberlands' frustration levels increased, the temptation to take tougher measures grew. But Shandwick recommended that the company's interests were best served by continuing to have NFA graffiti painted out rather than putting resources into trying to get NFA supporters arrested.

Arrests would have guaranteed publicity and undermined 'Timberlands current policy', which was 'to minimise publicity to protect the Sustainable Beech Management programme'. Shandwick's concern was that arrests would 'guarantee a marked increase in Timberlands related publicity and would act as a call to action'. Besides, the Timberlands strategy of employing contractors to paint out graffiti

In September 1997 Shandwick extended its public relations work to painting out poster messages. For the company that insisted on always having its say, freedom of speech was a one-way street.
Photo: Alan Tennyson

and posters had the support of the minister responsible for Timberlands, Jenny Shipley. 'The current erasure campaign has the support of the Minister of SOEs and Prime Minister,' Shandwick noted.[36] Writing on the walls of Wellington was having an impact at the highest levels of government.

Despite this advice, Timberlands appears to have increased its efforts to have the street critics caught. When young NFA people were filmed painting a wall on the TV current affairs programme *Assignment*, Shandwick finally thought they might have some evidence to support prosecutions. The minutes of the weekly PR teleconference noted 'Assignment – some individuals involved in graffiti now able to be identified? Shandwick to follow up.'[37]

With the possibility of arrests, Shandwick thought it wise to prepare a draft media release on the issue. 'Top drawer news release re protester apprehension has been redrafted,' their weekly teleconference minutes noted.[38] The 'reserve news release' marked 'not for publication' was headed 'Timberlands supports arrest of protester(s)'.

PAINTED OUT – Balaena Bay resident Lee Hatherly lies in front of a wall which once sported environmental slogans which she and some other local residents enjoyed.
Picture: CRAIG SIMCOX

Forest group and loggers wage poster war

By SUZANNE GREEN
Environment reporter

like this before. Every single thing that can be done to fight us [NFA] they are doing, apart from death threats."

break the law, vandalise people's property, deface it with graffiti [and think] it's all right because they have a cause.

est Action is not that important. Native Forest Action is just a small group of people trying to destroy us on the outside."

Residents in Wellington's Balaena Bay complained publicly about Timberlands' removal of environmental slogans. 'We regard it not as graffiti but more as a community noticeboard or a community statement of feeling,' Lee Hatherly said. 'We have developed quite a lot of local pride in it.'

In the draft release Timberlands announced its support for the hypothetical arrest of a protester: 'We're pleased to see that the Police have acted decisively and have taken action against those protesters who deface public property and therefore break the law.'[39] During this period one security company repeatedly harassed conservationists putting up posters in the central city; in one case this led to an assault complaint to the police after a young NFA member was dragged along the ground by the hair after being found by the security guards.

Still the graffiti kept appearing. Time at the Timberlands weekly PR teleconference meetings was often taken up with graffiti reports, with items such as 'Graffiti en route to Wellington Airport has been taken care of' appearing regularly.[40]

After the painting out of its posters began, Native Forest Action formally complained to the Public Relations Institute of New Zealand (PRINZ), pointing out that posters and even painting on walls were long-standing vehicles for freedom of speech. Never in memory, through numerous elections and public protest campaigns, had it been regarded as legitimate to remove opposition messages.

The letter of complaint pointed out that, at election time, all political parties put posters and signs around the country which, though not strictly legal, were tolerated as part of the democratic process. It pointed to the institute's code of professional conduct that required members 'not [to] abuse the channels of public communications or the processes of government'. The National Ethics Committee of PRINZ agreed to investigate and wrote to Shandwick and Head Consultants asking whether they had been involved in these activities.

Shandwick raised the complaint at the next teleconference: 'PR ethics committee meeting. Letter sent to Shandwick who will forward to HCC and Timberlands.' Far from considering the ethical issues, the teleconference minutes record a decision that Shandwick would 'compile a strategy for dealing with it and take advantage of it'.[41]

Citing client confidentiality, Shandwick refused 'as a matter of principle' to tell the National Ethics Committee whether it was involved in advising Timberlands to have posters and graffiti removed and 'strongly protested that the question should have been posed'. Head Consultants simply replied that it had not been involved. The committee subsequently concluded that it 'must accept that both consultancies have responded truthfully and appropriately.... [and] in the light of these responses, and the fact that you can produce no evidence of any sort', the committee concluded that it did 'not intend to take this matter any further'.[42]

The Timberlands Papers reveal that Shandwick was instrumental in proposing and executing the campaign of blotting out messages by groups opposing the company's activities. Although the NFA complaint was dismissed by the PR industry ethics committee, the defacing of posters did end abruptly after the complaint was made.

The graffiti removal continued, but although it reduced the number of conservation messages on the walls of the capital city, it did not stop them. During 1997 and 1998 Timberlands had sent a series of letters and made a series of calls to the Wellington City Council (WCC) requesting that it have critical graffiti removed. Eventually Bruce McLean from the WCC Asset Programming section was prompted to write to Timberlands' general manager operations, John Birchfield. 'It seems that without a change in your operations there will remain a small but committed band of graffiti installers which will not change,' he wrote. 'Whilst it is Council's wish to remove graffiti as quickly as possible, I will need to be far more strategic with my now dwindling resources.'[43]

Timberlands itself had spent tens of thousands of dollars on the political cleansing. For a company that could never afford to pay a divi-

Before

After: The state company paid for this mural in Balaena Bay, Wellington, from its sponsorship budget, after a complaint from the Prime Minister about graffiti critical of native forest logging. Photos: Beth Flinn

dend on its native logging activities to its government owner, it had plenty of money to wage war on graffiti – a curious use for a state-owned enterprise's finances. Many of the posters and graffiti did not mention Timberlands, but called generally for the protection of public native forests. Timberlands had made it its business to counter all the criticism.

Then Shandwick dreamt up a final solution. The most frequent source of irritation was graffiti on a large concrete retaining wall in Wellington's Balaena Bay, strategically located beside the route used by politicians to travel between Parliament and the airport. For many years it had served as a 'democracy wall' for critics of the government, and its messages were much discussed by locals, one of whom appeared in the *Evening Post* newspaper on behalf of residents complaining about Timberlands' removal of environmental slogans. 'We regard it not as graffiti but more as a community noticeboard or a community statement of feeling,' Lee Hatherly said. 'We have developed quite a lot of local pride in it.'[44]

In December 1997 Shandwick staff noticed a small article in a newspaper proposing a mural on the Balaena Bay wall. Timberlands and Shandwick spied an opportunity to deal with their troublesome critics once and for all. Anne Pearson of Timberlands wrote to the WCC's community arts development adviser, Neal Palmer, following up a phone call he had received from Jeremy Alston of Shandwick. 'It is our understanding that you are presently looking for sponsors for the mural and it is this aspect of the project that we believe could be mutually beneficial. As you are no doubt aware, the particular stretch of wall you have earmarked has been used for some time as "canvas" for anti-Timberlands graffiti.' Sensitive to possible accusations that it was trying to censor its opponents, the company said it was keen to offer financial support for more altruistic reasons. 'Political sentiment aside', Pearson wrote, 'we feel it is a shame for most international visitors to Wellington to be confronted by this eyesore on what is otherwise a very attractive approach to the city…. A possible idea we had in mind would be for us to provide the paints.' She concluded by saying that, although Timberlands' involvement in the project would be 'totally transparent', they would prefer that there was no 'visible indication' of the company's part in the mural or any other publicity. [45]

Timberlands' teleconference minutes record that Shandwick followed up with the council to suggest a 'native forest scene'.[46] Neal Palmer replied that he was keen for Timberlands to be involved but there could be some problems. The minutes of the teleconference noted: 'Will discuss with Mayor. Thinks there may be some resistance. Would like to see it done by end of February. WY [Warren Young, Timberlands board chair] may even discuss it with [Mayor] Blumsky.'[47]

Slowly the project progressed under the watchful eye of Rob McGregor and Klaus Sorensen at Shandwick, assisted by a second PR company run by former West Coaster Gerry Morris. His company, Morris Communications Group, had organised a publicity campaign that same year involving 'extremely eye-catching' posters being pasted up on walls and lamp-posts throughout central Wellington by a pirate poster-sticking company.[48] The Public Relations Institute ethics committee had pointedly asked whether the defaced NFA posters were legally placed, but the institute saw nothing wrong with illegal postering arranged by a PR company. The institute's website highlighted the Morris Communications postering campaign as an admirable example of successful 'limited budget' public relations.

The mural was to be painted by the School of Design with paints donated by Resene paints.[49] Timberlands had to contribute $2,500 to be paid directly to Wellington Polytechnic, as the total cost for 'designing and executing the mural'. Neal Palmer advised Timberlands that the mural would be going ahead 'with the $2,500 sponsorship from your company, which Wellington City Council will be pleased to accept'.[50] The work was completed in September 1998. According to WCC staff, without Timberlands' financial support it is unlikely the mural would have eventuated.

An important issue came up at the time of Native Forest Action's complaint to the PRINZ National Ethics Committee. In its letter dismissing the NFA case, the committee said that Shandwick had commented on the 'irony' of NFA complaining about the 'defacing' of its posters and graffiti when NFA was 'engaged in similar activity'. This attitude revealed a surprising lack of appreciation of the ethical issues surrounding freedom of speech.

Painting a message on a wall and painting out someone else's message have a superficial similarity. Both use a paintbrush. Both are illegal, although the charge is minor. Putting up a poster and taking down someone else's poster are also superficially similar. But ethically they could not be more different: one is exercising freedom of speech, the other is depriving someone else of their freedom of speech. Shandwick's equating of the two acts, repeated by the ethics committee, was false. The environmental groups had not been trying to stop the Timberlands managers or anyone else having their say on the logging issue.

This points to a wider issue. A familiar defence of a PR campaign like Timberlands' is to say 'but the environmentalists do the same things'. Both 'sides' write press releases, both lobby politicians, both approach journalists to cover their views and write letters to the editor. So what is the problem?

If Timberlands had stuck to providing complete and accurate information and stating its viewpoint, this would be true. But many PR tactics are specifically designed to prevent people with opposing views from having influence over decisions. Secrecy can be used to deprive people of the information they need to argue their case. Selective release of the information held by the organisation can be used to mislead the public. Public interest groups such as environmentalists can, of course, also make misleading and incorrect statements. The difference is that their statements can be tested in public debate; whereas when governments and businesses are secretive or control information, the purpose is to inhibit public debate.

Contrary to some people's perception, activism is not about protesting. Environmental activists are motivated to do something about the problems they see in the world around them. They have to be dedicated and professional, though few of them are paid. They are supported by many other people who act on their beliefs and seek to make a difference – people in scientific institutions, in businesses, in schools and all other walks of life. The cynical view ignores the right of such public interest groups to protest, to research, to publicise their views and to attempt to mobilise general support for their cause. They can be the ears, the voice and the drive of a democratic society and it is the public who should decide if they are worth listening to.

CHAPTER 5

GREENWASHING

*Unlike the opponents of sustainable management, this side
of the camp is letting the truth be known and providing
information in a composed and professional manner.*
Paula de Roeper, Timberlands corporate
communications manager, 2 October 1998[1]

Governments make policy, public servants offer 'impartial and neutral'
advice, managers of Crown-owned companies run profitable businesses
within the policies set by government. Right? Actually, wrong.

Timberlands had different ideas about accountability. Political campaigning by the senior staff of a government agency offers a stark example of how the processes of government can be undermined. It is also
an example of how many politicians and public servants seem happy to
ignore such abuse when it fits their personal political prejudices.

The determination behind Timberlands' campaign appeared to
come from two or three of the senior staff. These individuals, who had
come to Timberlands from its predecessor, the New Zealand Forest Service, had a lot at stake. Their whole professional careers had been based
around trying to maintain a native logging industry and the state company, built up over a decade, was their 'baby'. They were well paid too,
earning between $130,000 and $190,000 per annum. Yet by the late
1990s, after years of experience supervising the logging of rainforests,
they had seen the policies they supported fall from favour. Under pressure, they sought the expensive assistance of Shandwick.

Using literally millions of dollars of the state financial resources
they controlled under the State Owned Enterprises Act, these people at
Timberlands were able to build, from almost nothing, a significant political campaign to defend their native forest logging empire. In the absence of a strong pro-logging movement outside the company, a PR campaign was devised to manufacture the impression of a significant political

lobby, apparently including scientific, environmental and public support for the logging. Timberlands, on advice from Shandwick, opted for a multi-pronged strategy.

Timberlands set about cultivating political allies to act as spokespeople and using its public relations resources in an attempt to control news media coverage of the issue. The company also set out to reverse its declining support base on the West Coast, orchestrating pro-logging campaigning by locals through the creation of a pro-logging lobby group and bolstering its image on the coast through an expensive sponsorship and advertising campaign.

Because the ultimate fate of Timberlands would be determined in the corridors of power in Wellington, the company enlisted public servants in key government positions willing to join in the pro-logging campaign. It worked to orchestrate political backing where there would otherwise have been little.

Timberlands knew it was in dangerous territory. Convention dictated that the role of government agencies was to remain independent of political campaigns. As political activism is not the legitimate business of a government company, or of any company, many of the tactics have had to be executed secretly or with others acting as the public

The key objective of all the PR strategies was to gain government approval for a new beech forest logging scheme, starting here in the outstanding beech forests of the Maruia Valley. Photo: Rob Brown

front for the campaign. The Timberlands Papers reveal, however, that some government ministers were fully aware of the questionable public relations tactics being used to manufacture political pressure and attacks on environmental opponents.

Throughout its existence Timberlands had been working on plans to exploit the large areas of native beech forest on the West Coast. Foresters had long viewed them as a wasted resource compared with the rimu forests preferred by the sawmilling industry; they were waiting for some commercial use to be devised for beech. By 1998 the company had spent millions of dollars trying to put together an economically and politically viable logging scheme. It was the fourth attempt since the 1970s to win approval for a beech scheme, after each previous plan had proved to be both uneconomic and highly unpopular. The beech scheme was also Timberlands' main hope of maintaining native logging, involving a tripling of logging volumes by moving into beech forests as the available rimu forests ran out.

One of Timberlands' primary PR strategy papers, prepared in 1994, reveals the campaign planning that went into trying to win political support for what they always knew would be an unpopular idea. Timberlands set out under its 'goals' that it should 'Be prepared in the event of an anti-beech campaign to counter-lobby Parliament'. Lobbying in Wellington itself, however, would be insufficient. Its PR advisers decided it should 'develop key West Coast and national allies to publicly support sustainable Beech production as part of a counter-campaign by Timberlands'. To underpin its lobbying campaign Timberlands also had to reverse its poor standing in the eyes of the community and set out 'to create a positive public image for Timberlands West Coast'. [2]

To achieve its goals Timberlands developed detailed strategies. In its 'parliamentary lobbying' strategy, Timberlands candidly stated that it would 'establish reliable contact with Parliament to maintain current information as to environmental lobbying of Parliament'. Its own lobbying efforts involved 'a tiered approach to focus most information on most influential members... scaling up effort for MPs whose opposition [is] likely to be most damaging, and those whose support is likely to be most influential'.

Timberlands knew that, with its generally poor community image, a stand-alone lobbying campaign would be unsuccessful. It needed to spend time and resources 'developing beech allies'. To do this it should 'identify individuals/associations whose support would add credibility and authority to the beech scheme; Develop contacts, provide information and solicit support for a campaign'.

The company recognised that it was starting from a low base with declining support. It could not escape the fact that, with so much of New Zealand's native forests already gone, the majority of its citizens felt that those that remained should be protected. The West Coast was an area New Zealanders associated with tourism and national parks.

Ambitiously, Timberlands felt it should try to tap into New Zealanders' pride. 'Associate Timberlands West Coast closely with subjects, people, skills and ideas with which New Zealanders closely identify and value,' said its PR strategy. Timberlands hoped that, by doing this, it would be 'increasingly difficult to discredit Timberlands West Coast; and 'Mainstream light greens' (i.e. not affiliated with any environmental group) [would] feel justified/comfortable in supporting Timberlands West Coast'.

Timberlands knew that going public on its logging plans was only likely to increase opposition so, in order to 'Build Public Support', the company decided paradoxically to 'maintain a low profile until opposition campaign initiated'. In readiness for the campaign of those supporting the protection of the rainforests, Timberlands would 'Prepare a coherent and comprehensive public campaign including advertising, media features, stickers, fliers etc. on value of beech and its environmental acceptability'.[3]

By 1997 the mounting public opposition to the existing rimu logging operations in Charleston and elsewhere did not augur well for Timberlands' chances of gaining approval for moving into beech forests. In October of that year Shandwick completed a plan for Timberlands. Titled 'Sustainable Beech Management Project Communications Strategy', it bluntly stated Timberlands' objectives as 'ensuring sufficient political support and goodwill' for a beech scheme. Influencing government decisions was central to its beech logging ambitions. Shandwick argued that the key was to 'minimis[e] environmental opposition through a pro-active launch strategy'. To achieve this would require keeping details of the plans secret until the last minute and then carefully controlling the news media and orchestrating 'third party support' when they were released.

The PR papers were very clear about the importance of the PR campaign to beech logging: 'Developing more widespread public support for Timberlands West Coast will facilitate the implementation of all the company's strategies/plans. However, in no area is this support more crucial to the successful implementation of a scheme, and the develop-

ment of downstream operations, than in the area of the Beech resource.'
Shandwick summarised the 'key strategy elements' as:

1. *Build on the Timberlands business case (initially through the business media visit).*

2. *Commence West Coast local community support meetings.*

3. *Launch the Beech Project to a group of invited business and forestry media.*

4. *Hold a special briefing at the Beehive for all interested.*

5. *Follow this up with a cocktail function in Wellington ... hosted by the Chairman, for Wellington business people with a relevant interest in forestry to Timberlands, plus selected politicians and media....*

6. *Produce a range of information materials, bound in a Sustainable Beech Management Project Information Kit to be distributed to all media (Business Editors, chief reporters, editors, environmental and forestry reporters) politicians and commentators (talk-back hosts, environmental commentators etc.).*

7. *Develop an executive summary of no more than four pages, with emphasis on bullet points, for wide distribution.*

8. *Host several facility visits [West Coast PR tours] for key ministerial advisers.*

9. *Place strong emphasis on environmental prescriptions and research, with consideration being given to upgrading the predator control programme to coincide with the launch.*

10. *Identifying third party endorsers to publicly support the plan.*[4]

It was to be a tightly controlled programme aimed at getting quick approval for the project and minimising derailment by opponents of native forest logging. Shandwick believed that PR tours for hand-picked, sympathetic journalists and a series of public meetings in West Coast towns aimed at building local support for the plans were the essential foundations for a successful campaign. The plans would be launched at a set of invitation-only functions in Wellington, in which the company hoped to control the news coverage by inviting selected journalists, including some flown into the capital just for the occasion. Next there was a range of printed public relations materials including posters, booklets, brochures and a video.

To blunt the anticipated strong opposition from the major environment groups, Shandwick suggested that Timberlands 'place strong emphasis on environmental prescriptions and research'. One of the 'key messages', Shandwick advised, was that 'extensive studies on all native wildlife in the forest areas have been carried out and action will be taken to protect and enhance all species'.

Week after week, Shandwick and Timberlands laboured over the detail of managing the beech launch. Planning was everything. Shandwick had the task of detailing 'the political, media and green movement influences' in a draft that was 'sent to Timberlands to comment'.[5] Timberlands hoped to conduct a symphony of support from politicians, media commentators and even a couple of conservative environment groups that would drown out any opposition.

In late January 1998 the preparations began in earnest. The agreed 'Beech Management Communications Strategy' allocated tasks

Timberlands produced 500 copies of this PR kit in 1998, at a cost of $70 each – with 'sustainable resource logos and recycled look' – for lobbying politicians and to send to allies seeking submissions supporting its beech scheme plans.

to various parties. Christchurch-based Head Consultants got the job of preparing press releases. Shandwick was to use its Wellington networks to 'continue lobbying re SOE management of any announcements made.... Continue pressure for Parliamentary Caucus briefing.... Prepare for briefing at Beehive.... Continue encouragement to delay date of official announcement until ready.' Timberlands staff members Kit Richards and Dave Fraser had the task of finding 'third parties' who would be prepared to publicly endorse the beech scheme.[6]

Leading up to the launch Timberlands went to great lengths to keep the beech logging plans secret. Everyone involved had to return their numbered copies of the documents as soon as they had finished with them. Copies were given only to key allies, in preparation for their being 'third party endorsers'.

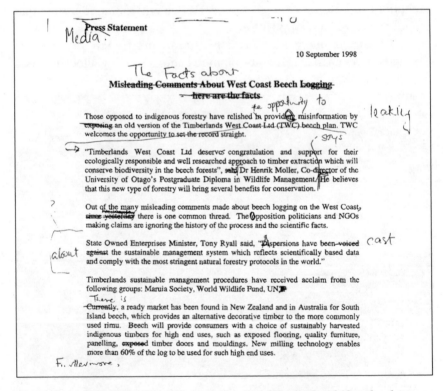

Environmentalists distributed a leaked copy of Timberlands' beech scheme plans in September 1998, derailing the carefully planned PR strategy. This draft Timberlands press release was part of frantic efforts to cope with the leak.

Timberlands had decided to limit opposition by ensuring that a 'Low media profile [was] maintained until appropriate timing'.[7] A 1997 Shandwick strategy paper on a completely different subject, the graffiti campaign, had urged care with Timberlands' public image in case bad publicity about its anti-environmental tactics 'provide[d] the rationale for an official sympathetic to NFA to leak the Beech report'.[8]

Shandwick's fears about the plans being leaked were well founded. The launch plans collapsed when the beech scheme papers were leaked to Forest and Bird and NFA in September 1998. Shandwick discovered that even the best laid PR strategies and crisis management plans can go awry. Shortly after the leaked plans were passed on to journalists in the Beehive Theatrette at Parliament, a journalist rang up the Timberlands headquarters for comment. The Timberlands staff were in such a state of confusion that they included her in an emergency telephone conference between the senior Timberlands management, gathered together in their boardroom, and Shandwick staff in Wellington. They seemed oblivious to her presence as people continued to speak over each other, despairing, angry and panicky.

The Timberlands Papers include the draft press release sent urgently back and forth to Shandwick that afternoon. To divert attention from the details of its logging plans, the company argued that an outdated version of the plans had been leaked. In fact they were only a few weeks old and identical in all important respects to the final plans. 'Those opposed to indigenous forestry have relished the opportunity to provide misinformation by leaking an old version of the Timberlands West Coast Ltd beech plan,' the press release began.[9] It cited the company's carefully cultivated scientific and environmental allies, attacked the groups involved in the leak and even attacked Opposition leader Helen Clark, who had spoken at the leaking press conference, as caring more about 'political votes' than conservation. But Timberlands knew it had lost the advantage, and was beginning its campaign to win backing for a beech scheme on the defensive.

'Greenwashing' – the environmental equivalent of whitewashing – is a phrase that has emerged to describe the way that environmentally damaging companies portray themselves as 'green' to try to divert public attention from their activities. Commonly, companies and politicians adopt the language of their environmental critics to promote themselves.

When Shandwick was planning a survey questionnaire, for instance, it advised Timberlands that all survey questions should be in 'neutral language, rather than using terms such as "logging" and "native trees", in order to avoid bias'.[10] Logging of old growth forests becomes 'sustainable harvesting of indigenous production forests'. Similarly, while the beech logging plans are referred to as a 'beech scheme' in various private PR documents, in all public documents they are strictly referred to as the 'Sustainable Beech Management Plans'.

This is language that carefully omits anything unhelpful, emphasising the trivial 'positive' aspects of their clients' activities while sidestepping the main and most negative aspects. As described by Peter Dykstra of Greenpeace, greenwashing corporations depict 5 percent of environmental virtue to mask 95 percent of environmental vice.

A 1997 'communications strategy' prepared by Shandwick considered in detail how to portray the company as being environmentally responsible. To enhance its image, Timberlands was advised to upgrade, not its actual environmental research, but publicity about this. Shandwick also proposed that it publish an 'Environmental Report', upgrade the company's self-promoting *Green Monitor*, host environmental media facility visits (to coincide with the launching of the beech plans) and establish the 'open forests' policy.[11]

Timberlands went further. Instead of responding defensively to the charges of its critics, it sought to position itself as the saviour of the forests.

Greenwashing: the company's publications, including this video cover, consistently used words such as 'sustaining', 'nurturing' and 'natural' in descriptions of logging. 'Sustainable' was used in virtually every written and spoken communication.

'Far from wanting to "wreck" the forests, Timberlands' vision is to keep them in perpetuity,' the company's PR manager, Paula de Roeper, wrote in a letter to the editor. In Timberlands' view, the only hope for the forests was to log them. 'Change is constant, preservation is unattainable,' she lamented, before concluding 'Timberlands works for conservation so that future generations will enjoy the magnificent forests'.[12]

With even greater PR boldness, many Timberlands statements adopted a 'we are the real conservationists' theme. In August 1997, for instance, Dave Hilliard wrote to Professor Alan Mark, 'As true conservationists we respect our global as well as our national responsibilities'.[13]

An article in the *Independent* which, like the letter to Alan Mark, was written by Rob McGregor of Shandwick and signed by Hilliard, made an even more audacious claim. If the environmentalists were 'to succeed in their aim, they would be responsible for a set of perverse outcomes that would impact not only on the physical landscape in this country but contribute to the havoc being inflicted on rainforest around the globe, causing social and economic dislocation. Timberlands is accused of environmental vandalism by a group of extreme activists who are self-appointed, misinformed, and politically motivated.'

And further on in the article Hilliard referred to his 'responsibility to run a profitable forestry business.... In doing so, we believe that it is Timberlands that has advanced the cause of the wider environment, and not our critics.'[14] Shandwick staff were obviously pleased with this line, having used it earlier that month in a letter to the editor of the *Evening Post*: 'However, Timberlands believes the company, not its critics, has advanced the cause of the wider environment'.[15]

In the Timberlands lexicon, logging became 'harvesting', which 'mimics natural forest replacement processes' and 'retains the protective forest cover'. Timberlands publications and letters were liberally sprinkled with reassuring and soothing descriptions such as 'sustainable', 'natural', 'in perpetuity', 'regeneration' and 'minimal impact'. Among 'key messages' in one PR paper, logging of native forests was referred to as 'nurturing ecosystems'.[16] 'Sustainable' is used in virtually every written and spoken comunication.

The word 'sustainable' has become a favourite of greenwashers everywhere. An example of this is the World Business Council for Sustainable Development, formed in January 1995, which describes itself as a 'coalition of 125 international companies united by a shared commitment to the environment and to the principles of economic growth and sustainable development'. Its members are drawn from 30 countries and include, in terms of their environmental records, many of the world's most criticised chemical, industrial, genetic engineering and mining companies.[17] The membership list contrasts unflatteringly with the list of members of the United States-based Businesses for Social Responsibility. When companies such as Monsanto, Dow Chemical, Waste Management and the world's biggest mining company, Rio Tinto, adopt the word 'sustainable' it is worth checking out what definition is being used.

With a little 'repositioning', mining in national parks becomes sustainable, nuclear power is touted as the answer to the greenhouse effect and genetic engineering as the solution to food shortages.

In the case of Timberlands, the problem with its sustainability claims was easy to see. The first point about sustainability is whether a particular 'resource' should be exploited at all. Everyone, environmentalists and corporations alike, agree that more sustainable practices are urgently required. But it is a corruption of the concept to suggest that 'sustainable practices' give companies a licence to start exploiting the few last wild places, such as rainforests, left on earth. The best option can be to strive to retain them in a natural state.

As part of its efforts to claim independent credibility for its logging plans, Timberlands went to the overseas standards certification company SGS International Certification Services seeking ISO 14001 certification – a

corporated • Eastman Ko... • Interface Inc...
rporation • Grupo IMSA, S.A. de C.V. • Petro-Canada • Procter & Gamble
Johnson • Noranda Inc. • Petro-Canada • Suncor Energy Inc • Suez Ly
ompany • S.C. Johnson & Son, Inc. • Suncor Energy Inc • TransAlta Corporat
roup • CH2M Hill • Dow Chemical Company • TransAlta Corporation • UPM-Kymn
itro • Monsanto Company • Ontario Power Corporation • 3M Company • Avenor
Arthur D. Little • DuPont • Rio Tinto PLC • 3M Company • Saga Petroleum A.S.
Inc • Shell International Ltd • Unilever N.V. • Saga Petroleum A.S.
• AT&T • Waste Management International • Time Warner • TXI •
Unocal • Westvaco Corporation • Weyerhaeuser Company • Xerox
Corporation • Lafarge • March Group • Fortum Corporation (formally
Neste Oy) • NestlÈ Ltd\ • Norsk Hydro ASA • Novartis Internationa
Nordisk A/S • PLIVA d.d. • RhÙne-Poulenc • Royal Philips
• SGS SociÈtÈ GÈnÈrale d

The World Business Council for Sustainable Development, which includes the world's most criticised chemical, industrial, genetic engineering and mining companies, epitomises the way the word 'sustainable' can be abused by greenwashers.

supposed test of environmentally sound forestry practice. In May 1999 Dave Hilliard announced that, following months of extensive analysis and auditing of the company's environmental systems, Timberlands had been 'awarded' the 'Green Dove ISO 14001 environmental certification for its forest management'.[18] The dove logo was from then on featured on the Timberlands letterhead and an issue of the *Green Monitor* declared that the company's 'reputation has been strengthened with the award of the prestigious Green Dove ISO 14001 certification'.

A letter to the editor of the *Press* explained how little the awarding of the certificate really meant. 'As a trained EMS auditor,' wrote Andrew P. Nichols, 'I am angered over Dave Hilliard's misleading claim that the ISO 14001 certification of Timberlands is some kind of endorsement of their forest destruction practices. The ISO14001 standard requires that an environmental management system complies with respect to the law, local regulations and a standardised documentation of its procedures (whether sustainable or otherwise).... SGS International Certification

Green Monitors, according to secret PR plans, were to 'provide information and confidence in Timberlands' decisions and operations, undermine extreme view credibility [and] promote the moderate view'. The 'extreme view' in practice included anything that questioned Timberlands' logging plans.

Services just checks compliance with this standard and does not certify ecologically sustainable management practices.'[19]

Timberlands attempts to give scientific respectability to its operations through a publication called the *Green Monitor*, which is published on ostentatiously recycled-looking paper. Peppered though its pages are stories about 'working with nature' and Timberlands' concern about the forest ecosystem and the fate of endangered bird species.

In the leaked internal documents, Timberlands is candid about the role of the *Green Monitor* in the debate over the logging of the forests. The objectives and aims of the publication were outlined in Timberlands' 1994 communications strategy. It was to 'provide information and confidence in Timberlands' decisions and operations, undermine extreme view credibility [and] promote the moderate view'. In practice, the 'extreme view' included anything that questioned Timberlands' logging plans.

Timberlands identified its audience as 'Ministers, advisers, relevant MPs, caucus leaders/spokespeople, key house committee members, local/regional government, key media'. The first issue in 1995 described it as a 'reference and briefing file for decision-makers'. The 1998 *Green Monitor* mailing list, which was among the Timberlands Papers, had 400 names including all MPs, parliamentary staff, central and local government officials, editors and journalists, libraries and a wide variety of individuals involved in the native logging issue.

The purpose of the *Green Monitor* was demonstrated by an issue distributed in early 1999, which replied to a scientific report by the Crown research institute Landcare casting serious doubts on the beech scheme management plans. The Landcare report, which had been commissioned by Forest and Bird, found mistakes in the Timberlands forest population model that meant the company had overestimated the number of millable trees by 95 percent over 50 years and by a factor of four over 200 years. 'The Timberlands model contains a systematic bias that exaggerates yield and contributes to the illusion of sustainability,' the author Murray Efford concluded. 'The bias was found to be large, and serious enough to call into question the validity of any economic projections for the scheme.'[20]

A few weeks after this damning report was released, Timberlands began circulating a draft *Green Monitor* to some of its key government and environmental allies in an attempt to reduce the damage of the Landcare criticism. The introduction said that there were 'serious lapses' in the Landcare report and that 'consequently, it should be viewed with scepticism and no reliance placed on its extreme conclusion'.[21]

The *Green Monitor* contained several pages of justification of its mathematics, finally coming to its real concern in the final paragraph of the report. 'The Landcare report has laid Timberlands open to abuse by the inevitable exaggerations of its opponents from the extreme environmental lobby,' it argued. 'Imbalances in the Landcare report have put years of careful work towards an ecologically and economically sustainable project, and the livelihood of West Coasters, at political risk.'

The Landcare report had been peer reviewed by other scientists before publication and, after Timberlands' criticisms, the Landcare management checked it again. That was the difference between the two publications: one was a scientific paper, the other a political document. The function of the *Green Monitor* was not to get to the bottom of the issue but to attempt to discredit this questioning of the logging plans. Timberlands' immediate response, the day after the report was released,

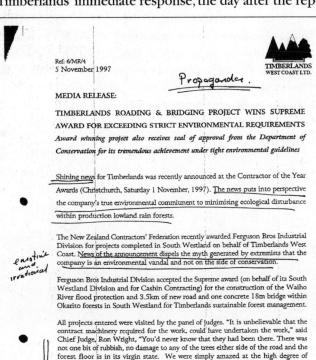

Ref: 6/MR/4
5 November 1997

Propaganda.

TIMBERLANDS
WEST COAST LTD.

MEDIA RELEASE:

TIMBERLANDS ROADING & BRIDGING PROJECT WINS SUPREME AWARD FOR EXCEEDING STRICT ENVIRONMENTAL REQUIREMENTS
Award winning project also receives seal of approval from the Department of Conservation for its tremendous achievement under tight environmental guidelines

Shining news for Timberlands was recently announced at the Contractor of the Year Awards (Christchurch, Saturday 1 November, 1997). The news puts into perspective the company's true environmental commitment to minimising ecological disturbance within production lowland rain forests.

emotive and irrational

The New Zealand Contractors' Federation recently awarded Ferguson Bros Industrial Division for projects completed in South Westland on behalf of Timberlands West Coast. News of the announcement dispels the myth generated by extremists that the company is an environmental vandal and not on the side of conservation.

Ferguson Bros Industrial Division accepted the Supreme award (on behalf of its South Westland Division and for Cashin Contracting) for the construction of the Waiho River flood protection and 3.5km of new road and one concrete 18m bridge within Okarito forests in South Westland for Timberlands sustainable forest management.

All projects entered were visited by the panel of judges. "It is unbelievable that the contract machinery required for the work, could have undertaken the work," said Chief Judge, Ron Wright, "You'd never know that they had been there. There was not one bit of rubbish, no damage to any of the trees either side of the road and the forest floor is in its virgin state. We were simply amazed at the high degree of sensitivity and understanding of the environment taken during construction."

He continued, "This is a first for environmental engineering projects as no other project has been submitted like it. It has surpassed everything we have ever seen and we were very impressed at the thorough manner in which this was handled such as discussions with the Department of Conservation. I believe it would do environmentalists good to have an look at the roadway and understand once and for all that we as New Zealander's can work in the forest, work to save our heritage and look after the environment. It is not everyday that you see the level sensitivity that was approached in Okarito forest."

This was too much even for Timberlands' own PR staff. Handwritten notes on the media release, distributed by Head Consultants, described it as 'Propaganda' and 'emotive and irrational'.

had not boded well for sensible scientific debate. General manager of planning Kit Richards had issued a knee-jerk press release dismissing it as 'asinine'.

Despite Landcare not backing down on its original findings, Timberlands subsequently sent a revised copy of the *Green Monitor* to everyone on the mailing list.[22] Although Efford had found that Timberlands' objections were not valid, the *Green Monitor* aimed to reassure supporters of the beech scheme and, for decision-makers, at least to muddy the waters enough that the criticisms would have less impact.

A 1997 issue of *Green Monitor* entitled *Ecologically Sensitive Engineering* was devoted to praise of a new bridge Timberlands had had constructed across a creek in Okarito Forest. Its theme was that 'potentially damaging engineering projects can, with innovation, care and co-operation, and "an eye to the greatest overall benefit" be successfully undertaken in lowland rain forest environments at minimal ecological cost'. Okarito is indisputably one of the finest rimu forests in New Zealand and the best coast-lagoon-terrace forest sequence left anywhere in the country. The purpose of the bridge was to allow a controversial new road to be pushed into the untouched half of the forest, opening it

The press release on the previous page praised a new bridge Timberlands constructed to allow logging in this forest at Okarito Lagoon. It was a classic case of emphasising the 5 percent of environmental virtue to mask 95 percent of environmental vice. Photo: Steve Phipps

up to logging. The Okarito road was being strongly criticised by environmentalists, who believed it was being bulldozed into pristine forest to head off conservation proposals. Publicising the ecologically sensitive bridge was a classic case of emphasising the 5 percent of environmental virtue to mask 95 percent of environmental vice.

School children have been another key target of the company greenwashing. For two years, from 1997 to 1999, production of PR materials for schools was a regular item at the weekly teleconferences. The idea began after Timberlands' annoyance over the May 1997 school students conservation rally at Parliament. Not content with letters of complaint to the principals, two weeks later Klaus Sorensen of Shandwick sent a seven-page strategy plan to Timberlands proposing how the company could get its message to 'year seven and eight schoolchildren'. The introduction explained that, following the rally, it had been decided that 'a more formalised approach' was needed to deal with 'environmental attacks' of this nature.[23] The plan was to produce a school resource kit to be provided free to every school in the country for use in the science curriculum.

The 'ecologically sensitive bridge' allowed construction of this new road, which environmentalists believed was being bulldozed into pristine forest to head off conservation proposals. Photo: Peter Russell

The paper proposed that the kit include Timberlands' beech scheme promotion video, laminated posters, maps, guide notes for teachers and information on 'Timberlands revenue contribution to the local community'. As a concession to balance, the final item in the kit was to be 'An environmental view'.

'The kit,' Sorensen explained, 'will use those Timberlands resources already available and with a relatively modest expense will develop these along with associated teaching materials into a kit which, because of its specific curriculum relevance, will be taken seriously within schools and will apply peer pressure to those teachers with an existing environmental position. The strategy is therefore to ensure that the kit cannot be discarded in the first instance and will be accepted as a useful and important teaching aid.'[24]

The draft covering letter to principals and heads of social studies and science explained that Timberlands was 'able to operate a long-term indigenous forest industry on the Coast with no environmental damage. We believe it is important that children have information which will help them to make informed choices on how NZ's natural resources are managed.'[25] The guide for teachers consisted of three pages of points justifying continued West Coast native logging, followed by a quarter of a

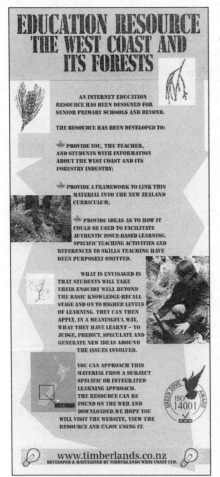

After the May 1997 school students' conservation rally, it was decided that 'a more formalised approach' was needed to deal with 'environmental attacks' of this nature. The result was this school resource kit to get the company's message to 'year seven and eight schoolchildren'.

page of arguments in favour of native forest conservation that were deliberately phrased to sound extreme.[26]

A year later the kit was still being worked on. The plan by June 1998 was to have a 'promotional postcard' sent to all schools advertising a school resource kit located on the Timberlands website, and a double-page poster in the school student magazine *Tearaway*. 'This poster would tell the Timberlands/West Coast forestry story and, by accessing students directly, bypasses the teachers who for their own reasons could choose not to use the School Resource Kit,' a Shandwick briefing paper explained.

In contrast to the small school conservation rally that started all this off, which had been organised openly and with parental permission, Shandwick believed that Timberlands should downplay its role in the school PR kit and make it appear, as much as possible, to be a legitimate part of the school curriculum. The paper noted that 'an outstanding issue relating to the School Resource Kit is how it is branded, the prominence given to Timberlands'. Shandwick knew the company would not be popular with school students and wanted as little sign as possible that it had provided the educational materials. 'To ensure uptake of the resource and to enhance its credibility,' Shandwick advised, 'we recommend the Timberlands branding be discreet rather than prominent.'[27]

The school resource kit, completed in mid-1999, included all the well-practised arguments for native logging. The 'environmental view' never made it into the final version. The list of 'School Resources' available consisted of the *Green Monitor* newsletter – 'a useful periodical with lots of interesting facts and figures about forestry on the West Coast', the company's beech scheme information kit, its 'sustainable forestry' promotion video and 'summary information' on Timberlands and West Coast forestry. The promotional brochure sent to schools stated that 'The Educational Resource was commissioned, and is maintained, by Timberlands West Coast Ltd. as part of its commitment to our communities'.

Production of materials for schools is a growth area for public relations companies around the world. Corporate interests realise the value of getting their spin into the classrooms of future customers and voters. Schools, perhaps more than any other area, deserve to be kept free of such commercial influence.

On the West Coast the two major threats to native forests are destructive human practices such as logging and introduced animals. Not surprisingly, Timberlands was keen to put the spotlight on the animal pests. One strategy developed with Shandwick was to claim that active conservation efforts by Timberlands, funded from the proceeds of its logging operations, would lead to the native wildlife and ecology being better off under a logging regime than in reserves.

Animal pests such as possums and deer feed on native plants, while rats, stoats and again possums feed on birds and other native animals. Exploiting legitimate public concern about these pests, Timberlands considered it had an argument to blunt environmental anxiety about its operations. As government spending on conservation management has always been inadequate, conservative industries, think-tanks and politicians have latched onto a new argument against excluding mining and logging from protected reserve lands. If we log a forest here, we can fund environmental protection there: for some, it is a seductive thesis.

Timberlands began to argue that the money it spent on control of possums and assisting research into stoat control more than compensated for the impact of its current and planned logging. To support its

Timberlands followed Shandwick's advice and made the 'pest control argument' central to its public justification of the beech scheme, but no more money was committed to predator research.

West Coast Times 7-1-99

Predator research is threatened by environmentalists' plans to derail the West Coast beech scheme, according to Kit Richards (pictured) from Timberlands.

Timberlands claims research only hope for wildlife

[By Ian Gill]

Environmentalists opposing sustainable beech logging on the West Coast could be hammering the final nail in the coffin of endangered wildlife.

Timberlands West Coast says predator research included in its beech scheme is the only glimmer of hope for wildlife threatened with extinction inside 60 years.

can't effectively control much either."

"What we are promising is that we are going to invest significant sums into research to try and find a method," he said.

Mr Richards said Timberlands has spent $200,000 on the beech scheme predator research programme over four years, despite not earning any money from these

argument that excluding logging would make things worse, Timberlands scathingly attacked the Department of Conservation about the neglect of pest control in reserved forests for which it is responsible. It went so far as to say that environmentalists could be 'hammering the final nail in the coffin of endangered wildlife'.[28] In a front-page article in the *West Coast Times*, Timberlands' general manager Kit Richards claimed that predator research included in its beech scheme is 'the only glimmer of hope for wildlife threatened with extinction within 60 years'. He proclaimed himself 'astonished' that the environmental lobby was 'prepared to sacrifice endangered wildlife'.

Timberlands' statements gave the impression that the predator control was a central part of its plans. 'The results of Timberlands research into predator elimination programmes have been encouraging and, if successful,' the company wrote in a briefing for the Minister of Forestry, 'these techniques will be applied to critical areas of the Sustainable Forest Estate'.[29] In reality, Timberlands' modest financial contribution to some predator research was quite separate from its logging plans.

The research in question was initiated by a small Dunedin-based consultancy, Ecosystem Consultants, in the mid-1990s. They have been experimenting with a technique of poisoning rats, mice and possums in native forests, which in turn kills stoats feeding on these animals. This was public-interest research that would once have been done by government scientists but, in an environment of privatised science, the Ecosystem Consultants researchers had had to seek money from a range of funders. They presumably welcomed sponsorship from Timberlands for their valuable work; at the same time, however, Timberlands got more than its money's worth by exploiting its support for the research in its PR campaign.

Possums, rats and stoats are very destructive of native forests. If a plan could be devised where a bit of logging provided the funds to control all these pests, would not it actually be better for the forests? Maybe – which was why the Ecosystems Consultants sponsorship was useful for Timberlands' PR campaign. Sadly, that was not what was happening and it was not what was intended. Near the back of Timberlands' beech management plans it was explained that, if predator control techniques could be developed, the company had no intention of ever funding the large expense of implementing them in its forests. The plans explained that this money would have to come from the government, which, of course, would not require logging the forests at all.

For a few tens of thousands of dollars a year ($44,000 in 1998 paid to Ecosystems Consultants and $41,000 on possum control[30]), Timberlands created a supposed link between its logging and protection of the forests, which it then referred to in almost every publication and public statement thereafter. This 'logging saves forests' argument has helped win over various political allies.[31]

The Timberlands spending on pest control in fact contrasted very poorly with the amount spent by the Department of Conservation each year on the West Coast forests in reserves. Tired by repeated Timberlands attacks about its neglect of pest control, in 1998 the director-general of DOC, Hugh Logan, circulated a letter taking issue with Timberlands' claims. He pointed out that his department was spending $3.7 million in that year on West Coast pest and weed control: 50 times more than Timberlands.

Shandwick's advice to Timberlands repeatedly emphasised the value of the predator argument. In its 1997 Beech Project Launch Proposal, for instance, the focus of the main media briefing at the launch was to be 'both on the business case and on the principles of sustainable management, ecological environment preservation and native species preservation and predator control'. The strategy document, which mentions the word 'sustainable' 19 times in its four pages, urged that 'strong emphasis' be placed on the predator control programme as a 'key message' and even proposed that 'consideration be given to upgrading the predator control programme to coincide with the launch'.[32]

Timberlands heeded Shandwick's advice that the pest control argument be central to its public justification of the beech scheme, but no more money was committed to the predator research. The argument was useful for countering environmentalist pests without having to spend any more money on the beech forest varieties.

CHAPTER 6

CONTROLLING THE MEDIA

*We need to be consistent with our strategy which is to let
them know we're aware of everything they say, and to
always insist on replying to them - having the last word.*
Rob McGregor, Shandwick New Zealand Ltd,
3 December 1997[1]

None of the greenwashing and other public relations tricks should work
if the news media are doing a good job. Part of the function of a free
press is that journalists can cut through attempts by vested interests to
mislead the public. Their job is to report all sides of an issue independently and fairly to inform their audience. Well, that is the theory.

In practice, few news organisations are willing to provide much
time and resources for their staff to probe and build up specialist knowledge of issues. The emphasis on making news organisations profitable
has seen the rise of specialist sections to attract advertising revenue at
the expense of general news sections. Investigative journalism has fared
worst of all. In comparison, public relations companies have considerable time and resources to put into trying to gain news prominence for
their clients' messages and, wherever possible, their spin. Timberlands'
'communications strategies', such as their letters to the editor system,
are all part of this effort.

There is nothing sinister about a company trying to promote itself
and its point of view in the media. Governments, political parties and interest groups, including environmental groups, all want and should be able
to have their say. In a healthy democracy, informed debate should allow
for the airing of many and diverse views so that members of the public
can decide for themselves. The important boundary lies between promoting strongly held views and trying to control or manipulate all the news
on an issue. Democracy is weakened when one interest seeks to bend all
the news its own way and to actively discourage other points of view

being heard. This was precisely what Timberlands and its PR companies tried to achieve. The PR strategy papers were quite blunt about the fact that their goal was to 'control the media as far as possible'.[2]

As far back as 1994, Timberlands planned its strategy for cultivating key supportive journalists. The objective, Timberlands wrote, was to 'develop close contact with a number of key individuals in the press industry whose support is likely to be most influential'.[3] Timberlands' main strategy for winning the support of influential journalists was an active 'Journalist Contact Programme'. Any journalists writing regularly on the issue, and especially potentially sympathetic environmental and business reporters, were invited on three-day tours of the West Coast as guests of Timberlands. Everything was very carefully planned and controlled, taking the visitors to model logging sites where it was hard to pick where the trees had been removed. More important, the journalists were accompanied by top company officials, allowing long hours of talking as Timberlands staff tried to convince their captive audience to their point of view. Evenings of wining and dining with the senior staff provided an opportunity to build up friendly relationships.

The journalists often rewarded this attention with large feature articles, in which only token, and sometimes no mention at all, was made of opposing viewpoints. Indeed Timberlands expected articles in return for its money. In one case when no article had appeared, Shandwick's Klaus Sorensen took on the job of ringing the business reporter from

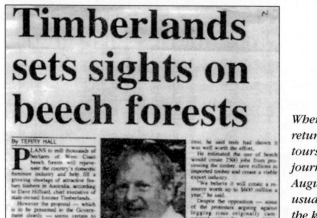

When journalists returned from the PR tours, here a business journalists' tour in August 1997, they usually wrote precisely the kind of uncritical, one-sided feature articles Timberlands' strategy plans had intended.

the *Press* 'to find out why they haven't produced articles as a result of the media visit'.[4]

Only the most sceptical journalists were not influenced by the tours. Three days of exposure to one side of an argument would rarely be balanced in a busy journalist's schedule by equivalent time for the other viewpoint: hearing, for instance, why the predator control scheme was not what it seemed, or seeing what real logging looked like. The treatment was persuasive. 'They think Timberlands is wonderful by the end,' Paula de Roeper told a colleague. 'But,' she complained, 'their stories get edited when they're back home.'

Not only did Timberlands PR staff plan where the journalists went and what they saw; they also planned what they hoped the eventual stories would say. When Pattrick Smellie of the *Sunday Star-Times* went on a Timberlands tour in December 1998, the PR staff also developed 'suggested story ideas/angles' for his article to guide their briefings to him. An internal PR document written shortly before his visit proposed that 'this is not a forestry story and should be aimed at the very average general public'. Paula de Roeper recommended that they encourage Smellie to focus on the 'misinformation angle: why is it that politicians and the general public are listening so closely to the "opposition" while experts have the scientific fact that proves that sustainable management systems work? Is there a conspiracy?!' She also hoped the story would describe how 'overseas experts [are] very impressed' and 'New Zealanders can be very proud of the systems in place here'.[5]

A note at the end of Smellie's eventual article pleaded its independence, saying that the newspaper had paid for his visit to the West Coast. Timberlands had, however, invested considerably more money in the visit, for instance flying him by helicopter on the same carefully chosen route it had used to impress various visiting politicians. It is interesting to look at the results. On any issues concerning economics, Smellie's area of journalistic expertise and interest, his reporting of the visit was critical of Timberlands, describing it as 'heavily subsidised, barely profitable and not commercially structured'. He noted that Timberlands was paying only about 3 percent of the market rate for the rimu trees it logged and was hoping to pay low prices for beech forest too.[6]

But on the ecological issues he had clearly been won over. In a superficially balanced feature article, over three-quarters of the space presented Timberlands' case, including the first third and the final section of the article. It was the kind of coverage that PR strategies work to achieve.

The only positive comment about environmentalists in the article was a quote from Body Shop chief executive, Ashleigh Ogilvie-Lee, describing Native Forest Action as the 'most effective and dedicated activists we've ever worked with'. But Smellie's next line was: 'She is unconcerned that Native Forest Action claims about the extent of logging under the beech scheme may be over-stated by a factor of six'.[7] It is obvious that it had been Smellie's question, not Ogilvie-Lee's reply, that suggested NFA's statements about the beech scheme might be highly inaccurate. In fact the NFA figures are confirmed by government papers, but Smellie had bought into the Timberlands 'misinformation angle' without checking the facts and NFA barely got a look in.

The expenditure on Pattrick Smellie's helicopter trip would have been judged very good value for money. He was flown over an area of otherwise unlogged beech forest where some logging trials had occurred. The purpose of the flight was to demonstrate how the forest appeared untouched from the air – and of course it was indeed unscarred after only a small proportion of one year's logging had occurred. What Smellie saw gave no impression of what a full-scale beech scheme, with its attendant road networks and log collection areas, would progressively do to the forests. But the flight had had the planned effect.

Smellie's article ended, half-apologetic about the PR motives of his hosts but still affected by them, with a description of flying over this

Visiting forestry experts laud TWC's management systems

Press 23/11/93

by Peter Christian
in Greymouth

Timberlands West Coast sustained forest management systems have received some unexpected high praise from visiting international forestry industry delegates.

The delegates were in New Zealand to attend the fifth International Forest Industry Roundtable conference at Rotorua. Their comments were made after a field trip to three of Timberlands' production and conservation forests.

Aspects of the management systems that came under scrutiny included attention to

because of the low value of harvested wood, he said. However, he believed that in the right conditions the Timberlands system was the most efficient he had seen.

Delegates from the United States and Canada also praised the level of commitment made to the systems, noting they were heavily weighted in favour of environmental considerations.

John Heissenbuttel, the forestry and wood division vice-president of the American Forest and Paper Association, said that in the United States, where most of the forest was in private hands, there were attempts to integrate not only environmental goals but also economic and social ones.

> **Harvesting could not be more selective or environmentally friendly.**
>
> Olav Henriksen
> Finnish delegate

A Timberlands PR teleconference arranged 'sympathetic media people' to provide positive news coverage of a visit by overseas foresters.

forest: 'Yes, these are the bits the company wants you to see. Yes, perhaps the heavy auditing which accompanies it will blow the scheme out of the water. In the meantime, however, this form of logging makes an extraordinary sight for this very simple reason – it is invisible.'[8]

Once they returned home, sympathetic journalists were identified for ongoing contact. When Timberlands was preparing for a public relations visit to the West Coast by the *Evening Post*'s environmental reporter, Suzanne Green, Shandwick was given the job of making contact with her after the trip to check out if she was sympathetic: 'Next Steps: Rob [McGregor] to follow up with Suzanne after the visit to establish her position'.[9] The minutes noted that, if appropriate, McGregor was to suggest that she do an interview and write a news story about one of Timberlands' allies.

Unknown journalists were screened. 'To check out Jo Mackay, NZ Business who has contacted Paula de Roeper re article on Timberlands', the minutes of another teleconference recorded.[10] After the first contacts, 'on side' journalists were regularly phoned by Timberlands PR staff to check they had all the information they need and to suggest story ideas. They were even sent Christmas cards personally signed by the senior Timberlands managers.

The Timberlands Papers quite openly identify certain journalists as being 'sympathetic' to the company, such as Peter Christian of the *Press*. So when a group of overseas foresters visited Timberlands in 1998, and the company hoped for positive news coverage from it, internal documents noted that Christian would be invited to accompany them and that Timberlands' second PR company, Head Consultants, would be asked to suggest 'other sympathetic media people'.[11] Christian joined the overseas foresters' visit, subsequently producing an article headed 'Visiting forestry experts laud TWC's management systems'. The article began: 'Timberlands West Coast sustained forest management systems have received some unexpected high praise from visiting international forestry industry delegates'.[12]

The presence in PR companies of former journalists such as Klaus Sorensen in Shandwick and Warren Head in Head Consultants is helpful for corporate media strategies. It not only provides detailed inside knowledge of how the media work, but it also allows access to networks of former colleagues still working as journalists, as well as political insiders and other sources. It delivers contact with 'sympathetic' journalists and, as we will see, access to senior news staff to complain about stories critical of their clients.

When Timberlands wanted lots of positive stories to appear, the PR staff could use their skills and contacts to try to build good publicity for the company. In 1998, as the beech scheme decision approached, the PR teleconference called for 'Generic articles to be pushed out in every possible publication. Trade, business, etc.'. [13] The following week the pressure was still on the PR staff for more positive stories. 'Proactive communications is [sic] paramount. Everyone to submit ideas on articles for publication and other ideas for proactive PR,' the minutes recorded. [14] One of de Roeper's ideas was to approach *Metro* magazine suggesting a feature with these story angles: 'This is a New Zealand resource that can be utilised through this innovative system forever. Lack of integrity of Forest & Bird. Jobs – forfeiting jobs and social structure of community through the population's innocent misunderstanding – orchestrated by F&B/NFA.' [15]

Another idea for proactive PR reached the newspapers in April 1999. Environmentalists had been pursuing Timberlands under the Official Information Act for material on the sensitive subject of the threatened plants and animals in forests open to logging. While it stalled on releasing this information, the company prepared a full-colour field guide of threatened plants and animals likely to be present in its forests to distribute to its logging staff. Under newspaper headlines such as 'Timberlands take on watchdog role', the project manager Karl Tolley explained that forestry crews were being asked to become 'conservation watchdogs' and keep a lookout for threatened species. This, he explained, would allow Timberlands to 'take special precautions' and, if necessary, 'evasive action' when logging in stands of trees where threatened species were spotted. [16]

When a letter to the editor appeared in the *Dominion* criticising the newspaper's lack of coverage of native forest conservationists and urging the paper to investigate the issue, Shandwick saw it as a chance to get good publicity for Timberlands. The 'in' was Klaus Sorensen's personal links with the *Dominion* editor. Shandwick faxed Timberlands suggesting that 'yesterday's letter to the editor from Susie Brow provides us with a potential opportunity to talk to the editor and brief him on the issue'. Rob McGregor's letter pointed out that 'Klaus knows Richard Long, the editor, well' and noted that 'Ms Brow challenged the editor to do some investigative journalism, a challenge we want the editor to take up'. He explained: 'We would want to ensure that the company perspective is presented, the environmental activists exposed as unreasonable and their tactics as unethical – not what Ms Brow had in mind'. [17]

All these examples demonstrate the 'positive' side of Timberlands' media strategies, using their PR staff and a PR budget to get better than balanced news coverage of their viewpoint. But just as much planning and effort went into attempting to block and discourage news organisations that covered their opponents' points of view.

Timberlands frequently used the line that the environmentalists were 'extreme' and perpetrating 'misinformation' to discourage journalists from taking them seriously. In many cases, the company went further, targeting journalists who included criticism of Timberlands in their stories and using legal threats in an attempt to scare off news organisations reporting on the environmentalists' case.

In one example, Timberlands had spent thousands of dollars on an all-expenses-paid PR visit to the West Coast for a group of business journalists. One of these, Richard Inder from the *National Business Review*, took the ordinary journalistic step of contacting someone from a different side of the issue, in this case Forest and Bird, for comment. Having heard about the trip, Forest and Bird took the opportunity to send Inder a briefing stating the case against logging; later, it sent this to other journalists too. When the Timberlands bosses found out, they were furious. Shandwick was given the job of investigating.

In a fax to Timberlands CEO, Dave Hilliard, Shandwick's Rob McGregor wrote: 're: Forest and Bird Propaganda. Here is the material that was sent to the Business Media following their return from the West Coast. We understand there is also another document but our contact has yet to locate it. You will be familiar with most of this, with the exception of the first three pages. They look as if they have been specifically cobbled together for the Business Media on the Timberlands tour.' Shandwick turned this into a conspiracy. 'If this is correct,' McGregor wrote, 'it suggests that Richard Inder of the NBR was working hand in glove with F&B as he accepted the invitation to be part of the visit.... We will try to deal with him separately. Klaus will be following this up.'

Typically, Timberlands also considered legal action against Forest and Bird. McGregor concluded that his 'reading of the [Forest and Bird] material is that it is not only factually incorrect, but that it was produced with the clear intent of impeding the company's ability to operate its lawful business. Therefore it is likely to be actionable.' He suggested that 'it could be sent to Pitt & Moore for an opinion as to whether we could successfully prosecute F&B'.[18] This was not pursued.

Shandwick used its media contacts to cause trouble for the journalist blamed for telling Forest and Bird about the trip. Klaus Sorensen reported a few days later that he was investigating the contact between the *National Business Review* and Forest and Bird 'through media channels'.[19] What this meant was that Sorensen got in touch with the editor of the *National Business Review*, where he had previously been deputy editor himself, to complain about the journalist. 'Spoken with Nevile Gibson about C Hutchings and R Inder and he was appalled at their behaviour,' the teleconference minutes recorded.[20]

Yet all that had happened was that a journalist had gone to the 'other side' for comment, as Timberlands continually insisted journalists covering environmentalists should do. Forest and Bird had taken advantage of hearing about the PR trip to have its say, again precisely what Timberlands itself attempted to do at every opportunity.

Then there was the case of Timberlands complaining to the editor of *New Zealand Geographic* after a journalist tried to visit Charleston Forest with Native Forest Action. The journalist, Derek Grzelewski, described his experiences in the cover story of the magazine's October 1998 issue. A Timberlands contractor had taken him into Charleston Forest 'on a tour through seemingly pristine forest, which, save for a stump here and there, I would never have guessed had been logged at all'. He was told how they could fell trees with no damage to the surrounding forest, 'like throwing a cricket bat through the wicket without disturbing the bails'. A small helicopter 'happen[ed] to be available' (the pilot was based far away in Karamea and had probably been brought in especially) and took him for a flight. Just like Pattrick Smellie, he found the logging impact was 'so small you can't even see it from the air.... I no longer feel guilty about working on a rimu table,' he concluded.

Grzelewski was chatting and joking with a couple of the loggers when, as he was about to leave, a Timberlands security guard turned up. This man had the job of patrolling the 'open forest' to prevent protesters coming and going. Earlier the guard had caught NFA spokesperson Annette Cotter guiding Grzelewski into the forest to show him the damage caused by logging and had ordered them both out with threats of trespass charges. The guard recognised the journalist and 'the so-far animated conversation [took] a sudden dive.... No more jokes, no more verbal shoulder slapping.' Kit Richards of Timberlands complained to Grzelewski's editor about the journalist's attempt to enter the public forest with NFA.

As it happened, Grzelewski was 'growing increasingly uneasy about the conflicting messages about low-impact heli-logging.... I made another appointment with Annette Cotter.' Defying the pressure from Timberlands, they tramped in, starting in the early hours of an Easter Saturday. Three hours later, after following rivers, they got to the logging areas that were not a part of Timberlands' PR tours.

'What I see is what I imagine an elephant graveyard looks like,' Grzelewski wrote, 'a jumble of broken limbs, the pipe cleaner branches of rimu drooping dead like weeping willow, dry and brown. What I see is as different from the earlier site as a Zen garden is from a rubbish dump. Beyond their first branches – though I was told repeatedly that all millable timber is taken – the left over rimu logs are about an arm-length wide. There are also stumps of smaller trees, mainly beech, chainsawed hip-high, their trunks left where they fell.'

The PR helicopter flight was also explained. 'Ironically, Nature herself is quick to cover up the scene of the crime,' he wrote. 'Deprived of competition, fern trees mushroom out of the debris, blossoming into huge green umbrellas. That's why, from the air, you can see nothing but the unbroken carpet of verdure.'[21]

If the complaints against the *National Business Review* and *New Zealand Geographic* journalists sound like an overreaction, in one case a man was pursued by Timberlands' lawyers merely because of a passing comment during a radio interview on a different subject. In the course of the interview on National Radio's *Kim Hill* show about logging of native forests in Southland, lawyer David Parker had said, 'You know, the

Away from the PR tours: 'What I see is what I imagine an elephant graveyard looks like…. [It] is as different from the earlier site as a Zen garden is from a rubbish dump' – Derek Grzelewski, New Zealand Geographic. Photo: Peter Wham

most serious environmental damage through logging is still being done by Timberlands on the West Coast.'[22] Shandwick heard about the comment and was quickly onto the case.

In a fax to Timberlands, Klaus Sorensen wrote, 'Note reference to Timberlands on p.15 of attached transcript. Do you want me to correct this with Kim Hill's producer and find out where to contact this joker Parker?'.[23] Timberlands did. Pitt & Moore drafted a public apology for Parker to sign, 'accepting' that the statement was factually incorrect and 'unreservedly' apologising to Timberlands West Coast Limited. The minutes of Timberlands' PR teleconference recorded that 'Pitt & Moore have forwarded letter to Mr Parker (Kim Hill's radio show) and a follow up letter will be done today. Copies to Shandwick and Head Consultants.'[24]

The following week Timberlands was still pursuing Parker over his comment. Although he had no involvement in the West Coast forestry issue and the public had presumably long forgotten his words, the company went to the trouble of putting pressure on him through his employers. Parker refused to apologise, but the following week's teleconference minutes recorded that 'the firm he works for was tracked down and they promised to ensure that a public apology was made'.[25] Finally Timberlands pressure worked: 'Retraction aired on Kim Hill's programme. Suggested a copy of the script be faxed to the Minister's office.'[26]

Cartoonist Tom Scott, on the other hand, got the softly-softly approach following a satirical cartoon about Timberlands' logging published by the *Southland Times*. Sorensen sent it to Hilliard with this note: 'The attached cartoon concerns me greatly. The inferences are pretty much as serious as that chap Parker on Kim Hill's show. However Tom Scott is not only a bloody nice bloke he is also something of a national icon, therefore any threats of legal action would be likely to attract considerable unfavourable publicity and attendant accusations of trying to muzzle cartoonists' right to comment etc.'

Sorensen advised that it would be counter-productive dealing with Scott the way they had dealt with Parker. 'I suggest we deal with this one in a NICE way, i.e. pleasant letter to the Southland Times, plus a letter from Dave personally to Tom pointing out that his cartoon was based on something of a misunderstanding.... Let me know and I will begin drafting same,' Sorensen wrote to Timberlands.[27]

When Forest and Bird and NFA publicised the leaked beech scheme plans in 1998, the media gave prominence to the story. Timberlands was furious not only that the plans had been leaked but also that the coverage featured environmentalists' criticisms of the plans. Shandwick was quick to prepare formal complaints for Timberlands.

'TV ONE COMPLAINT: I have drafted the following letter to TV One chief reporter making a formal complaint,' McGregor wrote. 'I will get this emailed to you so that Dave can sign it and fax it to Ms Green [TV1 news editor] today.'[28] It was a busy time for Shandwick. The same day they drafted a complaint to TV3. 'We believe that this news item was not balanced or objective or impartial,' Shandwick wrote to Jacinta Sutton of TV3.

One of the purposes of the complaints is obvious. As an example of TV3's lack of balance, objectivity and impartiality, Shandwick's letter conjectured that the reporter gave Forest and Bird, ECO and NFA 'credence in referring to them as the heavyweights of the conservation movement'. It then complained that the news coverage had not included comment from the two environmental groups that supported Timberlands logging plans – as if this should be part of the reporting of the leaked logging plans. 'We note that at no time did the programme make any reference to the Maruia Society or the World Wide Fund for Nature, both of whom support sustainable forest management.'[29] The tactic worked. The following night TV3 had a follow-up item including Guy Salmon of the Maruia Society, whose endorsement had long been part of Timberlands' beech scheme launch planning, defending the logging.

When an anti-logging protest was organised for outside Parliament in July 1997, Timberlands was ready. 'Prepared news releases, facts and fallacies sheet, morning report interview with Kit Richards or Dave

Even the long-running TV soap Shortland Street got the heavy word from Timberlands.

Hilliard on Tues morning,' their internal documents noted.[30] But Timberlands also got Shandwick to draft a letter of complaint to Paul Gittens at TVNZ because the six o'clock news had run a brief item on the protest. Hilliard wrote 'we noted with interest your support for the Native Forest Action Group's recent Rally on the steps of Parliament.... While we respect your right to support this action, we wonder whether you had the opportunity to hear the other side of the debate.... Did you know that the West Coast Rimu supply saves in the order of 1,000 hectares of tropical rainforest in Southern Asia and Pacific Island nations from destruction each year?'[31] Why was Hilliard describing news coverage as 'support' for the protest? The obvious aim of the letter was to discourage such 'support' in the future by seeking to undermine NFA's credibility.

Timberlands went to ridiculous lengths to censor any adverse media references to itself. Even the long-running TV soap *Shortland Street* got the heavy word. In mid-1997 the producers caused offence when during a small sequence, a Native Forest Action poster was sighted on the wall of the nurses' staffroom. *Shortland Street* publicist Reagan Holdridge said that Timberlands had 'reacted strongly' to the poster and it was removed. '*Shortland Street* can't get into political battles,' she told the *Sunday Star-Times*, 'but a number of the cast do have an opinion and, yes, most of them have signed the [Native Forest Action] petition.'[32]

The Timberlands/Shandwick partnership even succeeded in muzzling news stories entirely, as in the case of the fledgling Auckland-based *Spirit* magazine. For its first issue it planned to run a large article on West Coast native logging. Kit Richards and Dave Hilliard were both interviewed but became aware that the story was going to be critical of the company's native forest logging. They then threatened to sue *Spirit* which, as a new publication, could not risk the legal costs, so the article was pulled out just before it was due to go to print.

The minutes of the weekly PR teleconferences show Timberlands working, right from when the magazine first made contact, to check out whether the article was likely to be positive or critical. 'Shandwick have been following up with more information on the magazine. Provide Head Consultants with information on "Spirit" publisher,' the minutes said.[33]

After the initial interviews, Timberlands resolved to stay in contact with the magazine to make sure it got its point across. 'CR and DH have been interviewed by Spirit Magazine. Article to appear in February issue. Should follow up to ensure all information is available,' the next week's teleconference recorded.[34] Their follow-up enquiries were less than encouraging. The next week they discussed their concerns at their regular phone conference. 'CR [Kit Richards, Timberlands] is not fully confident with "Spirit" magazine article,' they noted.[35] The following week they noted, 'Media: Spirit magazine – draft article not satisfactory and editor has since withdrawn it'.[36] The article was not 'satisfactory' because it was critical of

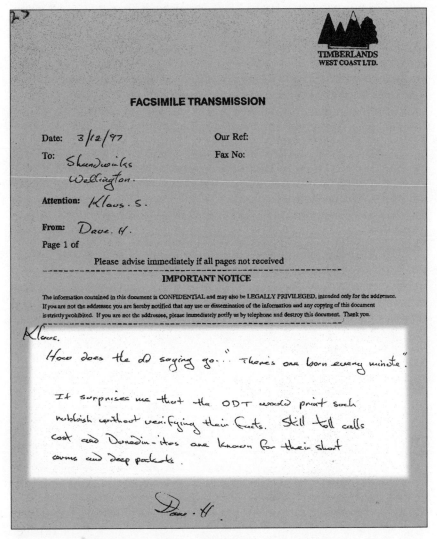

'Dunedin-ites are known for their short arms and deep pockets' – Dave Hilliard, a comment from the frequent correspondence between Timberlands and its PR companies on dealing with unfavourable news coverage.

Timberlands and gave prominence to the case for preserving the forests. The editor had not withdrawn it willingly.

Timberlands CEO Dave Hilliard was thin-skinned about any criticism of Timberlands in the media. When the *Otago Daily Times* published an article on rainforest and wetland conservation by Anthony Harris, including reference to Timberlands forests, Hilliard's reaction was abusive. He dispatched a fax to Klaus Sorensen at Shandwick in Wellington. 'How does the saying go…. "There's one born every minute". It surprises me that the ODT would print such rubbish without verifying the facts,' he fumed. 'Still toll calls are expensive and Dunedin-ites are known for their short arms and deep pockets,' Hilliard wrote, referring contemptuously to the Scottish ancestry of many in Otago.[37]

Later that day, Shandwick's Rob McGregor offered Hilliard a more strategic approach. 'Our suggested response to this nonsense is as follows. It consists of a letter to the editor and a contributed "opinion" article, which gives a big serve to Mr Harris. Please review, or get one of your people to review, the article.' The letter he drafted to the paper's editor said Hilliard trusted that they 'would want to provide balance to the extreme views propounded by Mr Harris'. McGregor's explanation of the reasoning behind this response also serves as a telling summary of Shandwick's overall media strategy: 'We do feel there is a need to reply, if we were to ignore this then they would try it on again. We need to be consistent with our strategy which is to let them know we're aware of everything they say, and to always insist on replying to them – having the last word,' he concluded.[38]

CHAPTER 7

MANUFACTURING POLITICAL ALLIES

We don't say, hey, will you come out and say nice things about us? No, we don't do that! As I say, we're a commercial entity, and we don't need nor want to get involved in that sort of stuff.

Dave Hilliard, 1999[1]

Back in 1994 Timberlands had acknowledged its isolation in the political landscape. On the West Coast, too, the senior staff had managed to sour relations with many influential locals. The company needed friends and allies if it was going to support its ambitious logging plans. 'It will be difficult for Timberlands to succeed as a "lone voice" against public / environmental opposition. The more allies the company has, preferably influential ones, who are willing to publicly support Timberlands, the easier it will be to counter opposition, and to exert counter-pressure at a political level. For this reason it is important that Timberlands develops its network of alliances and supporters,' stated an internal PR strategy.[2]

Timberlands then identified one of its objectives as being the need to 'maintain effective relationships with key influentials'. It therefore canvassed a strategy of 'Alliance Development' which would require it to 'develop contacts with groups whose interests are served by the implementation of Timberlands policies so that they become "natural allies" of Timberlands in times of conflict, and effectively act as spokespeople for Timberlands'. Given that many of those Timberlands would have called 'natural allies' were indifferent or even hostile towards the company, it was an ambitious plan.

Timberlands' list of possible 'allies' cited 'Trade Unions, West Coast Resource Users Group, The Forest Owners Association, FRI, Lincoln University, Forestry School – Canterbury, Rural Community....'. The strategy plan said the company should 'establish and prioritise which groups will be useful'.[3]

In its beech scheme PR plan, Timberlands recognised that it needed a specific strategy for 'developing Beech Allies'. 'Identify individuals/associations whose support would add credibility and authority to the beech scheme' the plan recommended. The company came up with a list that included some foresters specialising in native forests and a range of groups and institutions linked to native forest logging and conserva-

---

TIMBERLANDS WEST COAST

CORPORATE COMMUNICATIONS STRATEGY

The corporate communications strategy has been developed to support the achievement of the objectives set out in the Statement of Corporate Intent, and in particular, those outlined below:

To ensure that the company is:

- a commercial success;
- an industry expert and specialist in the area of management of indigenous forest resources;
- operating within ecologically sensitive environmental guidelines;
- an attractive joint venture partner;
- a good corporate citizen;
- an ongoing economic concern.

At the same time, effort must go into contact with the environmental movement to establish common ground and support for at least some of TWC's activities, so that it becomes increasingly difficult to view the company as an 'easy target'.

It will be difficult for TWC to succeed as a 'lone voice' against public / environmental opposition. The more allies the Company has, preferably influential ones, who are willing to publicly support TWC, the easier it will be to counter opposition, and to exert counter-pressure at the political level. For this reason it is important that TWC develops its network of alliances and supporters.

A significant pressure on both Government and public, is the extent to which TWC is viewed as a key figure in West Coast industry and employment. In addition to TWC promoting this fact to Government, the West Coast public and industry must be informed, and encouraged to support TWC.

The PR strategies included detailed plans for gradually winning over individuals in certain environmental groups.

tion: 'Denys Guild, Ian James, Academic Professors, Bird Researchers, Lincoln University, Canterbury University School of Forestry, Economists, Maruia, DOC/RF&B Scientists with TWC contacts, MOF, Udo Beneke'. The plan was to 'Develop contacts, provide information and solicit support for a campaign'.[4]

Allies can play a vital role in a company's public relations campaign. They can lobby government and participate in a political campaign, activities that Timberlands, as a government agency, can not be seen to be doing. Timberlands also needed allies who would add environmental 'credibility and authority' to the logging plans and 'effectively act as spokespeople for Timberlands'.

In the PR industry 'third party support' refers to the well-established device of arranging apparently independent and credible agencies to espouse the policies of the client. Corporations commonly rate as credible with less than 10 percent of the public while environmental organisations often rate in the 50-75 percent range. Using third parties to present the clients' case is much more effective than, for instance, paid advertising, which also has a low credibility rating. News coverage is seen to be more credible as the audience believe that the material has been sieved by journalists acting independently of commercial considerations.[5]

The people targeted by the company as possible 'beech allies' included native timber processors and users and 'experts' who could give the logging an appearance of professional respectability. It also set out to cultivate environmentalists from the World Wide Fund for Nature (WWF) and Guy Salmon of the Maruia Society. Environmentalists whose views could be used to undermine the standing of environmentalists opposing the logging would be particularly valuable. As we will see later, Timberlands also set out intensively to lobby and mobilise allies among public servants who advise the government on the issue.

As in the Journalist Contact Programme, the first, low-key step in the process of cultivating allies was offering visits to the West Coast to hear Timberlands present its arguments. In the three years from 1996 to 1998 Timberlands spent $100,000 from its PR budget hosting about 100 individuals and groups to the Coast for two-three day tours.[6] The guests were usually given free travel around the Coast, wine and meals – and for special guests helicopter flights – and received long days of well-practised talk from Timberlands staff justifying their operations. It was a convincing PR presentation for anyone who did not have detailed knowledge of the counter-arguments.

Timberlands said that such visits constituted 'consultation on the logging plans'. The Parliamentary Commissioner for the Environment questioned this. 'Timberlands appears to consider the consultation process consists of inviting stakeholders to visit sites and thereby understand,' he wrote. 'This process does not appear to have provided for the incorporation of any possible contribution by any visitors or commentators. There is little evidence to suggest that the groups so "consulted" have any impact on the plans.'[7]

Timberlands and its PR advisers worked hard to get native timber users to lobby the government in favour of continued logging. The management of these companies were regularly sent PR materials, brought to the Coast on all-expenses-paid visits to be sold the Timberlands line and

Lumber Specialties Ltd

115 MAIN SOUTH ROAD, CHRISTCHURCH, NEW ZEALAND
PO BOX 11211 • PHONE (03) 348-7002 • FAX (03) 348-7001

FACSIMILE MESSAGE

TO : SHANDWICK   DATE: 7/5/98

CITY/COUNTRY: FAX NO: 04-471-2278

ATTENTION: KLAUS SORENSEN   SENT BY: ALLAN SAYER

Dear Klaus,

For your information the following items appeared in the Christchurch Press yesterday and today

I have been writing and received replies from Shipley - Smith - and Ryall and would appreciate your thoughts on where now to head with consideration to the Media releases and if you require copies of letters received from the above three then please advise me.

Regards

Allan Sayer
Managing Director

ABS.NC

Timber industry allies: here the managing director of Lumber Specialties Ltd was co-ordinating with Shandwick on lobbying ministers.

included in strategy discussions about how to maintain the native timber supplies. Timberlands' PR strategy made it a priority to 'inform and educate potential natural allies as to the issues surrounding indigenous forestry management, and downstream industrial development, so that they can become "spokespeople" for TWC where implementation of TWC's plans appears threatened'.

Correspondence between Lumber Specialties Ltd, Christchurch, a firm using Timberlands' beech timber, and Shandwick in Wellington, indicated how useful allies could be. Allan Sayer, the managing director of Lumber Specialties, wrote to Klaus Sorensen at Shandwick passing on media stories from the Christchurch *Press*.

Sayer also wanted Sorensen's advice on lobbying ministers. 'I have been writing and receiving replies from [Jenny] Shipley – [Nick] Smith – and [Tony] Ryall,' Sayer wrote, 'and would appreciate your thoughts on where now to head with consideration to the media releases and if you require copies of letters received from the above three please advise me.'[8]

Likewise, Timberlands was provided with copies of letters from its main rimu customer, the Westco Lagan sawmill, to ministers lobbying for continued rimu logging. In one letter, Westco Lagan wrote to the then Prime Minister, Jim Bolger, to 'express the grave concern of our Company, Westco Lagan Limited, about the uncertainty surrounding the West Coast Accord....'.[9]

Westco Lagan worked closely with Timberlands in a major opinion poll that was used to lobby ministers in favour of maintaining native logging. The poll, which Westco Lagan funded, found that 90 percent of people agreed with a statement that native logging was acceptable provided it was done sustainably or in areas the government had set aside especially for forestry.

Environment groups pointed out that carefully worded questions had helped to ensure that the client got the required results. Native Forest Action said it was 'a sobering reminder that in the PR world money can buy anything'.[10] An UMR Insight poll conducted three months after the Westco Lagan one found that, on the specific issue of West Coast public native forests, only 22 percent of respondents disagreed that the government should 'put a stop to the logging of public-owned native forests on the West Coast'.[11] The Westco Lagan and NFA questions were so different that both could be accurate at the same time, but the message for the publicly-owned West Coast forests was clear.

The Westco Lagan survey produced good publicity for Timberlands, with headlines like 'Study claims 90% accept native logging'.[12] Westco Lagan director, Grant Carruthers, dismissed suggestions from NFA that the survey was a pro-logging public relations tool, saying that it was a marketing study 'to identify consumer attitudes towards purchasing native timber products'.[13] But a month before Westco Lagan publicised the survey, it had been circulated to politicians in Parliament on Timberlands letterhead. Here the results were presented in a Timberlands 'Political Briefing', headed '90% of New Zealanders nationwide are comfortable with the use of native forests for timber', with no mention at all of Westco Lagan's involvement.[14]

All of this had been planned in a Timberlands PR meeting with Shandwick shortly before the poll was completed. The minutes of the meeting noted that 'it was agreed that this research should be distributed to politicians in the first instance and possibly released publicly subsequently'. Shandwick was given the job of reviewing the research and preparing the briefing for the government.[15]

Joint research was referred to in the PR telephone conference minutes later that year: 'Kit Richards still to report back on discussions with Westco on research. To ring Rob McGregor [Shandwick] on this matter.'[16] After that, the poll was conducted six-monthly as a part of a programme to track shifts in public opinion.

When Timberlands was preparing the groundwork for the launch of the controversial beech scheme, Timberlands' 'friends' gained early information: 'Suggest that we start forwarding beech packs to our "friends" in parliament'.[17] Primed and well briefed, such allies could come out in support of the project so that Timberlands would not have to defend it alone.

The following month, Timberlands was mobilising support among its timber industry allies. 'Beech packs – to be distributed next week; FOA [Forest Owners Association], FIC [Forest Industry Conference] and Westco copies to be distributed immediately'.[18] A week later Timberlands reported that the distribution of the beech packs was progressing smoothly: 'Beech packs distributed to "friends": Eight to Ministers, Twelve to Westco etc.'.

Timber industry allies have also been regular recipients of the PR tours. When in 1997, the attempted attack by Timberlands on the Body Shop owners led them to stop all use of native timber and publicly urge other wood users to boycott rimu and beech, Timberlands feared a backlash. Within days of the Body Shop publicity, Timberlands ran a hastily organised all-expenses-paid PR trip to the Coast for Canterbury wood processors, on the weekend of 18-19 October 1997, to persuade them not to change to alternative timbers.

Allies in environmental organisations are especially valuable as they can give 'independent credibility' to logging plans. More important, they can be used to undermine the credibility of critical environmental organisations. Timberlands cultivated two organisations for this purpose, the World Wide Fund for Nature (WWF) and the Maruia Society.

In a letter to the editor of the *Otago Daily Times*, written by Shandwick and signed by Dave Hilliard, Timberlands proudly paraded its green allies. 'The extremists reject the concept of sustainable management, the cause of the mainstream conservation movement,' Hilliard

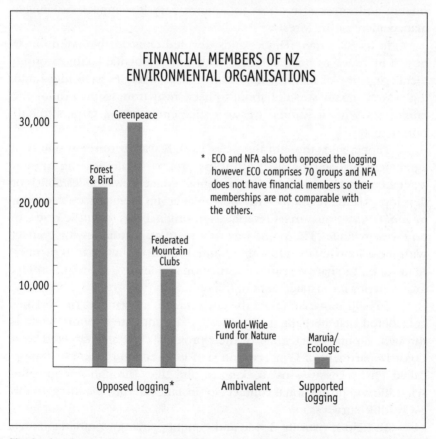

Timberlands sought to portray its environmental opponents as 'extreme' and 'fringe', and its few environmental supporters, the controversial Maruia Society and, for a time, the World Wide Fund for Nature, as 'mainstream'.

complained. Yet 'Timberlands has received accolades from organisations including WWF [and] the Maruia Society'.[19]

In a repeat of the age-old strategy of divide and conquer, WWF and Maruia were being used to undermine the work of other groups. Other supporters of environmental protection came in for the same treatment. When one wrote a letter to the editor of the *Otago Daily Times*, the Minister of State Owned Enterprises, Tony Ryall, had great pleasure in dismissing his concerns by citing Maruia and WWF's support for Timberlands. 'Mr Dougherty questions whether the beech plans will detrimentally affect other organisms inhabiting the forest. He might be interested to know that the Maruia Society and the World Wide Fund for Nature have publicly stated that Timberlands' proposal "represents a very sincere and impressive effort to achieve very low-impact sustainable management of the forest".'

In its PR papers Timberlands devoted considerable attention to how it intended to build alliances with 'Environmental Lobby Groups', identifying one of its most important initial strategies as 'bridge-building'. The company was not about to back away from its plan to log the rainforests. What it wanted was to entice environment groups to support its plans.

Timberlands thought the place to start was to 'develop points of agreement or commonality with these groups, ideally leading to joint agreements/statements etc.'. Timberlands' 'concept' was to 'establish or develop existing relations with individual group members on *common or non-contentious areas* [emphasis in original] eg. scientific research on forest wildlife'. The point was to 'Create opportunities for contact with these individuals'. From these initial contacts Timberlands planned to move on to 'share research information and involve them in developing scenarios for management in the wild'.

To help 'move alongside the environment movement', Timberlands considered that perhaps it should offer 'appropriate support' such as through 'support [for] some of their projects'.[20] (It also targeted West Coast Department of Conservation staff in a section of the PR strategy called 'Enviro-Discussions', seeking to find allies through 'encouraging scientific and professional contact', for instance during 'planning on forest wildlife surveys'.)

To help it plan its divide and conquer strategy, Timberlands felt that it needed to do some research on which of its current or possible opponents could be wooed. Of particular importance would be individuals who could be cultivated and would bring their organisation with them: 'Identify key opposition groups and the individuals within them who are likely to be more supportive/less opposed to Timberlands.'

Timberlands knew it could count on some support: 'Guy Salmon of the Maruia Society appears to be most open to this type of overture...'.[21] Support from Guy Salmon alone, however, would not be sufficient. Gaining the support of the WWF would be a significant prize.

Timberlands proposed methods of building personal contact with potential allies like the WWF. 'Obtain permission to use photos and personal quotes from a number of supporters and experts, in particular, bird experts, ecologists etc,' the strategy proposed.[22]

In the case of the WWF, Timberlands initiated co-operation with the organisation through some non-contentious surveying for the thought-to-be extinct South Island kokako in the Timberlands-controlled Maruia beech forest. Timberlands' PR discussions reveal that the company was delicately manoeuvring towards joint WWF-Timberlands publicity of the project: 'WWF has funded further kokako research.... To discuss with WWF a joint press release.'[23]

Although Timberlands staff were keen to be publicly associated with the WWF, they were a little nervous that this could undermine their longer-term plans. Behind the scenes they discussed the best strategy for using the WWF. 'Discussion of merits of gaining exposure for Timberlands at expense of jeopardising its relationship with WWF,' they noted. However they were reassured by Simon Towle, the WWF conservation officer. 'Simon Towle has little problem in being quoted in a joint press release with Timberlands,' the teleconference minutes recorded. Shelley Grell and Warren Head from Christchurch based Head Consultants would be delegated to follow through.[24]

Although it was unrelated to the kokako research, Timberlands invited WWF staff on a PR trip to the Coast. The company was delighted with the results. It later claimed in a briefing to its shareholding ministers that their visitors 'described their impressions of our management as for them "like children looking through a toy shop window".'[25]

Timberlands' PR strategy stated that it was 'Important to acknowledge the role different staff members and personalities can play in contacting and developing relationships with various groups'. In the case of Simon Towle, Kit Richards of Timberlands took on the task of building the relationship, maintaining regular telephone and mail contact with him.

The relationship was going so well that Kit Richards was confident enough to send the WWF an early copy of the controversial beech scheme plans.[26] Timberlands also gave copies of the still-secret report to the Maruia Society, the Parliamentary Commissioner for the Environment, a supportive academic at Auckland University, John Craig, and its community front group, Coast Action Network. Journalists, other environmental groups and Opposition politicians were not permitted to see copies of the report. Timberlands was keen to orchestrate support from its friends and starve possible opponents of information.

In 1997, Timberlands had its first success. Although the WWF had no policy on or involvement in the West Coast forest issue, Towle, along with Guy Salmon of the Maruia Society, agreed to appear on a five-minute Timberlands promotional video designed to sell the ecological virtues of the beech scheme. The piece of Towle's interview shown on the *Sustaining Our Natural Beech Forests* video is not about the South Island kokako or bird research or even ecology. Instead he is quoted saying that the shift to 'treating beech as a high quality, high value product is a very, very positive move'.[27] For Timberlands, having the words 'World Wide Fund for Nature' on the screen introducing Towle was likely to have been at least as important as anything he said.

Only three people spoke on the video. The second was Bernie Lagan of Westco Lagan and then Guy Salmon, who talked about Timberlands sustaining the wildlife and recreational values of the forests. 'Worldwide there is a huge concern about getting things on a sustainable basis to look after future generations,' he said.

The same process of relationship building was occurring with Dunedin ecologist Henrik Moller. Not long after the 1994 PR strategy plan was prepared, Timberlands agreed to provide some of the funding for the predator control research that Moller's private ecological consulting firm, Ecosystems, was conducting in West Coast beech forests.

Moller was also awarded a specific contract to prepare a 'bird research scoping report'; in this work he and his colleagues were involved in helping to plan Timberlands' wildlife research programme. It was an approach that echoed the proposals in the 'bridge building' PR strategy, where 'scientific research on forest wildlife... create(s) opportunities for contact with these individuals. Content: Share research information and involve them in developing scenarios for management in the wild.... Support some of their projects.'[28]

Later when the personal and funding relationships were well established, and the beech scheme was causing public controversy, Moller was more directly involved. In 1998 he was employed to help co-ordinate an in-house review of the beech scheme management plans before they were submitted to the government. He also assisted in preparation of some of Timberlands public relations publications. 'Meeting with H Moller on Tuesday who is reviewing the Green Monitor,' the minutes of one Timberlands' PR teleconference recorded.[29]

Links with another ecologist were also being fostered. David Norton, of the Canterbury University School of Forestry, is a well-respected university forest ecologist. Like Moller, Norton operates a private consultancy separate from his academic work and it was through this that he began to get contracts to work for Timberlands. He was employed during the 1990s to produce a series of audits of Timberlands' management plans for its logging in South Westland rimu forests.[30]

We are in no way questioning the quality or independence of Norton's work (and likewise Moller and the WWF), but it must be said that the effect of the contracts was to create a personal and professional interest in the continuation of logging (albeit attempting to make it as ecologically benign as possible). Timberlands' agenda was to involve credible individuals in the issues of how to conduct the logging to such an extent that they could be allies in the public debate over whether it should be occurring.

This approach also worked successfully with the Parliamentary Commissioner for the Environment (PCE), Helen Hughes. In 1995 Hughes undertook a technical review of Timberlands' beech logging proposals but avoided all questions of whether or not the forests in question should be used for logging. She also acceded to a Timberlands demand that, unlike the usual review procedure, the review be a closed process, with the public not permitted to obtain copies of the proposed logging plans.

Her successor, Morgan Williams, repeated this process in 1998, again choosing not to consider whether the forests should be logged and merely considering the issues of how the logging might best be done. This, too, was a closed review, with no opportunity for public input. Both Hughes and Williams have been hosted on Timberlands' PR tours and are supportive of the logging plans.

Timberlands was sufficiently pleased with Morgan Williams' views after he returned from the standard West Coast PR tour that Shandwick included him in one of its public relations action plans. At an August 1998 Timberlands/Shandwick PR planning meeting they identified the 'Parliamentary Commissioner for the Environment story' as an 'opportunity where public relations can be applied to further the interest of Timberlands'. Under 'work in progress', Shandwick was given the job of approaching a thought-to-be-sympathetic journalist to 'suggest that she interview the PCFE'.[31]

By far Timberlands' greatest public relations asset, though, has been Guy Salmon of the Maruia Society. As the Native Forest Action Council (NFAC), for the decade from 1975 to 1985 it had been the most active environmental organisation in New Zealand. Throughout this period, however, there were conflicts between many of the active members and the more conservative Guy Salmon and by the late 1980s other groups had become dominant. In 1988 NFAC's name was changed to the Maruia Society and during the 1990s – following a fall in membership and the winding up of the branches – the organisation's principal output was lobbying and writing by the chief executive, Guy Salmon.

There was no need for Timberlands to cultivate a relationship with Salmon as he had been promoting a beech scheme since before the company was created. In the mid- to late 1980s he liaised closely with a series of logging companies interested in logging West Coast beech forests, and openly supported logging proposals by Venture Pacific Ltd and Angel Harvest Ltd. With the Angel Harvest proposal, he lobbied other environmental groups in January 1989 to support its rimu and beech logging plans, which were aimed at exports to Japan.

Salmon travelled to the United States in 1989 and returned enthusiastic about 'third wave' environmentalism. This was the idea that, rather than opposing environmentally damaging activities, environmentalists needed to work closely with companies so that they would improve their development plans voluntarily. Instead of relying on environmental regulations developed by the state, 'third wave' environmentalists argued that 'sustainability' would be achieved by harnessing 'market mechanisms'. Later that year Salmon began to apply these ideas, persuading the Maruia executive to drop its advocacy of a ban on woodchipping of beech forests in exchange for a 'sustainability approach'.[32]

Also in 1989 Salmon infuriated other environmentalists by secretly lobbying against their policies on Antarctica, an issue in which Maruia had played no part. At that time environmentalists were making the last push in their successful campaign to have Antarctica declared a World Park.

Salmon wrote to the Foreign Minister Russell Marshall and offered to help him gain acceptance for New Zealand endorsement of the mineral exploitation regime that was being promoted by oil and mining interests. Salmon's letter to Marshall on Antarctica was leaked from the minister's office, at which point his own national executive found out about the lobbying and demanded that he write to the minister to explain that the views in the letter were not those of the Maruia Society.

It was clashes like these that irrevocably soured relations between Salmon and many other environmentalists and eventually led to the demise of Maruia as a membership organisation. Faced with declining membership and branches, the society saw salvation in corporate consultancy work. In a memo to its national executive in October 1992, Salmon recommended a financial strategy of increasing consultancy work as 'it enhances our credibility in sectors we are seeking to influence'. Salmon noted 'the latest inquiry is from an oil company in Australia that wants to employ us for a few days to train up its senior executives in environmental strategy'.[33]

By 1995 Maruia was pleased with its transformation. It proudly wrote to its members that 'our strategy of being the environmental group that works closely with business took off during the year. We are liaising closely with private sector interests on all the public policy issues on which we work; we are frequent speakers at business ... meetings and conferences; and we're starting to earn a proportion of our income from advising businesses on strategic environmental issues, and from training business executives in environmental awareness and values'.[34] Salmon found a receptive audience at business conferences. He appeared in immaculate corporate clothes, presenting a 'balanced' view that he contrasted with the policies of other environmentalists, whom he described as the 'woolly hat brigade'.

During the 1990s a substantial part of Maruia's income came from consultant fees paid to Salmon and Maruia's president, Richard Thompson, for work they did for organisations including the Fishing Industry Board and the Landfill Association.[35] In June 1999, at the society's annual meeting, it was decided to change the organisation's name from the Maruia Society to the Ecologic Foundation, to reflect its changing focus. Salmon announced that the organisation would like to increase its business membership.[36]

The Landfill Association contract graphically demonstrates the role an organisation like Maruia/Ecologic can play in corporate public relations strategies.[37]

The services and role Salmon offered to the Landfill Association appear little different to what Shandwick might have offered, except that Maruia's name and reputation provided a ready-made green front for the campaign. He proposed articles in major papers 'written by Guy Salmon', briefing of journalists to do in-depth pieces, 'briefing of Opposition politicians to raise the issues in Parliament', and 'assisting some selected local conservation or ratepayers groups' to make an election year issue of some substandard landfills, 'preferably in marginal electorates'. 'Campaigns always get higher media profile if there is conflict,' he argued. (Putting some obviously bad landfills 'at the sharp end of some publicity' would help make the association's standards look reasonable.) He urged that a core idea to get across in the campaign was 'that landfilling can be done well, so that it is a sustainable option'. These were all the kinds of things a real environment group might do in an environmental campaign, plus an obligatory claim of sustainability, but they were being carried out as a paid contract for an industry group.

Another of the businesses with which Salmon was working closely during the 1990s was, of course, Timberlands. All the same campaign strategies he offered to the Landfill Association as a consultant were used voluntarily in defence of West Coast native logging, including articles and briefings of journalists and politicians. He even used the 'good landfill – bad landfill' tactic, expressing outrage about an area of particularly bad native forest logging on Maori land in Southland – juxtaposed with his statements about what a good job Timberlands was doing in its logging. The National government responded in July 1999, offering compensation to end chipping of beech forests in Southland at the same time as it lifted a ban that had stopped Timberlands exporting beech chips.

Whenever West Coast native forest logging arose, Salmon commented on Timberlands' side. In December 1995, for instance, he had argued publicly for the government to allow woodchipping of West Coast beech forests and export of the beech chips as a necessary part of a viable beech scheme.[38] When the Native Forest Action tree-sitting protest began in early 1997, Salmon publicly criticised the action in a newspaper story headlined 'West Coast forest protesters using wrong tactics says Salmon'.[39] The article, copies of which Timberlands faxed to ministers, argued that the protesters should accept the logging as a necessary compromise dating from the 1986 West Coast Accord.

Later that year, after the Court of Appeal decided the government had no commitment to allow any further logging under the West Coast Accord, Prime Minister Jim Bolger promoted a proposal within the government to end all Timberlands logging. Salmon was tipped off about a secret government meeting on the issue and personally lobbied against Bolger's proposal. When news of this lobbying leaked out and was criticised by environment groups, Salmon replied that 'the allegation was representative of the paranoia within the conservation movement'.[40]

He said he 'was indeed lobbying – not very secretly – for native logging in the Buller to stop'. We have, however, since obtained copies of the faxes he sent to key Ministers the morning before the decision-making meeting, which said that Maruia supported Timberlands' 'high standard of sustainable native forest management' and that 'we do not support the [Timberlands'] production forests being allocated to conservation'.[41]

A separate section of Timberlands' 1994 PR strategy was devoted to the Maruia Society and Guy Salmon. Unlike the 'bridge-building' approach designed for groups like the WWF, the papers proposed the 'direct enviro-approach' for Maruia.

Timberlands' 'concept' for dealing with Maruia was 'when appropriate initiate direct contact for discussion on the overall environmental debate, its direction and its future (Maruia). Audience: Guy Salmon and similar thinkers.'[42] The view of the 'overall environmental debate and its future' shared by Timberlands and Maruia, as expressed in their respective public statements, was that the anti-logging environment groups were outmoded and that the real environmental issues were purely about how the logging was done.

Timberlands' publications talked of a 'very constructive dialogue' with the Maruia Society. Timberlands was pleased with Maruia as 'it has given open support for Timberlands West Coast's beech programme'.[43] Ironically, the Maruia Society had been named after the Maruia Valley of

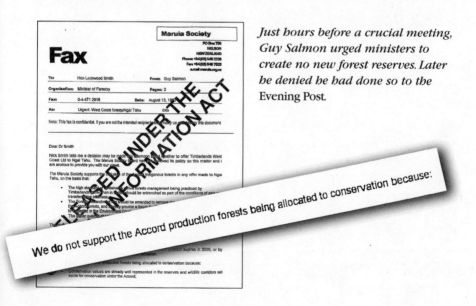

Just hours before a crucial meeting, Guy Salmon urged ministers to create no new forest reserves. Later he denied he had done so to the Evening Post.

North Westland which, thanks to its outstanding beech forests, was where Timberlands planned to begin its beech logging scheme.

According to a former Maruia office-holder, Salmon's 'main political significance today, sadly, is as an ally of organisations like Timberlands West Coast Ltd in opposing the efforts of the movement of which he was formerly a part'.[44] Forest and Bird's conservation director, Kevin Smith, in the same article, described him as 'the major public apologist for Timberlands', someone who had taken actions 'which have been extremely unhelpful, and bizarre really'.

CHAPTER 8

EXPLOITING THE ALLIES

Timberlands' proposal... represents a very sincere and impressive effort to achieve very low impact sustainable management of the forest.... The two groups also noted that Timberlands had made a significant contribution to scientific research into the conservation of endangered species such as kokako and kiwi, and into control of major pests such as stoats.

Guy Salmon, Maruia Society, and Simon Towle, WWF,
10 September 1997[1]

Environment groups are split over proposals to log native beech forests on the West Coast.

'Two environmental groups praise beech logging plan', *Press*,
11 September 1997 [2]

The test of Timberlands' programme of alliance building was looming with the planned launch of the beech scheme. The company had aimed to 'develop contacts with groups whose interests are served by the implementation of Timberlands policies so that they become "natural allies" of Timberlands in times of conflict.... so that they can become "spokespeople" for Timberlands where implementation of Timberlands' plans appears threatened'.[3]

In 1997-98 the environmental campaign to have the Timberlands forests protected had grown to a point where the beech scheme plans did indeed appear to be threatened. The day after the leak of the plans in 1998, Guy Salmon approached Simon Towle of the WWF after an early evening meeting and suggested they issue a joint press release, which was sent out the same evening. This stated that Timberlands' proposals for sustainable 'harvesting' of beech forests should be given 'serious and open-minded consideration'. Borrowing the industry phraseology, they said that the plans represented 'a very sincere and impressive effort to achieve very low impact sustainable management of the forest.... The two groups also noted that Timberlands had made a significant contribution to scientific research into the conservation of endangered species such as kokako and kiwi, and into control of major pests such as stoats.'[4] It is not known whether Timberlands approached Guy Salmon for assistance, but either way it was a classic case of allies acting in effect as '"spokespeople" for Timberlands where implementation of Timberlands' plans appears threatened'.

Predictably, the press release was reported as a division in the environment movement. The Christchurch *Press* ran the obvious line that 'environment groups are split over proposals to log native beech forests on the West Coast'.[5] It was as good as Timberlands could have hoped for. Without any prospect of getting all environment groups to back its plans, having some public allies would at least blunt the opposition. It fitted in neatly with Timberlands' public relations strategy:'The more allies the company has, preferably influential ones, who are willing to publicly support Timberlands, the easier it will be to counter opposition'.

Forest and Bird's Kevin Smith replied in the *Press* article:'I would ask WWF and the Maruia Society to look at the 12,000 hectares of out-

---

NEWS RELEASE 10 SEPTEMBER 1998

CONSERVATION ORGANISATIONS CALL FOR 'SERIOUS CONSIDERATION' OF SUSTAINABLE BEECH PROPOSAL

Conservation organisations the Worldwide Fund for Nature (NZ) and the Maruia Society today said the proposals for sustainable harvesting of beech forests should be given "serious and open-minded consideration".

Proposals of Timberlands West Coast Ltd for harvesting on 98,000 ha of beech forest were leaked and made public yesterday by other conservation groups.

WWF-NZ conservation director Simon Towle and Maruia chief executive Guy Salmon said the beech forest in question had been set aside for "a continuing supply of indigenous timber in perpetuity" under the West Coast Accord, which was signed by conservation organisations in 1986, and was a binding contract.

"The Accord document was a negotiated agreement between all the parties to the long-

---

Guy Salmon and WWF's Simon Towle leaped to Timberlands' defence after its beech logging plans were leaked. As the PR plans had intended, it was allies acting in effect as '"spokespeople" for Timberlands where implementation of Timberlands' plans appear[ed] threatened'.

standing beech forest on the east bank of the Maruia and ask themselves in all conscience if they want to see the bulldozers and loggers in there'.[6]

Timberlands' cultivation of the WWF's Towle had, if anything, been too successful. The WWF had no policy on the beech plans and Towle had made the statement without authority or checking it with his organisation. He was later rapped over the knuckles for putting his name to the statement and the WWF chairperson, Dame Cath Tizard, issued a press statement saying that it was 'regrettable that WWF-NZ's position on the Timberlands Beech Forest Proposal has been misrepresented'.[7]

The damage was done, however, and Timberlands had what it needed: the impression of environment movement support. Months later, despite the WWF writing to the government to correct his statement, the minister in charge of Timberlands, Tony Ryall, was still sending a copy of the Salmon-Towle press release to everyone who wrote to him concerning West Coast logging. In the eyes of the government it was proof that reasonable environmentalists backed the logging. It had no interest in the WWF undoing the damage.

In the week following the leak, Henrik Moller also spoke publicly for the first time in favour of the beech forest logging plans. He wrote a newspaper opinion piece entitled 'This time Timberlands is right' which attacked those advocating the cessation of logging, arguing that 'conservation needs to be protected from some of its friends'.[8]

The article gave unqualified support for Timberlands' logging plans and, picking up one of the company's main lines, argued that opponents

OPINION   THE PRESS, Christchurch

This time Timberlands is right

SATURDAY SOAPBOX

HENRIK MOLLER

Conservation needs to be protected from some of its friends. Having dedicated 20 years of my career as a professional ecologist to conservation, I have become increasingly alarmed at the extravagant public statements of some leaders of our conservation groups.

Exaggeration and distortion of the facts may win a few recruits to the conservation lobby in the short-term, but in the longer run it will alienate New Zealand society and turn-off supporters.

Take the looming controversy concerning Timberlands West Coast forests" into "plantation-type managed forests" and that "it is certain that any type of logging causes long-term changes in forest composition and structure".

None of these statements or implications even approximate the truth.

Timberlands' plans do not involve any clearfelling. Instead groups of one to 10 trees will be removed to create a gap in the forest of the size that naturally occurs when trees die or are blown over. On average only 15 trees will be removed every 15 years per hectare.

All the largest living trees and dead ticians should be welcoming the assistance of industry for conservation in this way, not spreading misleading half-truths based on out-of-date characteristics that all industry is a threat to conservation.

Devolving responsibility for conservation to local landowners, community groups and commercial enterprise is called "co-management". It is the way forward for conservation in the 21st century.

Conservation groups overseas like the International Union for Conservation of Nature and the World Wide Fund for Nature have captured enormous biodiversity benefits by encouraging co-management.

New Zealand lags well behind this international trend, partly because our conservation-group leaders have now. But now the emergency has passed. We are the envy of the world in our generous allocation of land to National Parks and reserves.

The new challenge facing the New Zealand conservation movement is to capture biodiversity gains outside the nature reserves by fostering wise land and natural resource uses. Conservation should not just occur within some line on a map around a reserve.

At its worst this misconception creates an environmentally damaging idea that if we have reserves for conservation then we can do what we like to the environment outside them.

Some of our conservation leaders have shown an inability to adapt to our new world. Among the conservation groups only WWF and the Maruia Society have avoided the

Timberlands had also cultivated a relationship with ecologist Henrik Moller, who first commented publicly on the beech logging proposals a week after Salmon and Towle.

of the scheme were 'seriously misrepresenting the facts'. As evidence of this he cited comments at a Christchurch meeting of Native Forest Action the month before which, he said, 'implied' that Timberlands was proposing to clearfell beech forests.

NFA had written extensively on the beech plans and never suggested it would involve clearfelling. Moller had not been at the meeting he referred to (he lives in Dunedin), but strangely this was one of the claims that were later made public by the Timberlands contractor who had been attending the meetings posing as an NFA supporter. At the time of Moller's article the contractor was still keeping his monitoring of the meetings secret and had presumably only been reporting on the meetings to Timberlands.

Moller's article went on to praise those environmental groups supporting the logging. 'Some of our conservation leaders have shown an ability to adapt to our new world,' he wrote. 'Among the conservation groups only WWF and the Maruia Society have avoided the temptation to undermine Timberlands.'

At the same time Moller wrote an eight-page letter to the Labour Party's conservation spokesperson, Jill Pettis, criticising a policy discussion paper she had written proposing that Labour end logging of public native forests (which includes all Timberlands forests). He said Timberlands' logging plans deserved Labour's 'utmost support'. 'Unfortunately some leaders of the conservation NGOs seem to be locked into ... an enflamed [*sic*] conflict-driven mindset.... Misleading public statements from some of these leaders on the Timberlands West Coast Ltd proposals have demonstrated [an] inability to adapt. Your thoroughly biased discussion paper has fallen into the same trap.'[9] The discussion paper had not been sent to Moller and his letter merely explained 'My attention has been drawn to your July 1998 circular...'.

It had clearly been drawn to many others' attention too. Jill Pettis received replies supportive of Timberlands' logging plans from various of the allies mentioned in Timberlands' PR strategy, including the Forest Owners Association, the New Zealand Institute of Forestry, the Farm Forestry Association, Therese Gibbens (of Coast Action Network), forester John Wardle and David Norton of the School of Forestry at Canterbury University.

David Norton who, like Moller, had long worked on contract for Timberlands, also went public defending the company in the weeks following the leaking of the beech scheme plans. In one statement he said that 'Timberlands had proposed perhaps the most ecologically sensitive forest management in the world' and 'biodiversity within managed native forests could benefit from the proposed management'.[10]

Similarly, he wrote to many Labour and National MPs after the beech plans were leaked, describing opponents of Timberlands' proposed management plans as 'outdated and misguided'. He again said that Timberlands was proposing 'perhaps the most ecologically sustainable forest management systems world-wide' and that 'We should be congratulating the company'.[11]

In neither the press statements nor his lobbying letters to MPs did Norton mention his personal links with Timberlands. To their recipients, the letters appeared to be from independent third parties.

David Norton's public comments were subsequently quoted in at least two press releases issued by the government in support of the Timberlands beech plans. A press release by minister David Carter pointed out that the WWF and the Maruia Society publicly supported Timberlands' plans and said 'their views are supported by eminent scientists such as David Norton, of the University of Canterbury'.[12]

The other scientist who lobbied Labour's Jill Pettis at that time was John Craig of Auckland University's School of Environmental and Marine Sciences, who was strongly supportive of Timberlands' beech scheme. Like the others, his relationship with Timberlands had been built up over time; it included Timberlands' sponsorship of an environmental conference he helped organise in Taupo a year before (the same conference after which Timberlands had attempted to cause problems for Cath Wallace). He sent Pettis an article he had written entitled 'Sustainable logging: achieving conservation without welfare'. The article was a re-run of the Timberlands 'logging the forests to save them' argument. 'TWC's plan involves achieving the conservation that DoC could not afford,' he wrote. 'A proportion of profits are returned to control pests [and] to monitor biodiversity.'

He also repeated the most important of the Timberlands evasions, that the vast majority of West Coast native forests are already protected: 'TWC propose a precautionary mix of 10% sustainable use to 90% lock up protection to conserve West Coast forests'. The figure for lowland forest – the ecologically rich forests of crucial importance for conservation – is about 50/50. Like Moller and Norton, his arguments were accompanied by a tone of contempt for other environmentalists and the Department of Conservation.[13]

The role played by these individuals and groups had been key objectives of the various Timberlands public relations strategies in the lead-up to the beech scheme. Mobilising credible third parties had been identified as a 'Key strategy element.... Identifying third party endorsers to publicly support [beech] plan'.[14] In another internal Timberlands document they had written 'Timberlands – Political: secure third party endorsements – Kit Richards and Dave Fraser.... Environmental and Media... prepare third party endorsements as above'.[15]

The privatisation of science in New Zealand has created a pool of people, such as Moller and Norton, who have the status of independent academics but also run private consultancies doing work for companies like Timberlands. The same scientists who act as independent judges of public interest issues can be in an undisclosed financial relationship with parties to those issues. Even in universities and Crown research institutes, scientists are encouraged to seek as much private funding as possible. Timberlands was spending several hundred thousand dollars each year just on research contracts related to the beech scheme.

A former consultant to Timberlands, who had helped to prepare one aspect of the beech scheme plans, was later hired by the government as the 'independent consultant' to judge which of the public submissions on the beech scheme were significant and summarise their arguments.[16] Other scientists, who did not support beech logging but who took research work where the funding was, found that their names were being used to give credibility to the scheme, in *Green Monitor* reports of their research, for example.

The PR industry generally takes the view that scientists used in a PR campaign should disclose their financial sources only if asked by journalists. Disclosure would undermine the perception of independence if there were a possible accusation of a conflict of interest. Information important to the public's ability to be able to make an informed judgement is often neither revealed by scientists nor requested by journalists.

Corporate-funded science does not necessarily mean that the science is of a lesser quality than publicly funded scientific research. Seeking disclosure of the funding is not a challenge to the integrity of the individual scientists but an essential protection of the ability of the public and journalists to judge what weight they will give to information these scientists provide.

The people who came to play roles in Timberlands' campaign did so willingly and their opinions were honestly held. The significance of Timberlands' calculated PR tactics of bridge-building and drawing them into involvement with logging plans was that, without this manoeuvring, few if any of them would have ended up making the public statements or lobbying the politicians at the times required by Timberlands. Their lives and work would simply have been focused elsewhere. And, by becoming personally and professionally involved in the detail of devising logging plans, they were developing a personal interest in the continuation of logging.

In August 1997 Native Forest Action had a feature article by Kate McPherson published in the *Independent* newspaper, criticising Timberlands and its operations. Although the article was directed entirely at Timberlands, the reply in the newspaper a week later was by Guy Salmon. The arguments in his article were indistinguishable from those of Timberlands and he revealed a contemptuous attitude to other environmentalists. 'In the tradition of religious tolerance in this country, McPherson is entitled to her beliefs,' Salmon wrote, 'but when she advocates they should become public policy, and be imposed upon others, we need a more compelling rationale than strongly-held minority beliefs.'[17]

Internal Timberlands papers reveal that Salmon faxed a copy of the article to the company three days before it was published,[18] and that, on the morning it appeared, Shandwick took on the job of sending the article around to other news media: 'NFA: will circulate "Independent" article to other media'.[19]

Shandwick then prepared Timberlands' own response to the NFA article. 'Dave, Copy follows – writing this was a pleasure!' wrote Rob McGregor.[20] It was published under Dave Hilliard's name in the follow-

Defender of the forest up the wrong tree

The Independent 15/8/97 p.8

GUEST COMMENT

BY GUY SALMON

Kate McPherson and her band of treetop protesters deserve credit for their achievement.

There is now a widespread view that the unsustainable logging of Buller rimu forests should be phased out. Nobody - not even Timberlands West Coast Ltd - defends the unsustainable logging in principle.

There is little doubt now the government will take action to bring it to an end.

But a much bigger question is raised by McPherson's article (*The Independent*, 8 August).

She proposes conservationists should use the momentum of that impending victory in the Buller to stop all logging of native forests everywhere, whether sustainable or not.

Her group's manifesto, the Kawatiri Declaration, says: "In recognition of the urgent need to conserve our nation's biodiversity, all remaining areas of native forest deserve full and immediate protection from logging."

Let us be clear what the implementation of that demand would mean. First, it means New Zealanders would no longer be able to have, in their own homes, the native timbers of their own country.

Second, it means the owners of native forest on private land would not be allowed to harvest or fell any area - presumably by a law expropriating their existing legal rights to sustainable use, as well as their Treaty rights.

Third, it means any collective benefit that might come to New Zealanders from wealth and employment creation in sustainable forest management, sawmilling, furniture-making and related industries based on native timber would be foregone.

Fourth, it means the sizeable existing demand for timber that has harder, stronger and more decorative qualities than radiata pine, and used for furniture-making, panelling, staircases, handcrafts and other specialist uses, would be met by expanding our imports of tropical hardwoods.

Sustainably-produced New Zealand timber, benefiting New Zealanders, would then be replaced by destructively-logged wood from countries like Papua New Guinea where the land is left derelict and the proceeds flow to the pockets of corrupted politicians.

Finally, implementation of the Kawatiri Declaration would mean abrogation of the carefully-negotiated West Coast Accord, a contract binding the Crown to set aside an agreed area of 120,000 ha of forest for the explicit purpose of producing native timber in

In the tradition of religious tolerance in this country, McPherson is entitled to hold to her own particular beliefs.

But when she advocates they should become public policy, and be imposed upon others, we need a more compelling rationale than strongly-held minority benefits.

In speaking of sustainability, and of biodiversity conservation, McPherson touches on principles that do command wide support as a basis for public policy.

But if those principles are understood from an effects-based perspective, as they should be, neither of them requires a blanket ban on native timber production.

There are, however, dire threats to New Zealand's native forests. Landcare Research has measured ongoing losses of about 4% every decade in the biomass of South Island forests. It

When Native Forest Action had an article published criticising Timberlands, it was Guy Salmon who, a week later, replied defending the company and attacking environmentalists. He faxed his article to Timberlands three days before it was published.

ing week's *Independent*.[21] (A few months earlier Professor John Morton had written a feature in the *New Zealand Herald* called 'Why logging of our indigenous forests has to cease',[22] which likewise was replied to in a piece by Guy Salmon, defending Timberlands, entitled 'Native forests can be preserved, and logged too'.)[23]

Salmon's comment about 'minority beliefs', like the public statements of Moller and Norton, illustrates how allies like these are useful not only for endorsing the company's logging plans but also for joining in the attacks on its opponents. Core message themes developed by Timberlands, along the lines of 'small, extreme and misleading', were being used by one conservation group against another. Through contact with Timberlands, otherwise reasonable individuals such as Norton can also be drawn into sharing the company's animosities and prejudices.

Maruia's crusade for beech forest logging did not finish there. The main article in the society's November 1998 magazine was devoted to justifying Timberlands' logging plans. Reusing parts of the *Independent* article and the subsequent Maruia-WWF press release, the article canvassed all the same arguments used by Timberlands: that New Zealand beech forest logging would reduce logging of the 'ravaged rainforests of the tropics', that logging provided jobs on the West Coast 'where sustaining employment in small rural communities is a ceaseless struggle' and that (like Timberlands) it was the Maruia Society, not the 'anti-Timberlands groups', that was applying 'the ethic of sustainability in its fullest sense'.[24]

The article featured two photos of current logging operations. One showed a Timberlands contractor next to a single moss-covered tree stump in otherwise untouched forest. The other, featuring a modest pile of about 20 small logs, was used to illustrate a scheme that would involve creating piles of over 1000 logs each week. Both photos were taken by Salmon, clearly during a standard PR tour of the Coast.

The following issue of the magazine went further, with an article addressed to Helen Clark over her party's native forest conservation policy. In it Guy Salmon claimed that it could cost a Labour government more than $120 million to compensate West Coasters and timber companies for ending Timberlands' native logging. 'Most informed conservationists, Maruia believes, would be concerned about that prospect,' Salmon wrote.[25] He quoted Labour MP Jim Sutton supporting his view that there were higher priorities for this money. But the argument was a fake. The National government had by then already announced that it was cutting short two-thirds of Timberlands' native logging, after a minimum of consultation with West Coast interests. National had been advised by the Crown Law Office that, provided no supply contracts to sawmills were broken, no compensation was required.[26]

Salmon also made a point of visiting various Labour MPs, including West Coast MP Damien O'Connor, and presenting them with arguments in favour of Timberlands' proposals. Salmon was helping mobilise other allies on behalf of Timberlands' logging project.

Salmon also offered Timberlands political advice on who it should be lobbying. The minutes of one of Timberlands' weekly PR conferences recorded Guy Salmon advising Timberlands to lobby Deborah Morris, the Associate Minister for the Environment: 'Kit Richards [Timberlands strategic planning manager] spoke with Guy Salmon at Taupo. GS believes D Morris is still an important MP target.'[27]

Another PR teleconference discussed where various National ministers stood on Timberlands: 'Political: Been some meetings between [Nick] Smith, [Lockwood] Smith and [Tony] Ryall. Could be some concern. Birch does not appear to be as supportive of Timberlands as previously believed.'[28] Earlier minutes had stated that Finance Minister Bill Birch backed Timberlands' beech scheme plans. A few weeks later, Guy Salmon arranged a meeting with Birch to discuss Timberlands and 'sustainable management of the Crown's beech production forests'. Notes prepared for Birch by Treasury staff before the meeting said that they understood Salmon would argue that there were 'environmental benefits to be derived from sustainable management of the beech forests' and that 'the Government should be cautious about other views (eg no sustainable management at all) put forward by some environmentalists'.[29]

Timberlands and Shandwick were also aware of Salmon's value as a conduit to National's Minister for the Environment, Simon Upton. Internal Shandwick notes, on a lobbying visit it made to see Upton, recorded: 'Guy Salmon is very influential as far as he [Simon Upton] is concerned and Guy endorses what Timberlands are doing.... I know that when Simon first took over responsibility for the Environment portfolio he wanted to appoint Guy as his environmental adviser but the PM's office counselled against this. It sounds very much as if Guy is fulfilling this role anyway and is providing him with contestable advice to counter the Ministry's input.'[30]

Early in 1999 Timberlands began privately promoting a proposal that would bring together many of its key allies in an initiative designed to overcome the ongoing opposition to a beech scheme. The plan was to arrange the creation of a panel of experts that would 'independently' review Timberlands' beech logging scheme to assess its environmental acceptability. The group would include respected scientists as well as some environmental movement credibility provided by Guy Salmon and/ or the WWF. The proposal did not involve any consideration of *whether* the beech scheme should proceed; its purpose was merely to review how well the logging was being done. The proposed name of the panel was 'Guardians of the Forests'.

The objective was obvious. If a believable Guardians of the Forests could be put in place before the possible election of an unsympathetic Labour government, Timberlands would have a better hope of keeping the beech scheme alive. Salmon had been continuing his role in 1999, liaising with Kit Richards over the Guardians proposal. At the same time, Richards was working to get the WWF's backing but after Simon Towle had gone beyond the WWF policy brief on the beech scheme, Timberlands had a task ahead of it enticing the organisation back into the fold. First it contacted Towle to get the lie of the land, then it wrote a letter to the WWF chairperson, Dame Cath Tizard.

'In the course of discussion with Simon Towle of your organisation last week,' Richards wrote, 'I raised the issue of whether WWF would be, in conjunction with other groups, interested in forming an "environmental committee" to assist in an independent, transparent, overview role of the management of beech production forests.'

Timberlands was keen to suggest that the committee would be happening anyway and to create the sense that it was an opportunity for the WWF, with its emphasis on science, to have a say in how the logging would be conducted. 'You may be aware that Professor John Craig of the Centre for Marine and Environmental Sciences has been circulating a letter amongst ecologists seeking support for the concept of Sustainable Management as espoused in Timberlands West Coast plans.'

To help entice the WWF, Timberlands resorted to gushing praise of Towle's past efforts to support Timberlands. 'Over the last couple of years Timberlands West Coast has been gratified by the fact that they could establish a constructive, science based dialogue with WWF staff, and we would be delighted at the opportunity to work more closely.'

Timberlands wanted the WWF chairperson to take part in a PR tour of the West Coast. The company also had a possible sweetener: 'We also recognise that funds in the NGO [non-governmental organisation] community are tight and would be prepared to assist in some part with the costs of any visit were you willing to accept the invitation'.[31] Dame Cath did not accept the invitation.

The political motivation behind the plan is clearly visible. Kit Richards claimed that John Craig had been circulating a letter among ecologists 'seeking support for the concept of Sustainable Management as espoused in Timberlands West Coast plans'. But this was not what the letter said.

Craig had indeed been seeking support for the Guardians proposal, but the scientists who signed his letter had had it put to them that, if the beech scheme proceeded, it was important that any monitoring of it be done independently. In fact half or more of the individuals who signed the letter opposed Timberlands' logging and simply wanted to help reduce the damage in the event that the plan could not be stopped. One signatory, Professor Alan Mark was a prominent public critic of the scheme and others had publicly opposed it.

John Craig's letter was written as if it were an initiative independent of Timberlands. But Kit Richards' discussions with Simon Towle on WWF participation in the Guardians occurred before Craig's letter proposing the panel was even sent to the prime minister and his letter to Dame Cath, quoting Craig's letter, was dated only one day after it.

The Craig letter was used for other lobbying too. Only three days after the letter was posted to the prime minister's office, David Norton faxed a copy of it to Damien O'Connor, the main Labour MP known to be fighting his party's policy of opposition to Timberlands' logging. Norton clearly understood the letter's usefulness in the political debate, as did O'Connor, who immediately circulated it widely to opposition MPs of various parties (with Norton's fax details still printed at the top).

O'Connor had been targeted for cultivation as an ally. A 1997 PR telephone conference noted a request to Timberlands to 'Send all clippings quoting D O'Connor to Shandwick'.[32] The hot-headed O'Connor had been on bad terms with the Timberlands management but by 1998 tensions had eased. According to Timberlands staff, the MP became a regular visitor at the Timberlands headquarters and was often in phone contact with the Timberlands senior staff and public relations manager. He was by then said to have 'a good relationship' with the management as he lobbied within his party to maintain the native logging.

In February 1999, Labour MP Jim Sutton, the other Labour MP backing Timberlands, circulated a list of the signatories of the Craig letter around his caucus colleagues. Sutton stretched the truth to claim that 'the following have written to the Prime Minister supporting the

Timberlands West Coast proposals'.[33] The names of the scientists who signed Craig's letter were being used to bolster the credibility of and lobby for a scheme that many of them did not support.

Timberlands' next step was to arrange a meeting in Wellington in March 1999 to try to move on the Guardians plan. Kit Richards invited Guy Salmon, the WWF and a Ministry for the Environment officer to a meeting at the office of the Parliamentary Commissioner for the Environment. Curiously the commissioner, who is an independent officer of Parliament, agreed to 'facilitate' the meeting but allowed Timberlands, a state-owned company, to control who was invited. Forest and Bird got wind of the meeting and decided to attend as well.

By the time Dave Hilliard and Kit Richards of Timberlands arrived late for the meeting, the various environmentalists, invited and not, were chatting amicably with the commissioner, Morgan Williams, around his conference table. Hilliard and Richards refused to come into the room with Forest and Bird's Kevin Smith present. Williams checked that the other guests were happy for the meeting to proceed, in what was after all supposed to be a discussion of an 'independent [and] transparent' process, and went out to negotiate with the Timberlands managers. After 15 minutes of talking, Williams announced that 'Timberlands want to prescribe the agenda, they did not invite Forest and Bird and they won't go ahead if you're here'.

Kevin Smith said he would leave, but Timberlands' attempt to control the meeting backfired. The two WWF representatives did not feel comfortable being part of a closed process and announced that they were leaving.[34] As they left, the WWF chief executive, Paul Bowe, asked Guy Salmon if he was going too. Salmon replied, 'I think it's up to Timberlands who they want to talk to'.[35] In the months that followed, Kit Richards and Shandwick's Rob McGregor continued to contact the WWF to invite the organisation into the plan.

The meeting went ahead anyway and proved useful for the Timberlands campaign. The company had sought the meeting because it wanted to prod the government into approving the establishment of a Guardians of the Forests group and wished to present a confidential plan about how it should be arranged. Following the meeting, the Parliamentary Commissioner, Morgan Williams, wrote to the SOE and forestry ministers explaining that he had facilitated a meeting between Timberlands and 'selected NGOs' on how to develop an 'independent audit' process for the beech scheme. 'While the meeting did not include representatives of several major environmental NGOs,' he wrote, 'some thoughts emerged which I believe are a valuable contribution to advancing the development of an independent audit.'

Williams said that the Guardians of the Forests 'must have the confidence of the New Zealand public', which meant their appointment must be 'via a very open apolitical process'. To enhance the 'credibility' of the group, he proposed it was established 'via a Parliamentary-based mechanism (ie select committee, Officer of Parliament)'. He then offered himself (an officer of Parliament) as willing to assist the 'development of the independent audit/stewardship group if that is desired'.[36]

The thoughts that 'emerged' at the meeting were the confidential Timberlands plan. Soon after, Timberlands prepared a confidential 11-page paper spelling out the Guardians proposal in detail. The proposal, which was circulated to the company's allies in Wellington, discreetly made no mention of Timberlands on the cover and did not give the author's name. Titled 'A Suggested Solution to Independent Audit of the Crown's Indigenous Production Forests', it was written by Kit Richards. The introduction explained that the proposal broadly reflected 'the views of some scientific circles that have supported, to a greater or lesser degree, the proposed beech management system' and was 'compatible with the consensus' at a 'venue attended by the Parliamentary Commissioner for the Environment, Ministry for the Environment and the Maruia Society'.[37]

The proposal was for a seven- or eight-person body made up of people with a 'demonstrated reputation for objectivity and commitment to the ethic of sustainable landuse'. In case it was not clear enough that this was intended to exclude the extreme opponents of the beech scheme, the proposal emphasised that the body 'would be accountable for "problem solving" rather than "problem finding"'. Timberlands had already demonstrated its belief at the meeting in Morgan Williams' office that opponents of native logging had no place in the independent and transparent process.

The political function of the Guardians was plainly stated. It would be 'a vehicle for transparent, independent and credible dissemination' of information about the beech forest logging, 'devised solely to provide public reassurance' about the management of the disputed public forests. It 'would not undertake physical audit' of the logging (i.e. investigate it for itself) and 'would not be involved in day-to-day management'. It would merely 'review and compile the results' of Timberlands' existing unchallenging audit processes. Nor would it 'release reports before mutual agreement of both parties had been achieved or a disputes process activated' – ensuring that the lap dog did not unexpectedly bite its master.

The final section, headed 'Political Considerations', explained that the new body would provide 'more than operational and financial gains'. The paper was quite candid about the objective of removing the beech logging issue from the domain of public debate and party policy and making it a technical issue that would be dealt with 'constructively'. The political 'gains' were said to be 'Depoliticisation of native forest management', where 'No specific government is responsible for any particular action of the manager as they are reported on independently by the new body'. Thus, the 'new body should relieve the temptation for political interference'. In other words, move the issue of native forest logging out of the democratic realm and dispense with the problem of environmental public opinion for good.

And who was Timberlands suggesting would administer the independent audit process? Part of the 'Depoliticisation of native forest management' was to be achieved by having it funded 'through the office of the PCE': the Parliamentary Commissioner for the Environment, Morgan Williams. 'Depoliticisation' for Timberlands meant someone who, in his letter to the government offering his assistance in developing and even appointing the Guardians group, had explained that 'as Parliamentary Commissioner for the Environment' he believed it was possible to do ecologically sustainable logging 'within parts of New Zealand's publicly… owned indigenous forest estate' (which could only mean the Timberlands forests).[38] Yet he had never investigated the case for preserving the forests or requested to hear the views of Timberlands' opponents. His only trip to the Coast had been to go on the Timberlands PR tour.

It had been a lobbying coup for Timberlands. The company had convinced the parliamentary commissioner to co-operate in a PR strategy which, if successful, would have had the effect of freeing the beech forest logging issue from troublesome government and parliamentary 'interference'; that is, from democratic decision making.

Henrik Moller, David Norton, John Craig, Guy Salmon, the WWF and Morgan Williams: nearly all the environmental allies Timberlands had identified and/or cultivated in the preceding years had been brought together in the Guardians plan. The company's supporters in government then played their part. SOE minister Tony Ryall organised for Ministry for the Environment staff to begin work on a paper to Cabinet seeking government approval for the Guardians plan.

Timberlands' intention from the start had been clear: to create the impression of scientific support where little existed. The proposal for the Guardians had other strategic benefits too. It was an attempt to take decision-making over the fate of the forests away from public and political party processes and make it instead a technical decision to be overseen by selected specialists. While the public and political parties might, and probably would, choose to have the forests protected for conservation, Timberlands' political strategy was to present logging of the forests as a fait accompli and seek to restrict the issue to a dialogue between specialists over the methods of logging.

The Guardians initiative illustrated another benefit of the ally-building strategies: that it takes only a few people in key positions to be able to create an impression of support. Large numbers of ecologists and forest scientists had publicly opposed continued logging of the West Coast forests. As the Moller, Norton and the Craig letter showed, however, a small number of people could be used, in a determined campaign, to claim that expert opinion was on Timberlands' side. Impressions are what matters in public relations.

Timberlands' efforts to develop and mobilise allies had yielded a handful of ecologists, some professional foresters, the Parliamentary Commissioners for the Environment, Labour MPs O'Connor and Sutton, Guy Salmon and, for a while, the WWF willing to sign on for their logging plans. Most of the company's PR initiatives and most positive publicity for its logging involved some combination of these. Where Timberlands had started out in 1994 isolated, its sustained effort had yielded it enough friends in the right places to help ensure 'third party endorsements' whenever the political need arose.

CHAPTER 9

USING WEST COAST LOCALS

Interviewer: Has your company ever approached Coast Action Network for assistance in your public relations campaign?
Hilliard: No, never. In actual fact we're at arms length to CAN for obvious reasons....We don't have very much contact with them at all. We delight in reading about things that they're doing, of course, but certainly don't contribute to them financially or in any other way.

Dave Hilliard, 1999[1]

When environmental pressure began to build against rimu logging and the beech scheme in 1996-97, Timberlands had to face up to the fact that many of its main natural allies, West Coast people, did not hold the company in high regard. Timberlands was perceived as having shown little loyalty to local sawmills over supply, pricing and credit for sales of state pines. It had severely antagonised residents of the Buller region by transferring the contract for milling rimu from the local Westport mill (which subsequently went bust) to its preferred mill 150 kilometres south. The relationship had deteriorated to the point that, in 1994, Westport locals, including sawmillers and the mayor, blockaded the logging road where Timberlands was bringing out 'their' logs to truck to Hokitika.

Asked by a television crew in 1997 about Timberlands' decision to move the Buller contract, the chair of the West Coast Regional Council, Jim O'Regan, had said: 'Yes, that hurts. It hurts West Coast people and it hurts badly. That timber which we allocated in good faith for the maintenance of the sawmilling industry in Buller has been taken away.' Asked if he blamed Timberlands for that, O'Regan replied, with a smile, 'No comment.'[2]

On top of this, there was resentment at the way the Timberlands management splashed out on new four-wheel drives and earned high salaries. The company was regarded as arrogant and insensitive to local needs. The local MP, Damien O'Connor, was barely on speaking terms with the Timberlands management and the mayors had highly ambivalent feelings towards the company.

In 1996 Timberlands had commissioned a survey by MRL Research Group to establish perceptions of the company by key audiences, including staff, customers, contractors, Coasters and the wider New Zealand public. The confidential results painted a negative picture, with respondents talking of poor communication (a feeling of 'being dictated to'), inefficiency ('perceived overstaffing and a large fleet of vehicles are the most visible signs of this') and a lack of sensitivity 'to the needs of the West Coast forestry industry'. MRL concluded that 'Moving perceptions of the company from the present non-existent or lukewarm image to a clear, positive one... will be a major undertaking. At this stage we do not feel that we know enough about Timberlands' goals to make a recommendation about the necessity of this.'[3]

As the anti-logging environmental campaign gathered strength in 1997, Timberlands' PR advisers saw that the company needed West Coasters as a source of political support against the environmentalists. Shandwick thought it had the answer. In a paper of June that year it urged that resources be put into a 'Community Unity Strategy' to overcome what they tactfully described as 'some of the unevenness in local support for West Coast forestry and Timberlands'.[4]

Shandwick and Timberlands were borrowing from the menu of tactics developed in the United States for countering grassroots environmental campaigns. Recognising that no one approach would guarantee victory, it decided to blend its approach to include both grassroots and what PR trade insiders call 'treetops campaigns': pinpoint precision lobbying. Grassroots mobilisation creates a political base for corporate demands and counteracts pro-environment grassroots activities. Treetops campaigning aims to deliver consistent messages to the small number of people who often make the major decisions in society.

Shandwick recommended some tried and true items. First it recommended the creation of a community front group as a 'West Coast voice' arguing for Timberlands' agenda. Commercial interests have turned to creating bogus community groups as an effective way of getting their message across; Timberlands was to become the first government agency to try this approach. Shandwick also stressed the importance of cultivating key influential local figures. In its 1994 PR strategy, under 'regional support', it suggested 'building allies at "influential" level and developing general support from regional population via Timberlands West Coast communications strategy'.[5]

Timberlands also decided to call in favours from local businesses reliant on the company and to seek to build influence among locals through a generous sponsorship scheme. As an overarching strategy, Timberlands decided to take its case directly to locals through intensive, and expensive, advertising in local newspapers and radio broadcasts. Key messages in the campaign, repeated frequently by Timberlands' spokespeople, would be the claim that 500 West Coast families relied on the forestry industry and that loss of local native forest logging jobs would destroy the social fabric of the region.

The strategy was to tap into old 'greenies vs locals' prejudices from the era when there were hundreds of native forestry jobs, not the two dozen now at stake. The strategists shrewdly judged that in an apparent struggle between local interests and 'outside' environmentalists, many people, and in particular older West Coast public figures, would feel they had to take an anti-greenie stand.

---

8.   Video
It was agreed that the video needs upgrading for both School Resource Kit and other corporate uses.

Responsibility
Head consultants to draft production brief and do costings. Shandwick and Head consultants to produce script nearer time.

9.   Forestry Trust
The concept of establishing a forestry Trust to create a single all inclusive body representing all West Coast forestry interests and supporters was agreed in principle.

Responsibility
Kit Richards to pursue informally during Beech Scheme meetings with Mayors, etc.

10.   Advertising
The proposal for TWC to carry out public information advertising to promote sustainable management and circumvent the usual information "filters" was discussed.

Responsibility
It was agreed that some specific advertising should be considered as part of the Beech Launch programme or following it, depending on activist reaction.

The idea of a pro-Timberlands group, which would become Coast Action Network, was dreamt up in a PR strategy meeting. The 'Forestry Trust' name was never used, but the idea was soon being implemented.

In the 1980s corporate-funded and directed front groups proliferated. In a study of corporate front groups in the United States, Mark Megalli and Andy Friedman wrote:

> *The rise of corporate front groups in the US is a recent phenomenon, a direct response to the burgeoning consumer, citizen and environmental movements. Before these movements took hold in the late 1960s, major corporations delivered their messages through their lobbyists in Washington. The names of these traditional associations told the stories – National Coal Association, Chamber of Commerce, American Petroleum Institute.*
>
> *But as public-interest groups began to win widespread public support, it became clear that new mechanisms were needed to deliver the corporate message. If Burger King were to report that a Whopper is nutritious, consumers would probably roll their eyes in disbelief... But when the American Council on Science and Health and its panel of 200 expert scientists report that Whoppers are not so bad consumers might actually listen.... Increasingly big business is creating front groups to influence legislators, the media and consumers. These corporate front groups advertise, hold conferences, publish newsletters and reports, write editorials and appear on talk shows in an effort to sway public opinion toward industry views.[6]*

Ron Arnold, from the Center for the Defense of Free Enterprise in Washington State, was one of the early exponents of corporations funding grassroots groups. As he told a pesticide lobby group in 1984, 'it takes a movement to fight a movement'. On another occasion Arnold said, 'Our goal is to destroy, to eradicate the environmental movement. We're mad as hell. We're dead serious, we're going to destroy them.'[7] In 1986 Arnold, a 'wise use' movement leader, toured New Zealand sponsored by the chemical industry. Describing himself as the 'Darth Vader for the capitalist revolution', he defended the use of the carcinogenic chemical 245-T, claiming that chemical manufacturers wanted to make sure their chemicals were used safely.[8]

This is precisely what Timberlands set out to do, planning a pro-logging group, soon after called Coast Action Network, which was made up of Timberlands contractors and other locals and actively supported by the company. Timberlands' first consideration of the idea of establishing a front group is recorded in a June 1997 document. In the 'Communications Strategy for Timberlands West Coast', Shandwick suggested 'Local community support and unity. Audience: West Coast public, Foresters and families, MPs and Mayors. Strategy: Demonstrate leadership in dealing with environmental opposition, Focus efforts of beech scheme. Implementation: Create new body "West Coast Forestry Trust"...'.[9]

At a meeting two weeks later between Timberlands and its PR companies, the idea was developed further. The 1 July 1997 meeting was a major face-to-face strategy session between several senior Timberlands managers and Shandwick and Head Consultants. The campaign was not going well for Timberlands, with Prime Minister Jim Bolger privately backing an end to all logging and the NFA tree sitters, far from being deterred by heavy tactics, settling in for the winter. This was a meeting to devise ways to boost the company campaign: the automatic letters to the editor reply system and weekly PR teleconferences were instituted, West Coast pro-beech scheme advertising and public meetings were planned and creating the front group was 'agreed in principle'. Minutes of the meeting noted, under the item 'Forestry Trust', that 'the concept of establishing a Forestry Trust to create a single all inclusive body representing all West Coast forestry interests and supporters was agreed in principle'. It was decided that Kit Richards was 'to pursue informally during Beech Scheme meetings with Mayors'.[10] The Forestry Trust name was never used, but the idea was soon being implemented.

The first public signs of a Timberlands supporters group appeared soon after this meeting. During the following fortnight a carload of West Coasters, consisting of Timberlands staff and contractors and Westport unionist Cotrina Reynolds, drove to Christchurch to heckle at an environmental rally and a *Westport News* story reported that a 'yet-to-be-named' pro-logging group had begun meeting.[11]

Coast Action Network (CAN) first appeared a few weeks later, in early August 1997, when an *Assignment* TV current affairs team visited the Coast to cover the native logging controversy. In his first and only media appearance, a Timberlands logging contractor spoke on film from the middle of a logging area in defence of Timberlands, as spokesperson for the hastily named Coast Action Network. For its first year and a half, the group's secretary and spokesperson was Cotrina Reynolds of Westport. Reynolds was also on Labour MP Damien O'Connor's electorate committee. During this period the group's main activity was writing letters to the editor in reply to pro-environmental letters.

From the beginning, CAN was supported by Timberlands and served as a tool in the company's public relations campaign. At the 31 October 1997 PR telephone conference, Shandwick staff were given the job of dealing with a proposal that had appeared in the papers suggest-

---

Shandwick

2 Woodward Street
PO Box 3095
Wellington 6015
New Zealand

Fax: 64-4-471 2278
Telephone: 64-4-472 4190
E-Mail: 100254.2140@compuserve.com

FACSIMILE TRANSMISSION

TO: Jacqui Low   **FAX:** Auto Dial
Timberlands West Coast

DATE: November 4, 1997   **FROM:** Rob McGregor

NO. OF PAGES (including this page):   Four

Jacqui

Diana, Princess of Wales

As discussed, the revised letter to the Minister of Conservation follows together with the letters I have just drafted for the editors of The Greymouth Evening Star and The Westport News.

As you will see, I have kept the copy to under 200 words and so have edited the letter somewhat to ensure we do not have any difficulties complying with their requirements.

I will now get the disk with these letters couriered to you. Any subsequent changes can then be made at your end saving time and cost.

Thank you with your help with this and for arranging for the Action Group to despatch the letters on their letterhead and in the name of their organisation. Better this salvo comes from them than Timberlands.

Kind regards

Rob McGregor
Shandwick New Zealand Ltd

Shandwick was writing letters that Timberlands had arranged for the front group to send.

ing that some of Timberlands' rimu forests be preserved as a memorial to Princess Diana. The company was unimpressed by the idea. Shandwick drafted letters to the West Coast papers and the Minister of Conservation opposing the proposal and faxed them to Timberlands. In its cover note Shandwick's Rob McGregor wrote that 'the revised letter to the Minister of Conservation follows together with the letters I have just drafted for the editors of the *Greymouth Evening Star* and the *Westport*

FACSIMILE MESSAGE

TIMBERLANDS
WEST COAST LTD.

Fax to: Shandwick

Attention: Rob McGregor   *Date:* 14 July 1998

Fax number: auto   *Number of pages:*   2
                                    (including cover sheet)

From: Paula de Roeper

Subject: Letter to Editor - Nelson Mail

Please advise immediately if all pages are not received

IMPORTANT NOTICE

The information contained in this document is CONFIDENTIAL and may also be LEGALLY PRIVILEGED, intended only for the addressee. If you are not the addressee you are hereby notified that any use or dissemination of the information and any copying is strictly prohibited. If you are not the addressee, please immediately notify us by telephone and destroy this document. Thank you.

☐ **Urgent**   ☐ **For Review**   ☐ **Please Comment**   ☐ **Please Reply**   ☐ **Please Recycle**

Rob,

Thanks for the fax re NFA in NZ Herald. Cotrina Reynolds of Coast Action Network will write a response letter to the editor.

Please would you draft a response to the attached letter which appeared in the Nelson Mail (?date), from Dean Baigent-Mercer.

Thanks.

[signature]

A July 1998 fax from Timberlands to Shandwick shows co-operation with the Coast Action Network spokesperson over a reply to a New Zealand Herald *article.*

News'. But these were not the regular Shandwick-Hilliard letters –
McGregor had written the letters for others to sign. Revealingly, he wrote:
'Thank you for your help with this and for arranging for the Action Group
to dispatch the letters on their letterhead and in the name of their
organisation. Better this salvo comes from them than Timberlands.'[12]

Shandwick took it for granted that CAN would do the company's
bidding. Timberlands had promised to arrange it. In an unprecedented
move for a government agency, Shandwick was arranging for Timberlands
to lobby a government minister through a front group.

It was not an isolated incident. The Timberlands Papers reveal the
level of co-operation between Timberlands and Cotrina Reynolds. In July
1998 the *New Zealand Herald* published a news story about Native Forest Action prompting Timberlands PR manager, Paula de Roeper, to send
a fax to Rob McGregor of Shandwick regarding the use of the front group:
'Rob, Thanks for your fax re NFA in New Zealand Herald. Cotrina Reynolds
of Coast Action Network will write a response letter to the editor....
Thanks, Paula.'[13] McGregor responded: 'Paula, Your fax arrived while I
was working on the New Zealand Herald letter. I'm sending what I've
done to you because, while it needs further work, it may help Cotrina
or at least provide some material she can use... Cheers, Rob.'[14]

Reading through the local newspapers it could have appeared that
there was a broad constituency throughout the West Coast in favour of
Timberlands' logging, but when we looked at 100 pro-Timberlands letters to the editor sent to Coast papers in 1997, 1998 and 1999, we found
that the majority had been written by Timberlands staff, contractors and
consultants and/or by CAN members.

In a 10-week period over the summer of 1998-99, a majority of
the professional staff at Timberlands' Greymouth headquarters had letters published in newspapers in Wellington, Christchurch and on the
West Coast. Even the PR manager's clerical assistant who compiles publicity materials sent a letter to various papers. Apart from the chief executive and the PR manager, none of these letters acknowledged their
link to the company. In a healthy democracy, expressing one's views
should be encouraged. But if the letters are manufactured as part of a
corporate PR strategy, this harms the democratic process. The purpose
of the local letters was obviously to encourage other West Coasters to
back the company campaign, while those sent to papers elsewhere gave
the impression that Coasters wanted the logging.

The most unpleasant CAN activity was an attempt to counter a
1998 Queens Birthday weekend gathering of Native Forest Action and

Forest and Bird supporters in Reefton. Timberlands staff were determined that the event would not succeed. They contacted landowners with land leading into their forests to ask them to block access to environmentalists and, where this was not possible, physically blocked access roads with heavy machinery. At the same time they worked with CAN to try to build local hostility to the Reefton gathering. Before the weekend, Reynolds visited Reefton to encourage action against the environmentalists. She visited a local sawmill, talking to workers and distributing inflammatory posters.

The posters, (see illustration next page), which were widely distributed around Reefton, stated: 'Do you realise the extreme environmentalists are having an "Adventurous" weekend in Reefton, Queens Birthday Weekend, at West Coast people's expense?... How do you feel about NFA attempting to destroy your future livelihood, your future community viability, and the future timber industry upon which the Coast's economy relies? How do you feel about these outsiders playing with our lives, and turning them into their own adventures?... DON'T LET THEM DESTROY OUR LIVES.'

The poster was also faxed anonymously to the local community paper from Cotrina Reynolds' fax number and was displayed in shops around the town. At the same time, two other local Labour Party activists were putting up anti-environmentalist hoardings all around the town, which, ironically, has no native timber jobs, with such messages as 'tarring and feathering greenies' and 'Save a whale, harpoon a greenie'.

This aggressive approach had the desired effect. The local college, which had been booked by the environmentalists for meals and a public meeting, received threats of damage if they allowed the buildings to be used. As a result, the board of trustees decided to cancel the arrangement and set up security for the buildings over the weekend.

There were threats of violence towards environmentalists if the weekend went ahead. Some Timberlands contractors let it be known through the community that they intended turning up at the public meeting and roughing up some greenies. Little reassurance came from the police. When local Reefton environmentalists contacted the police a few days before the weekend, concerned about possible violence, they encountered a lack of interest and were told that only one officer would be on duty. Locals reported that the town's motels were booked out by journalists coming to cover the conflict.

The day before the gathering was to begin, Native Forest Action moved the event to another West Coast town, Murchison, and went ahead

Do you realise the extreme environmentalists are having an "Adventurous" weekend in Reefton, Queens Birthday weekend, at West Coast peoples expense?

Do you realise they are gathering to share what they call their "Adventures in Charleston Forest", and now they will be in Reefton to plan some more?

Do you realise this group, NFA, have publicly stated they wish to stop the proposed beech scheme on the West Coast?

How do you feel about NFA attempting to destroy your future livelihood, your future community viability, and the future timber industry on which the Coast's economy relies upon?

How do you feel about these outsiders playing with our lives, and turning them into their own "Adventures"????

WEST COAST NEEDS OUR TIMBER INDUSTRY!!!!

West Coast people, we need to show NFA, Politicians, Beauracrats,and city people that we are not prepared to accept that the West Coast will be forced to become the green concience for the rest of NZ!

With the West Coast Accord, 79%
of our land was locked up for conservation
We only have 5.7% Crown indigenous production area
and only 1.3% of the land for exotics.....

SO WHO GOT THE BEST DEAL ????!

WHAT MORE DO THEY WANT!!!

DON'T LET THEM DESTROY OUR LIVES-
If you believe in the survival of the West Coast Future, and would like to join us,
please contact Coast Action Network, Ph 7896980, Westport.

These inflammatory posters were distributed and anonymous threats of violence and damage to school buildings were made leading up to an environmental weekend in Reefton.

with its gathering without the aggression that had been whipped up in Reefton. A counter-public meeting arranged in Reefton, with buses laid on to transport people in from other parts of the Coast, went ahead at the Working Men's Club, with MP Damien O'Connor and regional mayors grandstanding against environmentalists. Slowly, community leaders formerly hostile to Timberlands were being drawn into the company's camp.

A parallel element of Timberlands' efforts was mobilising credible local figures in support of its campaign. In a weekly PR telephone conference in August 1998, Timberlands and Head Consultants agreed to brainstorm 'local "champions" to be identified who would support Timberlands in media'.[15] Two prominent local West Coast women – Greymouth businesswoman Therese Gibbens and district councillor Jacquie Grant – played this role in the following months. Grassroots PR campaigns choose people who are genuinely concerned with the welfare of the community; Gibbens and Grant were not to know that their actions would be part of a carefully orchestrated corporate PR plan.

In October 1998 public submissions were called on Timberlands' beech scheme plans. The company became aware that environmental groups were intensively collecting submissions in the cities and so began urgently trying to arrange submissions from the West Coast in favour of the scheme. CAN sprang into action. Thinly hidden behind the front group, Timberlands staff worked frantically to mobilise local support for the logging plans.

Save our beech forests, cut down a greenie. Reefton, which has no native logging jobs, was mobilised against the 'greenies'. Photo: Michael Simpson

Timberlands had prepared a detailed PR strategy for the submission gathering period, including 'steps to take once consultation started'. 'Encourage public meetings (if we can't implement them ourselves)' the plan suggested. CAN helped out. Timberlands went on to list other actions to ensure a favourable response from possible supporters. 'One to one media briefings, Push out feature articles, Use Shelley's [Head Consultants] release on Timberlands as World Leaders on sustainable management (not as it is, must be revamped as appropriate), Increase lobbying if appropriate, Use local media'.[16] The core messages of the campaign were to be that 'sustainable management provides for the future; nurtures ecosystems etc, encourages a healthy forest, provides for pest control, encourages bird life etc.'.[17]

When asked about the company's role in the public consultation, Dave Hilliard said: 'We didn't encourage people to put in submissions in favour of the plans, we encouraged people to put submissions in on the plans, because we wanted to know what people thought.'[18]

In a small region such as the West Coast, the considerable amount of public money Timberlands is able to spend on sponsorship makes a huge difference to many sports and other organisations. It also creates a pool of indebted people who can be enlisted in a political campaign.

The objectives of Timberlands' sponsorship were candidly spelled out in a 1994 PR strategy paper:

> *The sponsorship policy is designed to meet the objectives set out in the strategic communications policy: A. Inform and educate on TWC policies and related issues; B. Encourage regional support for Timberlands. C. Establish strong corporate morale and support for TWC (including contractors). D. Develop a positive public image for Timberlands.... The main emphasis of Timberlands' sponsorship commitment should be focused on areas, which support the image of Timberlands as a leading edge progressive company, which is committed to environmental responsibility.[19]*

The objective of buying support for the company's operations became more urgent as decisions on the beech scheme approached. PR strategy papers identified the West Coast Principals Association as a key target for sponsorship money. Internal documents crudely explain the strategy as:

'Concept: To provide practical assistance to the West Coast Principals Association in return for gaining the opportunity to get the support of local schools for Timberlands and its operations. Format: Donation to Annual Conference. Timberlands presentation at the Conference. Costs: $2,500.'[20] In the three years 1996-98, $7,500 was given to the association.[21]

In October 1998, Timberlands needed all the third-party support it could get by way of submissions supporting expanded rainforest logging. Timberlands was calling in its favours. The president of the West Coast Principals Association sent a letter to all West Coast schools, accompanied by a pro-beech scheme form submission that CAN was circulating. 'Timberlands have been generous supporters of our Principal's Conference and schools on the Coast,' the letter said, 'so I invite you and staff to consider this submission.'[22]

Attached was a letter to 'West Coasters and Friends of the West Coast' stating the usual case for a beech scheme from 'A concerned West Coaster' and a form submission to be signed and sent to the government supporting Timberlands' beech logging plans. Copies of the form submission were circulated around clubs and taken through pubs. Eventually many people had filled in their names and signatures on a submission that read: 'over the last few weeks I have taken time to understand how Sustainable Beech Management works'.

Timberlands was also busy sending numerous copies of its expensive beech information kit to 'timber industry participants, architects, furniture manufacturers/retailers' and other presumed allies, urging them to write submissions in favour of the logging scheme. Dave Hilliard's letter said 'I believe that is a defining step in the progression of both forest management in NZ and the "fine woods" industry' and 'I would urge everyone to take advantage of the right' to make a submission. For further 'information or guidance' concerning submission writing, they should not hesitate to call Timberlands.[23] The government company was trying to drum up submissions on its own project.

Timberlands' motives behind an educational sponsorship scheme were equally blunt. In a meeting between Timberlands, Shandwick and Head Consultants, under an item titled 'Educational Support', 'the possibility of creating further educational sponsorships, possibly as a way of assisting local support for the Beech Scheme was discussed and agreed in principle'.[24]

Educational sponsorship was seen as having other public relations benefits too. A June 1997 'communications strategy', in the section on building community support, recommended expanding educational sponsorship and proposed a 'Panel of six persons who would select the successful recipients. The panel could comprise two High School Principals, the two mayors and two company representatives.'[25] The public relations targets were the mayors, who could be brought into contact with Timberlands management in an activity that presented the company in a positive, pro-West Coast light.

Timberlands local sponsorship for the three years 1996-98 amounted to $350,845.[26] As one would expect of politically motivated spending, the sponsorship expenditure in 1998, after environmental protests began, rose to almost double the level in the two earlier years. Approximately 60 organisations received funding in the 1998 year, including 36 sports clubs, 10 schools, the Timberlands University Scholarships and a tour of South Westland logging for Lincoln University students.

Money also went to the West Coast Principals Association, the Farm Forestry Association (whose support Timberlands was cultivating) and the conservation conference in Taupo where Timberlands clashed with academic Cath Wallace. As she pointed out, 'by agreeing to such sponsorship [they] were essentially allowing Timberlands to buy reputation rather than earning it'.[27] In a period when police were frequently being called to resolve confrontations between Timberlands and environmental protesters, Timberlands even sponsored a 'Police Hunting Competition' ($1,800).

Recipients of Timberlands sponsorship in previous years included the New Zealand Institute of Forestry and the New Zealand Joinery Manufacturers Association. Grey District councillor Jacquie Grant received $5,000 of sponsorship from Timberlands for her private tourist operation, the Moana Kiwi House and Wildlife Park. Grant was an outspoken supporter of Timberlands' logging plans. 'I'm on Mr Hilliard's side,' she told media. 'Mr Hilliard runs a very good company, and he is a very well-respected man here and we respect his opinions...'.[28]

The recipients of Timberlands sponsorship were understandably grateful for the funding. In small communities like those on the West Coast, sponsorship for important community projects is hard to come by and harder to replace should the donor cut sponsorship. But, just like the calculated funding of potential scientific and environmental allies, local sponsorship had the goal of turning previously indifferent third parties into enthusiastic supporters. The president of the West Coast Hockey Association, whose interest is assisting young people in sport, came out openly defending Timberlands:

Timberlands Support
Sir, – I take exception to the remarks of Elanor Rae (Letters, June 12) in relation to the financial support

Timberlands give to the junior sports teams on the West Coast....

I have for many years been involved in fundraising for our junior players and have found Timberlands to be most supportive....Contrary to the belief that Timberlands are hellbent on destroying the future of our children, I see the seedlings they plant as a positive step to ensure some of them will have a future on the West Coast apart from the dole, they care for those seedlings just as they care for children's future.

I sincerely hope people do not come between Timberlands and the people they are helping to be recognised at a higher level, the junior sports people of the West Coast.

ANDY GREEN, President, West Coast Hockey Association.[29]

The issue was not that junior sports teams should be deprived of funding, but whether the public money going to these clubs should be allocated as part of the support-buying strategy of a state-owned company.

Timberlands' strategies also involved gaining maximum publicity from the sponsorship. The 1994 West Coast Sponsorship Policy showed clearly that publicity is the priority: 'Timberlands should be guaranteed highly visible acknowledgment through signage, programmes, media etc....Ideally, one would like high profile sponsorship, which would run over a period of time, but in practice there will often be a trade off between visibility and durability. Some high profile but short-lived events may warrant support, while some relatively low profile sponsorship may be worthwhile if it will be seen by many people over this period.'

ii	West Coast Principals' Association	
Concept:	To provide practical assistance to the West Coast Principals Association in return for gaining the opportunity to get the support of local schools for Timberlands and its operations	
Format:	Donation to Annual Conference TWC Presentation at the Conference	
Time Frame:	September Annual	
Costs:	$2,500	

Timberlands' PR strategies cynically targeted the West Coast Principals Association in its sponsorship plans, with a view to gaining support for its operations.

WEST COAST PRINCIPALS' ASSOCIATION

GRAPEVINE
3 pages

13 October 1998

Timberlands have been generous supporters of our Principal's Conference, and schools on the Coast. So I invite you and staff to consider this submission.

Mary-Clare Murphy
President

To Ministry of Agriculture and Forestry
PO Box 2526
Wellington

Re: **Public Comment West Coast Sustainable Beech Plans**

Dear Sir / Madam:

I would like to make a submission, in support of the three Sustainable Management Plans, which have been prepared for forests allocated for production under the 1986 West Coast Accord.

Over the last few weeks I have taken time to understand how Sustainable Beech Management works. In making my decision to support the above plans I have tested it against two important values

- **The Environment**
- **The Community**

These plans clearly explained that the environment is very important. They have considered and made provisions for wild life, plants, soil and water.

The community is provided with long-term opportunities, continued forest access, research and education, development of a valuable asset and a future for Indigenous forestry on the West Coast.

Yours faithfully
Name...

Signed by...

As planned, the Principals Association felt indebted to Timberlands.
It circulated a form submission to West Coast schools suggesting they write
in support of the beech scheme plans.

Timberlands West Coast Ltd
Sponsorship expenditure for year ended 31 March 1998 (excluding GST)

Buller Junior Hockey	3,111
TWC University Scholarships	4,000
W C Junior Hockey	9,333
Blackball netball club	600
W C Junior Rugby	19,715
W C Rugby – Ranfurly Shield Challenge	8,889
Buller/WC Rugby Development Officer	5,600
Buller Junior Rugby	19,555
Hokitika Junior Rugby	600
W C Junior Rugby League	12,231
W C Principals Assn	2,500
Lincoln University students tour of Sth Wld	1,511
W C Junior basketball	500
W C Provincial Fire Brigade	600
Rotomanu School	100
Touch Rugby	300
Great Westland Marathon	3,500
Greymouth Trotting Club	3,000
Inangahua College	444
Karamea School	916
Sth Westland Area School	1,055
Westland High School	101
W C Junior Softball	7,000
Kumara Races	1,000
Sth Westland Lions Raft Race	178
W C Badminton	1,500
Grey High School	444
Reefton First Light Festival	1,120
Whataroa Primary School	1,050
L Bradley	350
The Order of St John	889
Karamea Bowling Club	300
S P C A	89
Buller Primary Schools Sporting Assn	3,422
W C Junior Football Assn	889
Whataroa Golf Club	444
W C Grommet (under 18) Surf Club	500
Westland RSA	355
G Cook	1,000
Karamea Rugby Club	889
Lake Brunner Yacht Club	889
Buller High School	1,000
Buller High School girls hockey	889
Buller High School boys hockey	1,000
Charleston children's club	620
Farm Forestry Assn	6,222
Greymouth Clay target club	175
Westport Junior Soccer club	2,350
Reefton Workingmens Club	222
Buller Bowling Club	1,000
W C Junior Cricket	5,000
Runanga School	200
Wests Rugby Club	180
Buller Cricket	3,750
Hokitika Primary School	150
Sth Westland A & P Assn	30
Conservation Conference in Taupo	4,444
Guiness Games	80
W C Tennis Assn	100
Wld D C – exercise books	150
Police Hunting Competition	1,800
Miscellaneous	5,972

$155,803

(Dave Hilliard, replies to supplementary questions, Primary Production Committee, 1997-98 Financial Review of Timberlands West Coast Ltd, 8 December 1998.)

1998 Timberlands sponsorship recipients. Although valuable for the local communities, local sponsorship was aimed at turning previously indifferent third parties into enthusiastic supporters.

This policy was apparent in the constant advertising that appeared in West Coast newspapers promoting Timberlands' sponsorship. A major part of the company's sponsorship spending goes to the accompanying self-promotion, with the aim of maintaining 'an overall presence in the community through sporting and cultural events... in order to encourage a feeling of involvement/inclusion in local community and identification of TWC with West Coast and its people'.[30]

The Timberlands Papers sum up the manipulative thinking behind these 'community front' activities. Notes from a meeting between Timberlands and Shandwick recorded that 'Discussion identified a number of opportunities where public relations can be applied to further the interest of Timberlands.'

The discussion between Timberlands and Shandwick revealed that the boundaries between attacking NFA and its sponsorship largesse were non-existent. 'Community Front: *Thank you TWC letters – from allies who have received TWC sponsorship; *Promoting Scholarships (Full page advertisement calling for entries, Full page advertisement congratulating successful people, PR story/photographs (just before – 2 hits)); *Develop a sponsorship policy/guidelines for Timberlands.... 3. Environmental Front: *Anti-NFA letter writing campaign (stock letters); *Thank you TWC for supplying my son's football team, etc.'[31]

Shandwick also recommended national sponsorship projects aimed at improving the company's image. The strategy documents make no attempt to hide their contempt towards the 'mainstream greens whose support Timberlands needs'. Timberlands canvassed two ideas for winning the hearts and minds of the public. First it considered the need 'To associate Timberlands closely with subjects, people, skills and ideas with which New Zealanders closely identify and value, so that "mainstream light greens" feel justified/comfortable in supporting Timberlands'.

The strategy proposes a Timberlands-sponsored nature photography contest ('photography is popular among the young, affluent, mainstream greens whose support Timberlands needs') and a woodcraft competition using Timberlands-logged native timber (which first took place in 1999). It goes on: 'There is little reason for a self-professed "mainstream" green to support a logging company. We have to give the public reasons to support Timberlands.... Very little mainstream environmental support is based on factual knowledge/reason, but more so on vague emotional support for the desire to "save the planet" or to fall in with the latest fashionable concern.'[32]

If anyone doubted the political motivation behind Timberlands' sponsorship, they need look no further than the company's sponsorship of new name-tags for the Grey District Council in April 1999. The local newspaper pictured Mayor Kevin Brown holding his new name-tag, which had the council's and Timberlands' logos side by side at the top followed by the words 'I support sustainable resource management'. The badges were made of native timber.

2. Community Front
- Briefing Notes for TWC staff
- Thank you TWC letters – from allies who have received TWC sponsorship
- Promoting Scholarships
  Full page advertisement calling for entries
  Full page advertisement congratulating successful people
  PR story/photographs (just before – 2 hits)
- Sponsorship Policy
  Develop a sponsorship policy/guidelines for TWC

3. Environmental Front
- Predation versus Conservation Estate
- Bird Song Story/Bird Surveys
- Parliamentary Commissioner for the Environment Story
- Anti-NFA letter writing campaign (stock letters)
  Dominion/Press letter re. NFA lies
  Sustainable Management versus Devastation (Evening Post/Press)
  Successful business story (NZH) – 15m to 109m, exotics, predation,

  Conservation Estate and TWC Predation Control (WC/Press)
  Thank you TWC for supplying my son's football team, etc.

An August 1998 PR strategy meeting planned letters to the editor attacking Native Forest Action and thanking Timberlands for its sponsorship. These began to appear soon afterwards.

Councillor Tony Kokshoorn, a member of the CAN executive and part-owner of the local newspaper, was reported in the accompanying article as saying he believed the name-tags were a great gesture and they were free. 'I support sustainable resource management and will wear this proudly,' he said. Councillor Jacquie Grant, however, backed Councillor Margaret Macdonald when she told the council meeting she was not elected by Timberlands West Coast and did not expect to wear a badge with Timberlands' name on it.[33]

In a letter to the editor a few days later, Y. Davison of Greymouth wrote: 'It is hard to believe that the majority of our district councillors could be so foolish as to accept those name tags from Timberlands....If councillors felt they really needed name tags, I for one would have been happy to oblige, but I would not have required my name to appear anywhere, let alone on top, on equal terms with the council logo...They should also bear in mind that while most people would support genuinely sustainable management of resources, many do not believe that Timberlands' version of the concept is credible.'[34]

The other area where money could be used to try to win West Coast support was advertising. Most companies use advertising primarily to promote products and services and build public awareness of the company brand. With Timberlands, nearly all the advertising has political purposes: using publicly funded advertising as another opportunity 'where public relations can be applied to further the interest of Timberlands'.

Shandwick put it bluntly. 'By creating an opportunity for the company to tell its "own story" in an environment where it has complete control of the message, Timberlands can use public information advertising to present a strong message.... Public information advertising provides the opportunity for the company to control its message and to deliver a strong message to a wider audience, without a counter perspective.'[35]

What this meant in practice was that the company, which knew it was not winning the debate when the public was hearing both sides of the story, could bombard the locals with its own PR messages. One Timberlands advertisement on Radio Scenicland, which broadcasts to most of the West Coast, featured children's voices:

Presenter: What do you like about Timberlands West Coast?
Here's what kids around the West Coast like about
Timberlands.

175

Child: The thing I like about Timberlands is the pruning.
Child: The thing that I liked about Timberlands was that all the people were kind and caring.
Child: The thing I liked about Timberlands was when we had a turn on the fire truck.
Child: The thing I like about Timberlands is they replant the trees.
Presenter: What did you like about Timberlands?
Child: The thing that I like about Timberlands is because they take care of our forests.
Child: The thing I like about Timberlands is that they take out their time to take people out to the forests and show what they can do.
Child: The thing I like about Timberlands is you learn quite a lot.
Child: The best thing I liked about Timberlands was pruning the trees.
Child: The thing I like about Timberlands was going to the skid.
Presenter: What a great impression Timberlands have left in these kids' minds.
            Next time you're out and about in the forest, have a think about what Timberlands are doing for the West Coast.[36]

Advertisements like this were played at saturation levels during the period when Timberlands was attempting to ensure a flood of local submissions in favour of its beech logging plans. Pro-Timberlands advertisements continued to play heavily over the following months.

An advertisement on the other West Coast station, Radio Fifeshire, gushingly emphasised Timberlands' environment credentials.

At the end of the day Timberlands West Coast Ltd is pioneering the development of complex sustainable management systems in the indigenous production forests on the West Coast. They are sustainably logged and are examples to other forestry regimes around the world. Some people dress up in white heron costumes and flap their feathers from a nest on top of a tripod cooing about our *beautiful rimu forests. The facts are that people needn't be concerned. Timberlands West Coast Ltd manages around 37,000 hectares of rimu forest and the best part of it is Timberlands has fully audited sustainable management systems in place, the first and most significant in the country, ensuring our forests are there for our children's future.... Forget the myths about forests being hacked because Timberlands West Coast Ltd are sustaining, researching, regenerating, caring for and loving our forests through planting and nurturing our kids' future now.*[37]

By December 1998, when this was being broadcast, CAN supporters were arranging funding for some of the advertisements. This one was paid for by a Greymouth business run by an outspoken member of CAN.

Spending many tens of thousands of dollars on advertising and promoting its sponsorship buys Timberlands a further type of influence in a small region like the West Coast. Because advertising revenue is what makes or breaks small media outlets, advertising provides Timberlands with considerable leverage over editorial content as well.

Timberlands, a small SOE based in Greymouth, decided it had to get its message out to an audience beyond the West Coast. It even considered television advertising in an attempt to influence national public opinion. A December 1998 public relations strategy paper proposed: 'TV commercial or programme... February, to run XX times a week for two months', followed by 'TV Advertising... May-July (once beech gets go ahead)', then articles in 'Magazines (Trends, Home and Building etc. Messages – Quality product; Family heirloom; Environmentally sensitive), trade publications....North and South, Metro, Political Review (February), NBR (New Year).' The television commercial or programme was envisaged as having a 'Celebrity to present, eg Sir Edmund Hilliary. Shot on West Coast (forests, community, sawmills). Tell story of sustainable management (simply, visually)' and the TV advertising was to present native timber as a 'Quality product, New Zealanders proud of their heritage, In perpetuity, Embodied in family heirloom...'.[38]

CHAPTER 10

TARGETING LABOUR

Helen Clark must visit. (Has she got a clear conscience that her knowledge is balanced?)

Confidential Timberlands PR strategy paper,
December 1998

'Helen Clark – Maybe it is time you came with an open mind and had a look for yourself instead of listening to wild extreme groups who play no part in our commu-nity.... THERE WILL BE NO TRADE OFF. Be assured Mrs Clark, the fight has just begun.'

Coast Action Network form letter to Helen Clark,
January 1999

By late 1998, Timberlands' public relations strategy had had some success on the West Coast. The local MP was by then strongly backing the com-pany and various locals were outspokenly supporting the company. Coast Action Network, first planned by Timberlands 18 months earlier as the 'West Coast Forestry Trust', had the active backing of local mayors.

Some of this may well have happened anyway, but Timberlands' PR budget had transformed the politics of forestry in a short space of time. The interests of even pro-logging West Coast locals are not the same as those of Timberlands; the fact that it was the company's agenda that prevailed is testament to the effect of the PR strategies.

In 1997, when public controversy over logging increased and it became possible that native forest logging would end, the local mayors' usual response had not been implacable opposition but simply to stress that there would need to be decent compensation for the local commu-nities. They went as far as putting their names to a suggested compensa-tion package in exchange for an end to native forest logging. It was sub-mitted to government by a grouping of West Coasters under the name

West Coast Resource Interests. Timberlands' campaign, of course, was based entirely on maintaining and increasing its native forest logging. This difference between local and company interests shows up how the local supporters, through close contacts with the company, were led into supporting Timberlands' preferred policies.

The issue came to a head in November 1998 when the Labour Party's annual conference voted overwhelmingly in favour of ending all logging of West Coast public forests. It was the only remit that the leader Helen Clark stood to speak to, arguing that Coasters be offered a generous compensation package. She spoke of transferring state pine forests held by Timberlands to the local councils (valued at over $80 million), state support for local infrastructure developments and other initiatives. In an era of minimal state support for regional development, it was a major offer from the leader of a party that a year later might be government.

Only a year after their West Coast Resource Interests proposal, however, the mayors had been moved entirely to Timberlands' position. In the *Press* coverage of the Labour conference, all the West Coast spokespeople who had joined the Timberlands camp spoke against Labour's decision. Labour MP Damien O'Connor, Cotrina Reynolds of CAN, who had attended the conference as a Labour delegate, Buller mayor Pat O'Dea and Grey mayor Kevin Brown lashed out at the decision. Timberlands' Kit Richards spoke out for the company too.[1]

Pat O'Dea described the Labour delegates as 'cotton-picking crazy. Timberlands' forests are acclaimed to be world

In mid-1997 West Coast mayors approached the government supporting an end to Timberlands' native logging in exchange for a compensation package.

Stop rimu logging on Coast, say councils

By CHRISTINE CESSFORD
Environment reporter

The Government is in the firing line as the battle over West Coast native logging edges closer to Wellington.

As tree-top protesters continued to halt logging in the forest near Charleston, local community leaders joined their call for SOE Timberlands to stop taking rimu.

Coast council leaders said the 1986 West Coast Forest Accord, under which Timberlands claimed the right to log,

Pat O'Dea – compensation.

New Zealanders.

"Like the Treat Crown made promise: that it didn't keep," I

179

class.' Perhaps unbeknown to O'Dea, it was a direct quote from Timberlands' public relations materials. Only 18 months earlier, shortly before CAN was created, O'Dea had been saying that 'A lot of people are quite happy to have the protesters there. They believe Timberlands has cheated on the [West Coast] Accord and the trees should stay there ... because there is no benefit [to Buller from milling them].'[2]

'Local champion' Therese Gibbens adopted a strident position after a CAN meeting in Greymouth. 'There will be no deals, no compensations or trade-offs for the accord. We need Timberlands jobs,' she said. The article went on: 'Mrs Gibbens said she had been accused of being a mouthpiece for Timberlands, which had saddened and angered her.'[3]

The fact that the local mayors, only a year before, had been proposing a compensation deal as a trade-off for ending native forest logging was forgotten. Also absent from their reaction was the obvious thought that since Labour was heading towards stopping the logging, West Coast interests might require that they work for the best outcome for local people. It was quite understandable that people like Therese Gibbens were worried: she spoke of six retail shops closing in Greymouth just that week. Although it was genuine concern for their region that motivated her and others, it was Timberlands' agenda that directed that feeling into a no-compromise position.

In January 1999 West Coast members of NFA launched a petition calling for a halt to native forest logging in exchange for transfer of exotic forests to the local government; state funding for new sewerage schemes in the main West Coast towns, which the councils were facing huge bills to replace; and a levy on coal produced on the Coast to go to the local councils instead of central government. They reported in an article in the *Westport News* that about half the people they approached in the streets of Westport were signing the petition. But, as with the Labour conference, CAN 'wholeheartedly' rejected the regional development package.[4] Ironically, the environmentalists were proposing precisely the compromise package that had been developed and promoted to the government by the West Coast mayors.

Timberlands' political agenda was steering the actions of local activists in another way too. The support of Labour leader Helen Clark for protecting the forests was troublesome for Timberlands. In December 1998 Paula de Roeper of Timberlands had produced a paper called 'Public Relations Strategy – Where to from here?' She was gloomy about the effectiveness of Timberlands' campaign. 'Despite all efforts of Timberlands to alter the negative public perception of the company,' she wrote, 'a recent survey shows that the large scale misinformation campaign by the "opponents" (Native Forest Action, Forest and Bird) has in general been absorbed by the public. Conversely, the facts from Timberlands appear to be treated with mistrust and, in the main, ignored....Time is running out....'[5] One of the main conclusions of de Roeper's paper was 'Helen Clark must visit. (Has she got a clear conscience that her knowledge is balanced and that she can categorically say that the Timberlands sust. man. system is not acceptable?).'[6]

Timberlands' problem was that, as a state-owned enterprise, it was in no position to approach the Labour leader and express these frustrations directly. The company knew that the election of a Labour-led government could mean the end of all of its native forest plans. CAN fronted for it again, making it their primary project to try to pressure Helen Clark to visit the Coast.

In early January the group produced a form letter addressed to the Labour Leader urging her to come to the Coast to 'look for yourself instead of listening to wild extreme groups who play no part in our community'. The letter ended: 'THERE WILL BE NO TRADE OFF. Be assured Mrs Clark, the fight has just begun.' Like the form submissions circulated about the beech scheme, it was signed 'A concerned West Coaster'.

Several weeks later the group announced that it had had a 'fantastic' response to its call for Coasters to sign the letter to Helen Clark, saying they had taken the letter to recent A&P shows and the Buller marathon.[7] Other news stories said that CAN had contacted Labour MP Jim Sutton and been offered his help in arranging a visit by Helen Clark.

'Local champion' Jacquie Grant gained publicity in December 1998 planting a beech tree on One Tree Hill in Auckland 'on behalf of West Coasters who support beech logging by State-owned enterprise Timberlands West Coast Ltd'. She used the opportunity to attack the Labour Party for its stand against Timberlands' logging and urged 'expatriot [sic] West Coasters to consider not voting for Labour'.[8] The following month she named three ostrich chicks at her wildlife park after Helen Clark and two NFA spokespeople 'because ostriches were famous for putting their heads in the sand'.[9]

In early 1999 CAN was expanded and announced plans for its own 'nationwide public awareness campaign', including financial support from local companies and publications aiming 'to promote sustainable logging in a professional way'.[10] Meetings were held in towns around the Coast inviting new people to join the group and, at an 18 January 1999 meeting in Greymouth, an executive committee was formed. The same week Timberlands invited all the new CAN recruits on a free bus trip to view its logging in South Westland, including free Timberlands caps and laying on a huge lunch at an RSA hall on the way. It was a flop, with only 10 people accepting the invitation.

FREEPOST

HANDS OFF THE WEST COAST FOREST ACCORD
Helen Clark Leader of the Labour Party &
All Labour Party Members of Parliament
Parliament Buildings
Wellington

Dear Helen Clark

In 1986 the Labour Government was a signatory to the West Coast Forest Accord, a contract representing a carefully negotiated agreement between the West Coast Timber Industry, local authorities, environmental groups and your Government.

You have now stated that if elected you have every intention of breaking that agreement. The West Coast needs real jobs and diversified opportunities for its sustainable future.

The approved sustainable beech management programme is an opportunity to ensure the continuation of our forest industry and to protect our forests.

This is a personal invitation to visit our forests and confront the reality of what has and is being achieved on the Coast with Sustainable Management.

It is time you came, with an open mind and had a look for yourself instead of listening to extreme groups who play no part in our communities.

THERE WILL BE NO TRADE OFF
Be assured Ms Clark, the fight has just begun

Yours faithfully

Name: ....

Address: ....

....

A secret December 1998 Timberlands PR plan stated that its political priority was getting Labour leader Helen Clark on a company PR tour. After the Christmas break, Coast Action Network announced that its priority was persuading Helen Clark to visit the Coast.

Although more locals were being brought into the group, if anything, Timberlands' control over CAN's activities increased at this time. The original group, based around Cotrina Reynolds and Buller people, where most of the logging and claimed potential jobs were, was taken over by new people living around Greymouth and Hokitika – Timberlands country.

The new person driving the group was Timberlands contractor Barry Nicolle, the same 'former Native Forest Action supporter' who had gained publicity attacking the environment group after infiltrating its Christchurch branch meetings in co-operation with Timberlands. Within days of his media publicity splash Nicolle, who had moved to the West Coast four years earlier, was the main speaker at a series of pro-Timberlands public meetings. A month later he was appointed as the chairperson and spokesperson of CAN and by April 1999 news stories were describing him as the 'founder' of the group.[11]

Nicolle had been co-operating with the Timberlands campaign for months. His elevation brought the group even more closely into the company's PR strategies. Although a range of new people had been brought into the group (many from local companies appreciative of Timberlands' business), new executive members found that the agenda for the monthly meetings had been set by Nicolle before they arrived and, as with the Helen Clark letter-writing campaign, the action proposals fitted neatly with Timberlands' agenda. For the first six months of 1999 almost all CAN's activities were directed towards trying to influence Labour's policy

Coast Action Network spokesperson, Barry Nicolle, rejected a compensation package proposed by the Labour Party – even though it was the same deal local mayors had proposed the year before. Nicolle was working for Timberlands at the time and planning all the 'independent' group's activities closely with the Timberlands managers.
Photo: John Kelleher

on native forests. Timberlands' corporate communications manager Paula de Roeper confided to public relations colleagues at this time that CAN was being 'very useful to us' in the company's campaign.[12]

Nicolle's public statements were inflammatory and strongly antagonistic towards environmentalists. In February 1999, after NFA had called for donations for fines following a quiet protest blockading the logging helicopter, he declared: 'The protesting radicals are not content with West Coasters paying for their dole while they try and take our jobs off us, now they want us to pay their fines for eco-terrorism. Everyone I've spoken to suggested that they stay chained to the helicopter and be flown out to sea.'[13] In March 1999, when Green MP Rod Donald presented a set of development ideas for the West Coast, Nicolle replied that Donald ' appeared to believe in the Easter bunny... These greenies have no regard for Coast peoples' livelihoods, only that one goal – close our sustainable forests and put hundreds more Coasters on the dole.'[14] A month later he said the Alliance Party's anti-logging policy would 'rip the heart out of the West Coast'.[15] The fact that there were only a couple of dozen jobs left dependent on native forest logging, and that National government decisions were phasing out most of these, was lost in the rhetoric.

The Greymouth newspaper ran a front-page story on the reformed CAN, quot-

CAN launched a PR blitz in April 1999 with this 16-page tabloid. Although Timberlands denied any involvement, it turned out that the company had provided the mailing list to which it was sent.

ing Nicolle: 'We want to be seen as a respectable group with credibility. We'll be upfront with the truth. We have nothing to hide.' Nicolle was keen to distance CAN from Timberlands, telling the paper that although he worked for Timberlands as a pest control worker, CAN had no connections with the state-owned company. 'One of the misconceptions is that we are a mouthpiece for Timberlands, but that is not the case,' he claimed.[16]

But the Timberlands Papers reveal that CAN had been dreamt up in a PR plan 18 months earlier and that, from the beginning, it was co-operating closely with Timberlands and its PR companies. When the group's 'nationwide public awareness campaign' began in April 1999, close co-operation with Timberlands was apparent. CAN produced 20,000 copies of a glossy leaflet and a 16-page tabloid newspaper, publications full of West Coasters admirably sticking up for their region – but still the underlying agenda was driven by Timberlands. While mentioning all aspects of the region's economy, the publications devoted by far the majority of their space to native forestry. In the tabloid, the first article was on the Labour Party conference's forestry remits, then one on the West Coast Accord followed by a two-page feature by forest scientist Ian James, not mentioning that he had designed Timberlands' logging systems and that the article was a reprint of a *Green Monitor* issue he wrote for Timberlands. The next article was by Timberlands' ally Guy Salmon. A map and various photographs had been supplied by Timberlands and so too, it emerged, had the mailing list to which the publications were sent.

A Wellington journalist, Graeme Speden from the *Independent* newspaper, wondered why a West Coast community group was writing to him by name in the parliamentary press gallery. He phoned Paula de Roeper at Timberlands to ask if the company, whose mailing list he was on, had assisted. She replied that Timberlands had 'nothing to do with' CAN. 'It isn't to do with Timberlands,' she said, 'it's the local community doing their own thing.... We provide them with information when they come to us and ask for it, but that's all.'[17]

'Asked if the *Independent* received CAN's supplement because it was on Timberlands' mailing list,' Speden wrote, ' de Roeper said she didn't know how Nicolle chose the recipients. "Perhaps he looked through clippings or something and got your name," she suggested.' Speden then phoned Nicolle, who admitted that the newspaper's address had come from Timberlands. 'They sent me a list of people maybe I could post some information to,' he said.[18]

The CAN publications were part of a PR blitz timed for the last week in April 1999, leading up to the presumed date of the final decision by Labour MPs on their conservation policy. The week the CAN publications arrived in Parliament, West Coast MP Damien O'Connor held a West Coast expo in the Beehive and CAN held a large public meeting in the Greymouth picture theatre, 'officially launching' the group.

The Invest in the West expo was organised by Gerry Morris, manager of the Wellington PR company, Morris Communications Group, who had previously been employed by Timberlands to arrange the graffiti-covering Balaena Bay mural. O'Connor explained that the event would give key West Coast industries an opportunity to 'give their views on contentious issues, such as sustainable use of resources, through displays and by meeting guests'.[19]

It was planned for both Barry Nicolle and Timberlands' Paula de Roeper to be present, with both spending the following day lobbying on the Timberlands issue in Parliament.[20] After news publicity about the Labour-lobbying motives of the Invest in the West expo, Timberlands and CAN kept a low profile at the event. Television producer Julie Christie was flown from Auckland to be guest speaker at the event and she, at least, assumed that the evening still had a Timberlands theme. Speaking before the presentation of awards to some West Coast businesses with no links to native forestry, her whole speech to the audience of politi-

Julie Christie flew from Auckland to be the celebrity guest speaker at MP Damien O'Connor's 'non-political' 'Invest in the West' industry promotion: 'Will the will of Damien O'Connor alone be enough to stop his own party closing down the forestry industry?' she asked. 'I wish CAN all the best.' No one mentioned that she was the sister of CAN frontperson Therese Gibbens.
Photo: John Kelleher

cians, journalists and businesspeople was about maintaining West Coast native forest logging.

'On the West Coast they absolutely love Damien O'Connor,' Christie began, 'no matter what their political opinions. Everyone thinks Damien O'Connor is working for them. He's a great man.' Later she came to the point: 'Will the will of Damien O'Connor alone be enough to stop his own party closing down the forestry industry?' she asked. She finished her speech by saying, 'I wish CAN all the best', the first mention made of the group that evening and with no explanation of what the acronym stood for. No one mentioned that she was the sister of CAN frontperson Therese Gibbens.

The CAN public meeting in Greymouth that week was the highpoint of the campaign to influence the Labour Party's policy. Newspaper advertising and free copies of the CAN tabloid delivered to every West Coast home attracted 400 people to the meeting. It also brought together many of the political allies Timberlands had been developing through the rest of the campaign, including National and ACT politicians and the West Coast Labour MP Damien O'Connor. This 'launch' of CAN received considerable TV, radio and newspaper coverage, even though it was the third time the group had publicity for 'launching' itself.

The advertising for the meeting did not mention Timberlands or forestry. Rather, the ads were headed 'Do you care about the future of the West Coast?' and said 'Do you have children or grandchildren who may want to spend their future here?'[21] But the politicians were well aware what the meeting was for and devoted their speeches to Timberlands. Introducing the meeting, Nicolle said that CAN was concerned about all West Coast resources but that the forum would emphasise forestry, which was 'facing a crisis'.

'We cannot stand to lose our industry,' Nicolle said. An end to 'sustainable forestry' would be the 'death knell' for the region and a 'real catastrophe'. 'People don't want to move out of their homes because some greenie tells us our forests are not sustainable.' He made the standard denial that CAN was linked to Timberlands, even though he himself had spent the afternoon before the forum in a meeting with senior Timberlands staff at the company's headquarters.

The star speaker at the forum was Guy Salmon, whose speech artfully presented the arguments in favour of continued logging. He told the audience he had come along to support Timberlands and that there were three reasons why he was prepared to be on the platform.

He began by acknowledging environmentalists' concerns about

preserving lowland native forest, the forest 'that is really important for conservation and for wildlife'. But he explained that 83 percent of the lowland forest – 'the land below 700 metres' – in the North Westland and Buller regions was already protected. 'Now that's actually a very generous allocation of native forests to reserves,' he said.

Salmon would have been well aware of the trickiness of this statistic, which is frequently used in Timberlands publications. The established definition of lowland forest used by ecologists, which he himself had used many times in the past, is forest under 300 metres altitude, not 700 metres. By using a definition of 'lowland' that included forests stretching almost into alpine areas, Salmon was using statistics to hide the crucial fact that about half of the high-quality lowland forests were still open to logging.

Salmon's next argument was about the West Coast Accord – 'one of the great accomplishments of my career as a conservationist' – in which he had helped to negotiate the creation of some important new forest reserves while maintaining the West Coast timber industry until supplies of pine timber were available. He criticised the environment organisations opposed to Timberlands' logging, saying that was 'clearly a breach of the accord' and commiserated with the audience that 'understandably you're pretty shocked that a document you thought you could rely on is suddenly being called into question'. But, like the definition of lowland

Timberlands' ally Guy Salmon was guest speaker at a pro-Timberlands public meeting in April 1999, the culmination of his divergence from the environment movement.

COAST ACTION NETWORK

A MEETING FOR SUPPORTERS OF C.A.N TO ATTEND THEIR OFFICIAL

LAUNCH NIGHT

to be held at the Regent Theatre, Greymouth on
Tuesday, 27 April 1999
at 7.30 pm

Special Guest Speaker will be

GUY SALMON
from the Mauria Society

Forestry Spokesperson from each major political party have been invited to speak on their parties Forestry policy

This is a MAJOR issue for the West Coast leading up to the November election, we cannot afford to lose our sustainable forest Industry!

STAND UP FOR THE COAST - COME ALONG AND BE HEARD

forest, the real argument revolved around the detail.

The agreement made in the 1986 West Coast Accord was to allow several fine native forests to be clearfelled to maintain supplies of rimu logs to West Coast mills until the mid-1990s, when they could transfer to cutting pine trees. West Coast sawmillers received their side of the deal in the form of logs from native forests that were cleared over the following decade. In exchange some forests were made into reserves and other areas remained in limbo, possibly open to logging. Both the High Court and the Court of Appeal have since confirmed that the limbo forests (including those targeted by the beech scheme) did not need to be logged. But it suited Timberlands – and some of its allies, including Salmon – to keep arguing that a beech scheme must proceed.

Salmon saved his main point for the last few minutes of his speech. 'The third reason I wanted to come,' he said, 'was to sort of, perhaps, bring a message to you about how you can win your cause.' He said the challenge facing CAN was how to stop the beech scheme being 'derailed' by 'some politician coming to office and pulling it out'. The end of his speech was devoted to Timberlands' chief concern, the Labour Party, and in particular to urging the audience to write letters to Helen Clark.

'Now there's a bit of a secret that I'll share with you about how you win campaigns like this,' he told the audience. 'I don't know how many people we have here, I haven't counted, but it looks a hell of a lot of people.

OKARITO ONLY HOME OF THE WHITE HERONS WILL BE LOGGED;

UNLESS YOU STOP IT:

help by coming to
PUBLIC MEETING
Tuesday March 2. 8pm
Horticultural Buildings
151. Cambridge Tce.

INVITED: Mr. V. Young
Minister of Forests

SPEAKERS:
GUY SALMON Ed. 'Beechleaves'
GWENNY DAVIS Nat. Secretary N.F.A.C.
PROFESSOR KNOX (Cant. University)
W.C. SAWMILLERS REP.
TOM HAY (Forest & Bird Prot. Soc.)

PLEASE COME!

Twenty years earlier Salmon had supported protection of Okarito.

189

If you can all write a letter, if you can all ask one other person to write a letter, Helen Clark will have had a more powerful voice from grassroots New Zealand than she's had on any other issue for a long time. And believe you me, that works in terms of all the campaigns I've been involved with.'[22]

At the end of the meeting a CAN member approached the National and ACT representatives, John Luxton and Ken Shirley, to ask them the question that had been on his mind throughout the meeting. He wanted to know whether, if they remained in government, they would privatise Timberlands and the beech forests. Both, without hesitation, said yes. They explained that, with the beech forests, they would only be selling the long-term cutting rights, not the forests themselves, but the meaning for any West Coaster willing to think about it was obvious.

Nothing highlighted the deception of CAN supporters by Timberlands' PR campaign more than the issue of privatisation. There was nothing permanent about Timberlands. Ever since the company was created the government had been looking towards its eventual sale. Treasury officials had already been working on details of the sale and the Timberlands management had been holding talks with three possible Japanese buyers. But when challenged publicly about the possibility in January 1999, SOE minister Tony Ryall had said it was 'neither for sale nor being readied for sale' and Dave Hilliard of Timberlands had said the claim, made by Native Forest Action, was 'a load of rubbish'.[23]

Guy Salmon spoke at a pro-Timberlands rally: 'The third reason I wanted to come,' he told the meeting, 'was to sort of, perhaps, bring a message to you about how you can win your cause.' He urged the audience to write letters to Helen Clark.
Photo: Sunday Star-Times

Compared with CAN's foolish claim that ending native forest logging would be the 'death knell' of the region, privatisation of Timberlands really did have the potential to be a 'catastrophe' and 'put hundreds more Coasters on the dole'. If Timberlands' pine plantations were privatised, as had happened in most of the rest of the country, the new owner would have no obligation to process the trees on the West Coast. Commercial forces would decide. Hundreds of sawmilling jobs could go as logs were exported whole from the ports in Nelson or Christchurch. It would be the same for beech forest timber. Despite Timberlands' PR materials about beech logging providing New Zealanders with 'family heirlooms' so they could be 'proud of their heritage in perpetuity', the beech scheme was aimed at export markets. Under foreign control, there would be few jobs for locals in chopping down the trees and shipping them out of the region.

Was CAN making angry statements or organising letter-writing campaigns about the threat of losing their forestry industry through privatisation? Not a squeak. The issue was never mentioned as the campaign over native forest logging grew in pitch. The Timberlands managers were working towards the sale of the company but did not want public debate over what privatisation would mean for locals. The West Coast Accord had promised pine forestry in perpetuity once native for-

Timberlands logs loaded on a train to Christchurch, taking local jobs with them. CAN made no comment on any issues where West Coast and Timberlands' interests were obviously not the same. Photo: Peter Russell.

est logging was phased out. That commitment from the government, which affected hundreds of families, was best forgotten while spurious claims about accord commitments to ongoing native forest logging were being broadcast.

Two weeks before the Greymouth public meeting some locals had seen an ominous sight. They watched as whole beech logs were loaded into a closed shipping container in the yard of Frank Croft's transport company at Stillwater, near Greymouth (T. Croft Ltd is Timberlands' main log carting contractor.) The workers explained to them that the logs were being shipped to Tasmania for processing trials. It struck the locals that processing trials in Australia did not bode well for their jobs. Already, most of the beech timber processing trials were happening in Christchurch. It was concerns about this that led to the question about privatisation after the Greymouth meeting.

When Timberlands had released its beech scheme plans the year before, Dave Hilliard had said, 'the native timber will be processed locally to be used to manufacture high quality products'.[24] Guy Salmon had chimed in, saying that 'if these plans are approved, New Zealanders will at long last be able to use native timber with a clear conscience'.[25] When the Tasmanian-based timber company Gunns subsequently bought one of the main mills processing Timberlands native timber, the Carter Holt Harvey mill in Christchurch, and mentioned a general interest in the beech timber,[26] NFA questioned whether the local beech scheme jobs would really eventuate. Hilliard replied that the suggestion that 'Australians would take West Coast jobs' was 'bizarre, distorted and ignorant of the facts'. 'What will it be tomorrow?' he said. 'Probably the CIA landing spies from ships on Hokitika beach.'[27]

It is likely that Hilliard knew better. On 11 November 1998, the Auckland forestry consultants Groome Forestry Consulting Ltd had sent a fax stamped 'Confidential' to Minister of State Owned Enterprises Tony Ryall on behalf of its client, Gunns of Tasmania. The fax stated that Gunns were 'interested in creating an international market for beech' produced by Timberlands on the West Coast. It noted that Gunns wanted to buy the Carter Holt Harvey mill in Christchurch to use in processing Timberlands' logs, which it subsequently did. The fax also stated that Gunns were interested in Timberlands' pine plantations.[28] While CAN rallied to Timberlands' cause, the company was not returning the favour.

Timberlands and CAN maintained their pressure right up to the Labour Party decision. Out of the blue, one of the organisations Timberlands PR papers had identified as a potential ally, the Furniture Association of New Zealand, sent a report to all Labour MPs and the media in late May, entitled 'The Value of the West Coast Accord to New Zealand Furniture Manufacturers'. It argued, in alarming terms, that should the West Coast Accord be repudiated 'it is anticipated' that 1200 people would lose their jobs in the furniture industry and 270 people would lose their jobs on the West Coast (the latter figure was much higher than even CAN was claiming). Lest their political point not be clear enough, the report said their concern 'would become valid on adoption of policy, not simply after an election'.[29] The association followed it up two days later with a second press release headed 'Furniture Manufacturers Call on Labour to Honour the West Coast Accord,' and in that short time the number of jobs at risk had risen to 'some 1800 to 2000'. It 'endorsed calls by the West Coast Action Network for the Labour Party to stand behind the West Coast Accord'. [30]

Objective A: To Inform and Educate on the Activities of Timberlands West Coast and Related Issues

Audience

6   **Special Interest Groups (Supportive of TWC)**

[NZ Forest Owners Association, Furniture Manufacturers' Association, West Coast Resource Users Group, Trade Unions]

Strategies

✧   Inform and educate potential natural allies as to the issues surrounding indigenous forestry management, and downstream industrial development, so that they can become 'spokespeople' for TWC where implementation of TWC's plans apperars threatened.

Delivery

1   **Provision of Information**

Concept: To provide information to enable natural allies to speak on behalf ó Timberlands

Content: -   impact of TWC on regional economy;

Timberlands' PR plans had identified the Furniture Association as one of the allies that could become 'spokespeople' for the company.

In the same week as the Furniture Association lobbying, Timberlands tried to get more Labour MPs to come to the Coast for a PR tour. At the Beehive expo in April, CAN's Barry Nicolle had boasted to a journalist that one of the Labour MPs, who had grown up on the West Coast, 'seems to think he can get Labour MPs down there'. Four weeks later, all Labour MPs received an invitation from this MP to join

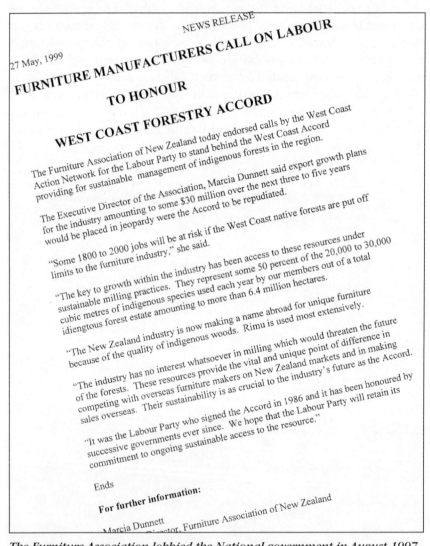

NEWS RELEASE

27 May, 1999

FURNITURE MANUFACTURERS CALL ON LABOUR

TO HONOUR

WEST COAST FORESTRY ACCORD

The Furniture Association of New Zealand today endorsed calls by the West Coast Action Network for the Labour Party to stand behind the West Coast Accord providing for sustainable management of indigenous forests in the region.

The Executive Director of the Association, Marcia Dunnett said export growth plans for the industry amounting to some $30 million over the next three to five years would be placed in jeopardy were the Accord to be repudiated.

"Some 1800 to 2000 jobs will be at risk if the West Coast native forests are put off limits to the furniture industry," she said.

"The key to growth within the industry has been access to these resources under sustainable milling practices. They represent some 50 percent of the 20,000 to 30,000 cubic metres of indigenous species used each year by our members out of a total idiengtous forest estate amounting to more than 6.4 million hectares.

"The New Zealand industry is now making a name abroad for unique furniture because of the quality of indigenous woods. Rimu is used most extensively.

"The industry has no interest whatsoever in milling which would threaten the future of the forests. These resources provide the vital and unique point of difference in competing with overseas furniture makers on New Zealand markets and in making sales overseas. Their sustainability is as crucial to the industry's future as the Accord.

"It was the Labour Party who signed the Accord in 1986 and it has been honoured by successive governments ever since. We hope that the Labour Party will retain its commitment to ongoing sustainable access to the resource."

Ends

For further information:

Marcia Dunnett
..stor, Furniture Association of New Zealand

The Furniture Association lobbied the National government in August 1997 and later the Labour Party in May 1999, both times arguing Timberlands' case when decisions were pending.

an information-gathering trip to the West Coast.

'Timberlands and the continued harvesting of timber from the West Coast is a controversial matter, with varying claims being made from all angles,' he wrote. 'I am writing to offer you the opportunity to be part of a visit to the West Coast to see the forests first hand; to smell the bush and hear the birds.... Having enjoyed the visit, you will be better informed.' He explained that they would travel by helicopter, visiting Okarito in South Westland and beech forests in the north. But there was

---

MEMORANDUM

TO: Labour Caucus

FROM:

DATE: 26 May 1999

SUBJECT: Forestry Visit

Timberlands and the continued harvesting of timber from the West Coast is a controversial matter, with varying claims being made from all angles. In my experience, comments are often made with no actual experience or first hand knowledge.

I am writing to offer you the opportunity to be part of a visit to the West Coast to see the forests first hand; to smell the bush and hear the birds. The trip will be for one day and travel will be by helicopter so you can see the rimu forests in South Westland around Okarito and the beech forests in the north.

An independent forestry consultant will provide commentary. An expert in forests, Ian James lives in Okarito and is a consultant for the Department of Conservation.

Believe me, an aerial trip across Westland will be a memorable visit. The strip of land to the west of the Southern Alps is beautiful and from the air you will get an appreciation that is just not possible from the road.

Having enjoyed the visit, you will be better informed.

Can you please register interest by contacting Karen in my office on x9927 or by email.

Travel details will be arranged to find a best fit.

Labour
New Zealand 2000

Labour MPs were invited to investigate the logging issue but no mention was made that Timberlands had sought and arranged the visit as an opportunity to lobby the MPs.

no mention of who would be paying for the helicopter, no mention of Timberlands and no mention that the itinerary would be the standard company PR tour.

'An independent forestry consultant will provide the commentary,' he wrote.'An expert in forests, Ian James lives in Okarito and is a consultant for the Department of Conservation.'[31] Ian James may have done work for the Department of Conservation, but his main job, of course, was developing and overseeing Timberlands' logging plans for Okarito and the beech forests. He had also for several years been the main person used by Timberlands to host a stream of journalists and politicians on its PR tours of the Coast. His *Green Monitor* writings had defended the logging plans he had developed. He was a forestry consultant, and an expert on forests, but he could not have been less independent. The MP was being used by Timberlands to get his colleagues down to the West Coast where they could be given the company's PR presentation.

Meanwhile on the West Coast the radio ads and sponsored items continued day after day, such as this one in May on Radio Scenicland:

> *Send a little note to Helen Clark, care of freepost Parliament Buildings, and let them know about what your thoughts are on the severe danger of not being able to sustainably manage our own forests. And Timberlands have helped so many people through sport and it would be nice to turn around and help them, wouldn't it? Every sporting club that has had sponsorship, at least, should be putting pen to paper. Helen Clark – and Jim Anderton for that matter – freepost, Parliament Buildings in Wellington. Do it today, it's so easy.*[32]

A desperate edge was creeping into the communications as Timberlands used all the tools and mobilised all the allies possible. Not everything was going its way. In July 1999 the National government introduced to Parliament changes to the Forests Act which, among other things, lifted the ban that prohibited Timberlands from exporting beech woodchips. Timberlands knew that talk of wood chips was not good for public relations. Hilliard told reporters that 'Timberlands is not involved and will not be involved in indigenous wood chipping.'[33] Barry Nicolle said that the suggestion that Timberlands would use the legislation to export chips was 'absolute rubbish'.[34] Guy Salmon, of the renamed Ecologic Foundation, said he thought Timberlands beech chipping was 'extraordinarily unlikely'.[35] But the minister responsible for Timberlands, SOE Minister Tony Ryall, clearly unaware of their denials, issued a press release explaining that the legislation would 'help improve the economic viability of the... sustainable beech production that supports growth, investment and jobs on the Coast'.[36] Timberlands had long denied any interest in chipping beech timber, but there was clear evidence that this was not true.[37]

Two months earlier, in May 1999, the main native timber sawmill, and the principal employer of native timber workers on the West Coast, Westco Lagan, had accidentally cut the ground from under the Timberlands and CAN campaign. After news that planning controls under the Buller District Plan might end most of Timberlands' rimu supply at the end of 1999, managing director Grant Carruthers had been relaxed and said that their Ruatapu mill 'was in a position to cope'. 'You have to adjust to any situation you are faced with,' he said. 'We are designed to cut wood. It doesn't matter what species it is. So long as pine is available we will cut it.'[38]

Less than two years earlier Carruthers had written to the National government expressing 'grave concern' at the possibility of the Buller rimu supply ending. 'Our company could founder,' he had written, because only with access to native timber were they 'able to maintain a viable economic operation'.[39] Native timber milling was undoubtedly a very lucrative business that Westco Lagan preferred not to lose but, when faced with the likely inevitability of losing the rimu supplies, the company got on with adapting. So much for the 'death knell' for the region Barry Nicolle had spoken of at the Greymouth public meeting. The gap between Timberlands and West Coast priorities was widening.

The chapter should finish with a good word for CAN members, whom it would be wrong to dismiss as company stooges. Although the organisation was a creation of Timberlands' PR campaign, the vigour of its campaigning eventually attracted a range of people who had no personal or commercial links to Timberlands and were motivated by genuine concerns about their communities. Like other West Coasters, they had seen unemployment rise and government services cut in their towns during the free-market years. None of this could reasonably be blamed on environmentalists,[40] but the idea of a group devoted to sticking up for the West Coast and encouraging local development was very attractive. CAN members believed Timberlands' arguments and bought into its fight. Those aware of the quiet support Timberlands was giving to CAN were presumably just grateful for the help. It was, after all, the kind of com-

CHAPTER 11

SINGING FROM ONE SONG-SHEET

Hilliard: We don't lobby Parliament, that's full stop, that's what it is. We do not lobby.
Interviewer: Has Shandwick ever approached ministers on your behalf?
Hilliard: It depends on what 'approach' means. If it's to lobby, the answer is no. If it's to pass information, the answer is yes.
Interviewer: What about to gather information?
Hilliard: Not to my memory has it occurred the other way.
Interviewer: So you don't gather information from ministers? Or ministerial staff?
Hilliard: No. They send us information. But the contact's very arm's-length. They don't interfere in what we do and we don't try to influence what they are doing. Except if we are asked. Which is very seldom.

Dave Hilliard, 1999[1]

Who can be relied upon to act in a neutral manner and uphold the public interest in the midst of a political struggle like this? Traditionally, an important part of the answer to this question is public servants, that great pool of people who, once removed from party politics, are tasked with maintaining the public infrastructure of the nation. Public servants look after everything from passports to prisons, from Treaty of Waitangi negotiations to education policy.

They also administer indigenous forestry policy and serve as advisers in the offices of ministers whom Timberlands wanted to influence. Shandwick knew that the most influential allies for lobbying ministers can be their own staff and departmental advisers. These people became the target of Timberlands' most direct lobbying efforts.

The Public Service Code of Conduct requires public servants to act neutrally and impartially 'in a manner which will bear the closest public scrutiny'. Political neutrality is emphasised in the code 'in order to maintain... public confidence in the impartiality of the advice given, and actions taken, by public servants'.[2] Ministers, assisted by their personal staff, are also expected to act, in many of their duties, as servants of the public, albeit elected, maintaining and overseeing good processes of government. Timberlands' campaign activities invited ministers, their staff and public servants to compromise their official roles.

The documents Timberlands has made available to the government or public do not mention embarking on major lobbying campaigns but the secret PR papers are quite explicit about this being a priority activity. Government ministers, Opposition parties and all their advisers became key targets in the company campaign.

Timberlands' 1994 PR strategy devoted a section to 'parliamentary lobbying'. High on Timberlands' action list was the need to 'establish reliable contact with Parliament to maintain current information as to environmental lobbying of Parliament'. Having friends and allies in the Beehive was vital. Timberlands also decided that it would be most effective for its lobbying efforts to 'develop a tiered approach to focus most information on most influential members'. Most lobbying effort was to go into those MPs who could potentially cause the company problems: 'Provide information to MPs, scaling up effort for MPs whose opposition is likely to be most damaging, and those whose support is likely to be most influential.'[3]

Timberlands and Shandwick staff concentrated much of their lobbying effort on building up personal links with public servants in key roles or close to key ministers. They devoted resources to winning public servants' sympathy for the company's case, including during specially arranged PR tours of the West Coast. They used public servants as sources of political information about individual ministers' views and Cabinet discussions and for arranging lobbying of the ministers, either directly or via allies.

When the West Coast logging issue became publicly controversial in early 1997, the government set up a small, informal group of ministers to discuss how to resolve the issue. This group met secretly from March 1997 for two years before reaching decisions in December 1998. It was made up of the Prime Minister, the Ministers of State Owned Enterprises, Forestry, Environment and Conservation and, at times, the Treasurer. The secrecy of the process, designed to exclude the public and even other ministers from decision-making until this group had agreed on a plan, was initially not at all to Timberlands' liking.

The State Owned Enterprises Act gives state companies a good deal of the autonomy of private companies, which is why the Timberlands managers could get away with spending large sums of public money on their PR activities. But, as an independent company, Timberlands did not have formal access to government decision-making, just as the 'shareholding ministers' overseeing it were not supposed to interfere in the day-to-day running of the company. Timberlands was frustrated by the secret ministerial process because at first it made it difficult for it to find out what was happening. The company wanted political intelligence to use in planning its campaign. It wanted the benefits of being a state-owned enterprise without its limitations.

Shandwick was given the job of approaching public servants in key positions to collect what the internal papers refer to as 'political intelligence'. This work had been anticipated in earlier PR strategy plans – 'Beehive Contact: Establish a Wellington based contact who can reliably up-date Timberlands when environmental lobbying of Parliament occurs. Resources and Costs: Wellington based, to be identified; $2,500 retainer'[4] – and now Shandwick took on the role. There are dozens of examples in the Timberlands Papers of Shandwick staff reporting on meetings they had held with public servants and even ministers on Timberlands' behalf.

When the group of ministers had been meeting for some months, Timberlands got its first detailed report of what was going on from SOE Minister Jenny Shipley's private secretary, Cath Ingram. Rob McGregor of Shandwick described her as his 'key informant' in the following message to Timberlands in Greymouth: 'I have taken some soundings about the progress of the Officials report, the Ministers have a draft copy but my key informant has not yet had an opportunity to read it. I'll report further when I know what is happening.'[5]

Three days later Ingram provided him with a full briefing. She gave details of a secret meeting that Timberlands was, officially, not entitled to know about, and commented on another minister, Nick Smith, who was said to be unsupportive of some native forest logging. Ingram also offered McGregor advice about where Timberlands should 'focus attention'.

Shandwick's Rob McGregor wrote a 'File Note' for their client, Timberlands, recording the main points from the discussion. Entitled 'Conversation with Cath Ingram, SOE Secretary, Minister of SOE's Office, 9.30am, Thursday, 19 June 1997', the notes were full of helpful intelligence on the 'Cabinet Sub Committee to review Accord Appeal and Buller forestry policy'.

Cath Ingram had been generously forthcoming for the Shandwick PR man. 'Cath says there is not an official Cabinet sub-committee. There are however a group of Ministers who have an interest in the issue and who have responsibility for political management of the issue. This group was formed earlier this year when the newer Ministers felt that the issue was not going to go away and they needed to take control of the issue,' McGregor wrote.

Ingram had asked McGregor to reassure Timberlands. According to McGregor's file note, 'Cath has seen all the minutes and reassures us that Timberlands have no need for concern – tell them to relax'. Ingram was able to inform McGregor who exactly was involved in the decision-making: 'The group consists of the Ministers of: SOEs; Forestry; Environment, and his associate Minister (New Zealand First's Deborah Morris); Conservation; and the Prime Minister'. Further, McGregor reported that

Shandwick

2 Woodward Street
PO Box 3095
Wellington 6015
New Zealand
Fax: 64-4-471 2278
Telephone: 64-4-472 4190
E-Mail: 100254.2140@compuserve.com

File Note: (Timberlands West Coast)

Subject: **Cabinet Sub Committee to review Accord Appeal and Buller forestry policy.**

Conversation with Cath Ingram, SOE Secretary, Minister of SOEs Office, 9.30 am, Thursday, 19 June, 1997.

1. Cath says there is not an official Cabinet sub-committee. There are however a group of Ministers who have an interest in the issue and who have responsibility for the political management of the issue. This group was formed earlier in the year when the newer Ministers felt that the issue was not going to go away and they needed to take control of the issue.

2. Cath has seen all the minutes and reassures us that TWC have no need for concern, tell them to relax.

3. The group consists of the Ministers of: SOE; Minister (New Zealand First's

6. The Ministers will talk to TWC once they have the report.

7. The protest movement put the issue onto the agenda but the Minister of SOEs has been following it closely and is "in control".

8. Nick Smith is the worry. He isn't keen on non-sustainable/over-cutting.

9. We were told that the Ministers would not countenance over-turning the current contract. Those contracts expiring after 31/12/1999 could pose a problem. This is where Shipley, CCMAU and TWC need to focus attention.

Jenny Shipley's secretary, Cath Ingram, briefed Shandwick on secret ministerial meetings. 'Cath has seen all the minutes.... the Minister of SOEs [Jenny Shipley] has been following it closely and is "in control".'

Ingram told him that 'The group decided to do nothing until after the Appeal Court decision [which ruled on the government's remaining obligations under the West Coast Accord]. Once announced, they have called for a report from officials on the options...' and that 'The Ministers will talk to Timberlands once they have a report'.

McGregor and Timberlands were wondering what impact the campaign by environment groups was having. Ingram told him that 'The protest movement put the issue on the agenda but the Minister of SOEs has been following it closely and is "in control"'. She told McGregor that 'Nick Smith is a worry. He isn't keen on non-sustainable/over-cutting.'

Ingram was, however, able to give some relief to Timberlands' concerns. She reassured him that 'the Ministers would not countenance overturning the current contract. Those contracts expiring after 31/12/1999 could pose a problem. This is where Shipley, CCMAU and Timberlands need to focus attention.' (CCMAU, the Crown Company Monitoring and Advisory Unit, is the agency that assists the Minister of SOEs overseeing government-owned companies.)

Ingram advised Shandwick on the best PR strategy. 'Timberlands can best help at this point by keeping a low profile and keeping in close touch with Angus Napier (ex WWF for Nature) at CCMAU,' McGregor recorded in his file note. Keeping the issue out of the news would help their cause. McGregor recorded the meeting as finishing on an up note. 'Timberlands should take heart from the fact that no one has spoken out on the issue. They have been told to breathe through their noses and leave it to Jen and Lockwood,' Ingram had told him.[6]

The ministers had agreed that these meetings would be completely secret, but Jenny Shipley's staff were breaking this agreement in order to advise Timberlands' PR firm. Throughout the native forest controversy, Shipley had refused to meet environment groups and had even refused to allow her private secretary, Cath Ingram, to meet these groups and hear their views.[7] Ingram was, however, prepared to describe confidential meetings to a private PR consultant. It is not known whether Shipley approved this contact.

This was just the beginning. The relationship between Shandwick and Jenny Shipley's office grew rapidly and soon there was regular contact. The Timberlands Papers record numerous conversations and meetings between Rob McGregor of Shandwick and Cath Ingram. These contacts cannot be explained away as formal SOE business, because after Shipley became Prime Minister and ceased being Minister of SOEs, the contacts continued.[8]

The purpose was lobbying and day-to-day co-operation in political campaigning between state company and minister, much of it at the
petty level of trying to counter individual acts by environmental groups.
One internal Timberlands document, for instance, recorded that 'Cath
Ingram just called. NFA has just released a new run of posters and pamphlets which have been sent to all politicians – she asks you to ring her
if you haven't got copies'.[9] The Minister of State Owned Enterprises has
a formal role set out in the legislation for the overseeing of government
companies, yet in practice she spent part of her time condoning and
co-operating in Timberlands' political campaigning.

Environment minister Simon Upton also declined to meet with
NFA, but was prepared to give inside information on the secret ministerial meetings to Shandwick's Rob McGregor. In a file note to Dave Hilliard,
McGregor wrote that he had 'had a lengthy discussion with Hon. Simon
Upton' that morning. Upton had told McGregor which ministers were
most important to Timberlands' interests. 'Lockwood Smith, as Minister
of Forestry, and Jenny Shipley, as SOEs, are the two main drivers regarding Timberlands,' McGregor recorded. Although the post-election coalition agreement between National and New Zealand First had included
a commitment to review Timberlands' management of West Coast beech
forests, Upton explained that this was not the reason for the government meetings. McGregor recorded Upton as saying that 'The interest
in Timberlands is motivated not so much by the Coalition Agreement
undertaking but by the actions of NFA....'.

NFA had succeeded in putting the issue on the agenda, but Upton
told McGregor that 'The government will not want to be seen to capitulate to NFA'. NFA's campaign would have a hard time influencing Upton.
McGregor recorded in his note of the meeting that 'Guy Salmon is very
influential as far as he's concerned and Guy endorses what Timberlands
are doing'. Upton was keen to reassure McGregor that 'as he read the
situation, the company had no need for concern as far as NFA was concerned...'. For McGregor it was reassuring: 'The good thing about this
information from Simon is that it is consistent with the messages we
are getting from Cath Ingram in Jenny's office'.[10]

Shandwick staff were busy lobbying and seeking information from other
officials too. One of them was the public servant Dr Mary-Ann Thompson,
who was on posting from the Treasury to the office of Treasurer Winston
Peters. Peters was one of the ministers supportive of ending native forest logging, but the Shandwick record of discussions with Thompson

Shandwick

2 Woodward Street
PO Box 3095
Wellington 6015
New Zealand

CONFIDENTIAL

Fax: 64-4-471 2278
Telephone: 64-4-472 4190
E-Mail: 100254.2140@compuserve.com

FACSIMILE TRANSMISSION

TO: Dave Hilliard **FAX:** Auto Dial
Timberlands West Coast

DATE: October 2, 1997 **FROM:** Rob McGregor

NO. OF PAGES (including this page): One

Dave

This morning I had a lengthy discussion with Hon. Simon Upton. The major points to emerge were:
- Lockwood Smith, as Minister of Forestry, and Jenny Shipley, as SOEs are the two main drivers regarding Timberlands.
- The interest in Timberlands is motivated not so much by the Coalition Agreement undertaking but by the actions of NFA.
- Simon has not been actively involved in the current review, the Ministry for the Environment's interest is not directly related to the review but rather in terms of what goes into District Plans.
- The Government will not want to be seen to capitulate to NFA.
- The Government has a moral obligation to the Accord.
- The Government is not of a mind to break the current contracts.
- Simon does not appear to know about the Beech Management Plans! He said we'd need to talk to Jenny's office about those operational type matters.
- Guy Salmond is very influential as far as he is concerned and that Guy endorses what Timberlands were doing.
- His final comment was that, as he read the situation, the company had no need for concern as far as NFA was concerned.

I know that when Simon first took over responsibility for the Environment portfolio he wanted to appoint Guy as his environmental advisor but the PMs office counselled him against this. It sounds very much as if Guy is fulfilling this role anyway and is providing him with contestable advice to counter the Ministry's input.

The good thing about this information from Simon is that it is consistent with the messages we are getting from Cath Ingram in Jenny's office.

Kind regards

Rob McGregor
Shandwick New Zealand Ltd

Minister for the Environment, Simon Upton, who refused to meet NFA, was prepared to brief Shandwick privately on the government's secret plans.

shows her co-operating with the pro-logging campaign. Ironically, the discussions included her being strongly critical of Forest and Bird lobbying in Parliament at the same time as she was talking to and giving advice to a paid PR company lobbyist.

At the time of the contact, Timberlands was concerned about a policy paper being prepared by an inter-departmental officials group for the ministers on options for resolving the West Coast logging controversy. According to McGregor's file note on a conversation with Thompson, he began by explaining Timberlands' concern 'that the drafting of the policy paper was being carried out by people with various green allegiances'. The note records that Thompson replied 'she was interested to hear that, said Forest and Bird were intense lobbyists in parliament and that she would "look out for that" when she received the policy paper'.

Thompson had some words of advice for McGregor as well. According to his file note, 'Her strong advice was that Timberlands should visit the various ministers, especially Mr Peters and Mr Birch, since she felt there was a lack of up to date information on the issues and understanding of them'.

Timberlands knew from past experience that one of its best lobbying opportunities was getting people on tours to the forests. One of its hurdles, however, was getting busy people to make time for the trip. Timberlands was aware that if the suggestion of a tour came from an impartial adviser it would carry more weight. McGregor recorded: 'I sug-

---

Conversation with Dr Mary-Ann Thompson, Senior Policy Advisor, Treasurers Office, 4.45 pm, Monday June 23 1997.

1. Had not had an opportunity to further inquire regarding the policy paper, however was very interested in and expressed concern at, the details of those ministerial officials involved in drafting the policy paper.

2. Would be interested in joining the CCMAU and Treasury officials on a facility visit, however this week and probably next is out for her. Will contact Anne Pearson to discuss an appropriate date, probably late next week or the week after that.

3. Stressed that she felt that Timberlands should be lobbying more strongly among all ministers and parties to put their position and explain the issues of sustainable forestry, "we see the chairmen and CEOs of SOEs all the time".

4. Indicated that she would follow up with other officials including John Wilson of Treasury.

Mary-Ann Thompson, a Treasury official in Treasurer Winston Peters' office, advised Timberlands to lobby all ministers and parties more strongly.

gested to Dr Thompson that it might be better if rather than Timberlands offering facility visits and seeking meetings it would be useful if the Treasurer's office were to request information from Timberlands, and seek a visit (say for Dr Thompson). She said she would talk to Birch's office tomorrow afternoon when she had time.' Thompson repeated her personal views about Forest and Bird. 'She reiterated that Forest and Bird are "always in the Beehive" and that she likened them to the worst of the American lobbyists,' McGregor wrote.

Thompson also passed on political intelligence to McGregor. 'She warned that there appeared to be a mood to offer some form of concession to the greens, which sounds like Buller could be the victim. I stressed Timberlands' concern that any concession could, if they weren't careful, also endanger the long term and sustainably managed forestry on the West Coast and this was undoubtedly Forest and Bird's ultimate ambition. She said she would take this on board.' Thompson sought to reassure McGregor that 'She is no stranger to these matters having been the principal government negotiator on the Ngai Tahu [South Island Maori tribe's] claims'.[11]

Once contact was established with Thompson, Shandwick kept in touch. A week later it made a file note of a follow-up conversation. According to McGregor, Thompson 'Stressed that she felt that Timberlands should be lobbying more strongly among all ministers and parties to put their position and explain the issues of sustainable forestry."We see the chairmen and CEOs of SOEs all the time".' Thompson volunteered to help: 'She indicated she would follow up with other officials including John Wilson of Treasury'.[12]

Thompson, a public servant, saw it as her role to advise the PR consultant that his client should be lobbying ministers more strongly, and recommended that special lobbying attention be given to her own minister and Bill Birch.[13]

Internal Timberlands papers explained the value of building a personal relationship with important lobbying targets. 'Use personal contact to establish a sense of familiarity and recognition between Timberlands and key politicians,' a PR strategy paper urged. This, it explained, might make key decision-makers more 'objective' towards an opposition campaign.[14]

The Timberlands-Shandwick telephone conference minutes show that the political intelligence being gathered by Shandwick from public servants was often about their own and other ministers. After Tony Ryall replaced Jenny Shipley as SOE minister, Shandwick went into overdrive to establish good contacts with the new minister's staff. 'Rob McGregor will introduce himself to new Minister's staff when appointed,' one set of minutes noted.[15] A few weeks later the minutes said, 'Beech Launch Strategy: Shandwicks are waiting until 26 January when Ryall's communications advisor commences'.[16] Soon afterwards, Shandwick managed to get a meeting with Ryall's staff to discuss the beech launch strategy. Internal Timberlands minutes note 'Rob McGregor has briefed Alec McLean [Tony Ryall's private secretary].'There was worrying news:'Tony Ryall and Nick Smith are good friends'.The friendship between the Minister for Conservation and the Minister for State Owned Enterprises could cause problems with public statements affecting forests policy. Smith was considered by Timberlands to be hostile to its interests.

Shandwick sought to make sure that all public statements came from the SOE minister's office. The lobbying bore fruit. 'Alec will do his best to ensure announcements come from the SOE office,' the Timberlands minutes noted. Leaving nothing to chance, Shandwick 'also met with Communications Adviser, Evan Boyce in the Prime Minister's Office'.[17]

Soon Shandwick was getting a regular flow of political intelligence from its variety of sources.Timberlands' PR teleconference minutes noted 'Political: Been some meetings between Smith, Smith and Ryall. Could be some concern. Birch does not appear to be as supportive of Timberlands as previously believed.'[18] With the political controversy over Timberlands' activities heating up, Shandwick was kept busy. 'Political: Klaus Sorensen and Rob McGregor met with Minister's staff... Shandwick to contact C Ingram [i.e. Mrs Shipley's office],' another set of internal minutes noted.[19] Soon the new minister was backing Timberlands against another minister. 'Political – Rob McGregor has been in contact with the Minister's office. Lockwood Smith is not getting his own way as T Ryall is being firm on issues. Suggested that T Ryall visit Timberlands'.[20] Lockwood Smith had been proposing a compromise that would cut off some Timberlands rimu logging.

The public servants appeared to be unaware that they were themselves part of Timberlands' PR strategies.The company had decided that initial meetings would be used to build up personal links between the officials and those involved in Timberlands' campaign. The minutes of one Timberlands phone conference candidly recorded the purpose of these meetings. 'Series of meetings set up between Paula de Roeper / Rob McGregor and ministerial staff on 17 July 1998. A rapport building exercise.'[21] Key public servant allies were offered trips to the West Coast for Timberlands' PR tours. In the view of Shandwick, these were a 'key strategy element'.To build better working relationships Shandwick suggested Timberlands 'host several facility visits and briefings for key ministerial advisers'.[22]

Shandwick's Rob McGregor succeeded in getting the Minister of State Owned Enterprises' press secretary, Simon Taylor, to 'broker' a meeting between the Shandwick consultants and Matthew Hooton, press secretary to Minister of Forestry Lockwood Smith – at the time when Smith was backing a compromise solution to the logging controversy that did not suit Timberlands. In a fax to Taylor, McGregor wrote 'Thank you for agreeing to broker the meeting. We intend it to be a get to know one another whereby we can acquaint Matthew with TWC's position, answer any of his questions and encourage contact between the senior management team at Timberlands and himself. We'd obviously like both of you to have the opportunity to visit Timberlands, and the sooner the better.'[23]

Conventional public service protocols required Timberlands staff to communicate to the government through formal channels, via their board of directors to the shareholding SOE and finance ministers, but

---

Matters Arising

Annual Report - to fax down document for further discussion.   KS

RM has made contact with C Ingram.

Political

RM has been in contact with the Minister's Office.

Lockwood-Smith is not getting his own way as T Ryall is being firm on issues. Suggested that T Ryall visit TWC.

WY indicated announcement of future of beech and rimu to be around late March due to overseas travel commitments by Lockwood-Smith. Back in NZ around 10/11 March.

To forward beech release with video to Ministers. Preferable to add our audit report if available.   AP

Media release on beech is to be updated.   WH

HCL to organise a presentation to Forestry Ministers adviser by WH/RM/DH/CR. WH to discuss with DH.   WH

Need to be prepared for possible closure of a local mill.

Reports of 'political intelligence' from Shandwick in Wellington became a regular feature of the weekly PR teleconferences.

Timberlands had decided otherwise. Here Timberlands' PR consultants used the SOE minister's press secretary to 'broker' a meeting with another minister's press secretary in order to lobby him and set up contact between the Timberlands management and the forestry minister's staff.

Private Timberlands papers made no secret of the purpose of the planned meeting. In a fax from Shandwick to Timberlands' PR person, Paula de Roeper, McGregor described his plans for the meeting with Hooton: 'The approach I intend to take, and which I have discussed with Simon Taylor from the [SOE] Minister's office, is to organise a meeting with Hooton with Taylor and I. We would discuss the Government's planned communications with Hooton in an attempt to ensure a greater degree of co-ordination in the future. Our objective is to get all parties singing from the one song-sheet. Simon thinks there is considerable merit in this approach.'[24] The intended song-sheet, of course, was Timberlands'.

Each contact with the public servants was carefully planned to assist Timberlands' PR objectives. The Timberlands Papers show some of the efforts that went into cultivating a useful relationship with Matthew Hooton. Timberlands' internal notes record the first move as being an 'Informal approach to be made to M Hooton'.[25] Two weeks later, 'Warren Head [Head Consultants] to meet M Hooton on 3 July 1998. Possible Hooton visit to Timberlands to be discussed then.'[26] Next a Shandwick meeting was arranged, and Timberlands and Shandwick planned their strategy. 'Simon Taylor/Hooton meeting with Shandwick scheduled for 19 June. Aim: to ask open-ended questions; what is going on. Warren Head to reinforce messages of this meeting when he meets Hooton. Simon Taylor/Hooton to be encouraged to visit Timberlands.' They noted that background information on beech was 'to be used as appropriate during lobbying'. [27]

The actual meeting with the two key Beehive press secretaries, Simon Taylor and Matthew Hooton, went well. Shandwick reported on it in a telephone conference with Timberlands later that month. 'Simon Taylor/Hooton meeting with Shandwick went very well.... Nick Smith says indigenous forest logging should stop. As compromise, Lockwood leans towards cessation of overcut in December 2000. Hooton's interpretation of this is that beech should start asap. Govt will decide. Lockwood concerned that activists should not get credibility. Timberlands to develop support via ongoing and active communications programme. Hooton will work with us (support). Middle NZ must not be captured by environmentalists – Klaus Sorensen/Rob McGregor.'[28]

Once again, public servants were busy passing on political intelligence about ministers to assist the Timberlands campaign. The Shandwick consultants were pleased with themselves, reporting that the primary goal of the meetings had been achieved: Hooton was on side. 'Hooton will work with us (support),' they noted. A shared political prejudice was agreed: 'Middle NZ must not be captured by environmentalists'. The Timberlands Papers contain many other references to Timberlands' lobbyists co-operating closely with these ministerial staff.[29]

The actions of Shandwick and other PR organisations not only compromise individual public servants who get drawn into their plans, but also do more fundamental damage to the functioning of democratic government. It would be possible to think that these contacts are not too bad; after all, surely government functions by lots of people talking to each other. The trouble is that too much official business can become informal: the contacts can occur without official records being kept, ministers do not need to know, information can be given out selectively by public servants and so on. Often nothing goes on the file and so none of it can be accessed under the Official Information Act, or

---

Dear Paula

Briefing the Minister of Forestry's Office

As discussed earlier today, a copy of the background briefing notes for the meeting with Matthew Hooton follow.

The approach I had intended to take, and which I have discussed with Simon Taylor from the Minister's office, is to organise a meeting with Hooton with Taylor and I. We would discuss the Government's planned communications with Hooton in an attempt to ensure a greater degree of co-ordination in the future.

Our objective will be to get all parties singing from the one song-sheet. Simon thinks there is considerable merit in this approach. We will also be encouraging both Simon and Matthew to make an early visit to Timberlands.

Could you please check that everyone is comfortable with what I propose before I take this any further. I would also like the fact sheets reviewing once again, particularly the two-page background for the Minister of Forestry's office.

Thank you and kind regards

Rob McGregor
Shandwick New Zealand Ltd

'Our objective,' Shandwick wrote, 'is to get all parties singing from the one song-sheet.'

by parliamentary select committees or in other review processes.

Secretive, informal government is naturally prone to unethical and undemocratic behaviour. That is why public service bureaucracies have evolved strict procedures for keeping records of meetings, correspondence and systems of accountability. When public servants operate in an informal environment, where their actions cannot be reviewed, it is much harder to resist pressures from ministers or outside influences like Timberlands to act in a partisan way. Eventually, like some of the public

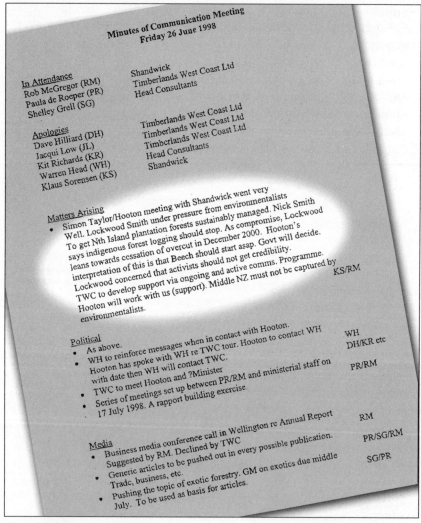

Minutes of Communication Meeting
Friday 26 June 1998

In Attendance
Rob McGregor (RM) Shandwick
Paula de Roeper (PR) Timberlands West Coast Ltd
Shelley Grell (SG) Head Consultants

Apologies
Dave Hilliard (DH) Timberlands West Coast Ltd
Jacqui Low (JL) Timberlands West Coast Ltd
Kit Richards (KR) Timberlands West Coast Ltd
Warren Head (WH) Head Consultants
Klaus Sorensen (KS) Shandwick

Matters Arising
- Simon Taylor/Hooton meeting with Shandwick went very Well. Lockwood Smith under pressure from environmentalists To get Nth Island plantation forests sustainably managed. Nick Smith says indigenous forest logging should stop. As compromise, Lockwood leans towards cessation of overcut in December 2000. Hooton's interpretation of this is that Beech should start asap. Govt will decide. Lockwood concerned that activists should not get credibility. TWC to develop support via ongoing and active comms. Programme. Hooton will work with us (support). Middle NZ must not be captured by environmentalists. KS/RM

Political
- As above. WH
- WH to reinforce messages when in contact with Hooton. DH/KR etc
- Hooton has spoke with WH re TWC tour. Hooton to contact WH with date then WH will contact TWC.
- TWC to meet Hooton and ?Minister PR/RM
- Series of meetings set up between PR/RM and ministerial staff on 17 July 1998. A rapport building exercise.

Media
- Business media conference call in Wellington re Annual Report RM Suggested by RM. Declined by TWC.
- Generic articles to be pushed out in every possible publication. PR/SG/RM Trade, business, etc.
- Pushing the topic of exotic forestry. GM on exotics due middle SG/PR July. To be used as basis for articles.

Shandwick reports on the success of its lobbying of government advisers: 'Hooton will work with us (support)'.

servants quoted in this chapter, they can lose sight of the fact that the public pays them to be neutral and impartial. Public relations strategies work best when democratic institutions are weakest.

The same thing happens if, as Shandwick wrote, someone like Guy Salmon can serve informally as adviser to environment minister Simon Upton, 'providing him with contestable advice to counter the Ministry's input'. No minutes of meetings, no due process, no access to documents under Official Information Act, no possibility of review, no accountability; open and democratic government is the loser.

Rob McGregor, as Shandwick's director of government and corporate relations, regularly guided Timberlands' PR manager, Paula de Roeper, around the halls of power (most recently on 18 June 1999). Some of the key public servants targeted by Timberlands are evident from the itinerary for a lobbying trip to Wellington arranged for de Roeper by Shandwick:

> *Wellington Visit, Paula de Roeper, Friday 11 December 1998. 8.45am Coffee at Shandwick. 9.00am Simon Taylor and Tricia Husband, Minister of SOE Office. 10.00am Bryan Smith and Janine Holland, Forestry Advisor and Press Secretary, Assoc Minister Food, Fibre, Biosecurity and Border Control. 11.00am Peter Wood and Cath Ingram, Prime Minister's Office. 12.00 noon Lunch Angus Napier, CCMAU. 2.00pm Review work in Progress and Issues Arising: Native Forest Action/News Media; Market Research; Education Resource; Profile Document; Business Front; Community Front/Sponsorship; Environmental Front; Political Front; Industry Front; Beech Marketing strategy. 5.00pm Debrief and Next Steps.[30]*

CCMAU, the Crown Company Monitoring and Advisory Unit, does not come out of the Timberlands Papers looking good. This agency, which is based in the Treasury Building in Wellington, is supposed to monitor the financial performance of the state-owned companies and provide policy advice for the SOE minister on the 'ownership objectives and targets for SOEs'. In the case of Timberlands it appeared to be uncritical in its scrutiny of the company's dubious finances and instead had been enlisted as part of a lobbying campaign for the company. In inter-departmental meetings CCMAU staff lobbied vigorously in defence of continued native logging, with meetings degenerating into angry argument on some occasions. The strength of CCMAU staff feeling is seen in the following report by Rob McGregor of Shandwick: 'Warren Young [Timberlands board chair] met with Minister March 12. CCMAU "spat the dummy" and were asked to leave meeting. Meeting went well. Nick Smith still causing trouble. He's out of control. People are distancing themselves from him. Public consultation problem still brewing.'[31]

The whole point of a 'monitoring and advisory' unit would be to give the ministers an independent source of advice. CCMAU often served as little more than a channel through which Timberlands' perspective could be presented to ministers as fact. The Timberlands Papers show how in 1997, when members of the public wrote letters to Jenny Shipley as Minister of State Owned Enterprises complaining about Timberlands, CCMAU (which was tasked with drafting ministerial replies) prepared her replies with help from Timberlands.

A letter from Timberlands to CCMAU provided 'points of reply' the unit had requested on various subjects from the company 'by way of response to a series of letters to the minister from various F&B branches and members'. An example of the 'points of reply' concerned the 1997 episode where Timberlands' logging helicopter tried to smash the treesitters' platform (which the Civil Aviation investigation confirmed occurred). Timberlands wrote: 'All the persons [present] have sworn that no such incident occurred and that at no time was any individual in danger'.[32] Timberlands was helping to write Shipley's replies on controversial subjects such as this.

Some staff in the Ministry of Agriculture and Forestry (MAF) have also played a partisan role, notably in their design of a public consultation process on the Timberlands beech scheme plans. There are well-developed guidelines within government on what it takes to conduct genuine public consultation; MAF broke almost all of them.

Ever since the threat of a beech scheme had emerged over a decade earlier, successive governments had promised a full public consultation process on what would be the single biggest native forest logging scheme in the country. In co-operation with Timberlands, MAF kept everything about the scheme secret until the day submissions were invited in October 1998. After years of highly secretive preparation of the logging plans, MAF gave the public and environment groups just four weeks, later extended to six weeks after public complaints, to try to analyse the many hundreds of pages of management plans and write submissions.

The process was stacked in favour of the logging. The management plans and a summary of them prepared by MAF for the public were entirely one-sided, containing not a single argument or piece of evidence in favour of preserving the forests. No government resources were used to present information supporting the conservation case. In the past, other conservation-focused government departments played this role. Instead all the public got was hundreds of pages of justification for logging. On top of this lack of balance, the ministry announced that public submissions should not comment on whether there should be logging, but merely on 'the way in which Timberlands proposes to manage the West Coast beech forests'.[33] The option of and issues surrounding preserving some or all of these nationally significant forests was not to be part of the public consultation process.

To the dismay of pro-Timberlands officials, and despite the obstacles, public submissions poured in opposing the whole idea of allowing the beech forests to be used for a logging scheme. The level of interest was almost unprecedented, with over 12,000 submissions arriving during the six-week period. MAF staff, however, set about trying to play down the level of public concern.

Rather than simply reporting to the government on the submissions that had arrived, which were overwhelmingly opposed to the beech scheme, MAF hired a private consultant to analyse and summarise the submissions. The analysis found that 10,298 submissions opposed the scheme and 2038 supported it. But the independent consultant was asked to make a subjective judgement about which of the submissions were 'substantive', defined those that contained 'well-informed' comment and were 'typically at least 10 pages long'. His analysis managed to come up with only 36 'substantive' submissions out of the 12,354 received, which he declared to be evenly divided between support for and opposition to the plans.

Having failed to discourage public input to the process, the public servants emphasised the 'well-informed' submissions, declaring in the introduction to the analysis of submissions that 'The submission process was clearly <u>not</u> intended as a referendum on the future of the beech forests. In seeking comments on the Plans, the government considers that reasoned comment should carry more weight than numbers in support or opposition.'[34]

The analysis of submissions was remarkably shoddy. Leaving aside the many good submissions that would not have made it into the 'substantives', we found that many of the so-called substantive submissions in favour of the beech scheme did not even comment on the detail of the management plans. Timberlands' allies Henrik Moller, John Craig and David Norton were among the substantives, but only Moller's discussed the plans. Craig's one-page submission and appendices (one of which was an e-mail he had sent out urging the recipients to write submissions supporting the plans) included no discussion of the management plans and instead centred on attacking the views of environmental groups.

Norton had not even written a submission, but MAF staff had included a two-and-a-half-page lobbying letter he had written to Bill Birch as a submission and then declared it to be substantive. Norton's letter, again an attack on the environmental groups' approach to conservation, was written before Timberlands' management plans were released and made no mention of them.[35] When NFA asked to be able to look through the public submissions and review MAF's analysis, the officials refused, saying that they did not want to give NFA 'ammunition' to claim their analysis was 'shonky'.[36]

MAF's actions on the closing day for submissions summed up the staff's attitude to the public. NFA had contacted the head of MAF's Sustainable Resource Use policy group, Mike Jebson, and explained that the group, accompanied by some members of Parliament, would be delivering a bundle of submissions to their main entrance on that day. When the small group arrived with the MPs and submissions, they noticed various large security guards near the doors and asked them what was going on. Jebson had hired six Armourguard staff for the day, plus a senior Armourguard manager to oversee operations, to protect the ministry from the environmentalists.

As with the ministerial staff, it does not matter whether the motive for partisan behaviour by MAF was the public servants' personal prejudices or because ministers expected it of them. They were paid by the public to act professionally and do an impartial job.

In early December 1998, following the shock of so many submissions against its logging plans, but before the MAF analysis was completed, Timberlands sent an internal PR strategy paper to Simon Taylor, the helpful official in SOE Minister Tony Ryall's office with whom Shandwick had been building a relationship. Timberlands' PR person, Paula de Roeper, wrote: 'I have put together the attached PR strategy.... I have sent it to Simon Taylor and Trisha Husband [SOE secretary] for their thoughts and have asked them for their input when we [she and Rob McGregor] meet them.'[37]

De Roeper's strategy paper proposed the following plan for using Taylor's and Husband's minister to counter the influence of the public submissions against the beech logging: 'Setting the record straight –

Beech. Stage 1. Audience: General Public, Politicians. Medium: Media Conference at Beehive [Parliament] (TV, newspapers, radio) with press release. Possible angle: Tony Ryall to indicate that there are only approx. 30 substantive submissions out of 10,000.... The public are not fully informed about sustainable forest management. This is <u>not</u> a numbers game, but must be based on factually correct info and informed opinion – too much is at stake.... Duty of Government to fully inform public on such matters.'[38] De Roeper's suggested strategy had an uncanny similarity to the MAF analysis of submissions above, completed a few weeks later, both with their emphatic 'not'.

Later that month, on 23 December 1998, cynically timed for the Christmas rush to minimise public reaction, a junior minister, David Carter, got the job of announcing what they described as a conditional 'green light' for the beech scheme. Although the scheme still had various hurdles to cross before approval, the main purpose of the announcement appeared to be to make it clear to the public that the huge number of submissions was not going to have any influence on the final decision. This was achieved in Carter's press release by simply ignoring them. The government made no mention at the time, nor has it since, of the public consultation process and the 10,000 submissions it had received, only a month earlier, opposing the scheme.[39]

The Timberlands Papers state the company's lobbying plans plainly. The key targets were '1 Shareholder – Ministries of Finance and SOEs', the company's own ministers and their departments; '2 Advisors and government officials', the influential public servants and ministerial staff targeted by Shandwick; and '3 Caucus leaders / Relevant spokespeople', in particular the key Opposition MPs who might one day be in government. The strategy included maintaining a 'political resource file' with 'up to date details on all Members of Parliament, caucus leaders, etc., their portfolios, interests and influences'. The aim was to 'Identify relative influence among key players, their respective portfolios and viewpoints', 'facilitate easy exchange of information with those concerned' and 'develop personal contacts'.[40]

Shandwick lobbied the Cabinet ministers directly and indirectly. Shandwick's McGregor lobbied environment minister Simon Upton directly, while indirectly Shandwick prepared a letter for the front group Coast Action Network to sign and send to conservation minister Nick Smith over a proposal to commemorate Diana, Princess of Wales, by creating a forest reserve.

> *Hon Dr Nick Smith,*
> *Minister of Conservation*
> *Parliament Buildings*
> *WELLINGTON*
>
> *Dear Sir,*
> *I understand that you recently received a proposal, which*
> *I presume to be inspired by Native Forest Action, to re-*
> *name thousands of hectares of native forest after the late*
> *Diana, Princess of Wales.*
> *It does not escape the attention of those living on*
> *the West Coast that.... this is another attempt by Native*
> *Forest Action to shut down indigenous forestry on the West*
> *Coast....*
> *West Coast communities, unlike our opponents, 'can*
> *see the wood for the trees'. We denounce this proposal and*
> *trust that others will see it as another shallow attack on*
> *our livelihood co-ordinated by outsiders.*

This was a state-owned company's Wellington-based PR consultant posing as concerned West Coaster to lobby a Cabinet minister who disagreed with the company's minister.

When a conservation rally was planned in front of Parliament, Shandwick got the job of sending a letter to all the key ministers the day before, to limit any political impact. Hilliard's letter, drafted by Shandwick, warned ministers that 'As you will be aware, Timberlands West Coast is the target of an ongoing campaign by a small group of extremely dedicated environmental activists. We have found these activists to be persistent, obstructive, time-consuming and, this is perhaps the most worrisome aspect, to have a blatant disregard for the facts and perpetuate misinformation.'

Defending its direct intervention in the public debate, rather than leaving it to its minister, Hilliard wrote: 'This is not a situation we can ignore.... We now believe the company needs to become more pro-active. Accordingly we have prepared the accompanying material for your information and intend to release it to the media to pre-empt the proposed parliamentary Rally tomorrow....'[41] The letter was written by Shandwick and signed on behalf of the Timberlands CEO by Maree Procter, the same Shandwick employee used to write to NFA posing as an interested member of the public seeking information on the group's plans.

In September 1997, Timberlands asked Shandwick to prepare a strategy paper on political party policies. It was 'undertaken to identify which political parties have explicit positions on key issues relevant to the company [Timberlands] and whether these policies are opposed to its business interests'. The paper recommended that Timberlands 'Develop an information strategy to target each political party in turn', noting that 'Bringing the other parties "on-side" as far as possible first would enable an approach to the Alliance to be made from a position of strength'. It also proposed that 'We need to discover where the Alliance acquired the belief that sustainably managed Podocarp Forests are not ecologically viable. Once this has been achieved, a strategy can be developed to counter or disprove this evidence.'[42]

The Timberlands Papers show detailed preparations for meetings with each of the Opposition parties in Parliament, 'scaling up effort for MPs whose opposition is likely to be most damaging, and those whose support is likely to be most influential' as the strategy documents intended. Shandwick had the job of liaising with each party in turn to

---

Objective B: Maintain Effective Relationships with Key Influentials

Audience

1   **Shareholder - Ministries of Finance and SOE's**

2   **Advisors and government officials**

3   **Caucus leaders / Relevant spokespeople**

Strategies

✿   Remain informed of political personnel changes.

✿   Identify relative influence among key players, their respective portfolios viewpoints.

✿   Facilitate easy exchange of information with those concerned.

✿   Develop personal contacts.

Government agencies are not supposed to lobby the government. The PR strategies, however, contained detailed lobbying plans.

propose and arrange briefings. Unlike many PR activities, these contacts could not just be kept secret. The last step in the arrangements was Shandwick legitimising the lobbying by asking the party representatives to seek clearance from the SOE minister's office for the contact with Timberlands executives.

The first the chairman of the Timberlands board of directors knew about the approaches to Opposition parties was after they were arranged. When a Shandwick consultant phoned him to ask if he could be part of the briefings, he replied that it was 'the first he knew about the proposal' and that 'he would have expected to be consulted'. Shandwick's McGregor sent off a quick fax to the Timberlands chief executive: 'Expect to hear from him about this issue'.[43]

By far the most effort went into lobbying the Labour Party, including close contact between Timberlands and the two Labour MPs with least sympathy for the environment, Jim Sutton and Damien O'Connor. The main focus of company PR efforts in the first half of 1999 was the attempt to change the Labour leader's mind on native forest logging. The ACT Party MPs were seen as sympathetic; the company even approached an ACT MP for help in discouraging a Labour MP, Pete Hodgson, from asking probing parliamentary questions about the company's operations.[44]

Briefing of Opposition MPs by a state-owned company might be constitutionally acceptable but, as the strategy papers showed, the intention was lobbying, not just briefing. Timberlands was trying to influence the policies of parties that might one day be part of the government which controlled it. Constitutionally, it was all wrong.

Overall, Timberlands and Shandwick behaved like an aggressive private lobby group – except that it was a state company using public money to pursue the policy preferences of its senior staff. The public servants who supported this lobbying were perfectly entitled to support Timberlands as individuals; but when they did it in work time they compromised their role as professional public servants.

The ultimate responsibility for accepting a state-owned company playing politics in this way remains with the government. The National administration was allowing a PR company to circumvent the official channels through which the company should maintain its relationship with the government. Ministers and their officials were willingly co-operating in keeping the public out of decisions over the fate of the publicly owned native forests.

CHAPTER 12

SECRETS AND LIES

Shandwick New Zealand Ltd... has acted for Timberlands on a completely transparent basis for some years. Our involvement is simple: to assist Timberlands to explain to the public the facts of sustainable forestry in New Zealand against the barrage of misinformation from environmental groups.... Shandwick New Zealand Ltd is a locally operated company that has never sought any advice or input into the work it does for Timberlands from any of its international affiliates....

Now Mr Sage and NFA's conspiracy theories extend to the Coast Action Network (CAN). Let Mr Sage be assured that we have never had any dealings with CAN.... Unlike Mr Sage, we deal only in facts and have advised Timberlands that this is the best tool to use against the environmental misinformation peddled by NFA and its supporters.

Klaus Sorensen, managing director, Shandwick New Zealand,
16 June 1999[1]

We're always accused of being secretive but we never are. Like any other state organisation we're open to the Official Information Act, and all the information that we have is available to the public anyway except for that that is commercially sensitive.

Dave Hilliard, 13 July 1999[2]

Timberlands' public relations campaigning appears cynical, manipulative, unscrupulous and anti-democratic. It is a government-owned company: who should have to take political responsibility for it?

The main person must be Jenny Shipley who, first as Minister of

State Owned Enterprises and then as Prime Minister, was the staunchest supporter in government of Timberlands' rainforest logging. She not only supported the company uncritically in all the secret ministerial meetings held on the issue, but she also was aware of, and in some cases personally involved in, much of the covert political campaign described in this book.

The first meeting on the issue was held in Prime Minister Jim Bolger's ninth-floor office on 1 April 1997, with all the relevant ministers present and a ring of officials around the walls. Bolger began the meeting arguing that Timberlands' native logging should be stopped. He said that National could win public approval for doing this as it had when it stopped logging in the Central North Island's Pureora Forest 20 years earlier. He noted that King Country farmers were annoyed that they needed all sorts of permissions to cut down a few native trees while a state organisation could cut down thousands every year. Even if there were not protesters in the trees, he said, it would still be worth reconsidering the issue 10 years after the West Coast Accord.

Jenny Shipley was the only minister present to argue in favour of the logging. An SOE official who had accompanied her to the meeting put up a series of arguments for why the logging had to continue. But Shipley presented a more ideological case, saying that it would send a bad signal to business if the green movement were seen to be influencing government policy. Sensing that the meeting was not going her way, she eventually went quiet, as officials were instructed to go away and prepare an options paper about how the government could end some or all of the logging. Everyone was instructed to keep the discussions completely secret.

Jenny Shipley – Timberlands' main political supporter throughout the controversy – told Parliament her staff were not involved in any way in relations with Timberlands:

Parliamentary Question for Written Answer Number 005619 to the Prime Minister.[3]

Have the staff in the Prime Minister's office been involved in any way in relations between Timberlands West Coast Ltd and the government; if so, what has been the nature of this involvement?

Rt Hon Jenny Shipley, replied: No.

Jim Bolger made a tactical mistake. He left it to Shipley's staff to write the options paper, since they had most knowledge of Timberlands, which allowed a long process of bureaucratic stalling and obstruction. For the first 10 weeks after the Bolger meeting, Shipley's Crown Company Monitoring and Advisory Unit staff oversaw drafting of the paper for ministers, eventually presenting the ridiculous conclusion that it could cost the government several hundred million dollars to end the rainforest logging.

It was around that time, in June 1997, that Jenny Shipley's secretary Cath Ingram began giving Shandwick staff quiet briefings about the ministerial meetings, allowing Timberlands to know what was happening in the secret meetings. She reassured Shandwick's Rob McGregor that her minister was 'in control' and said to tell Timberlands not to worry. In the following months Jenny Shipley fought Jim Bolger in the ministerial meetings, while Forestry and Treasury officials produced a series of ministerial papers full of advice about the problems and dire consequences of ending the logging. The secrecy served Shipley well, as Bolger could not rally public opinion behind him and there was no opportunity for independent checking of the biased advice coming from officials.

On 1 October, when Bolger's leadership of his party had become shaky, the ministers held a meeting without him present. Without Bolger's knowledge, his options paper was ditched and Shipley took control. She got agreement from the other ministers that Timberlands' beech scheme would be allowed to proceed and instructed the officials to prepare a new Cabinet paper to this effect, with all the forest conservation options removed. Ministers who could see that their political futures relied on her patronage were hardly about to disagree with Shipley over a

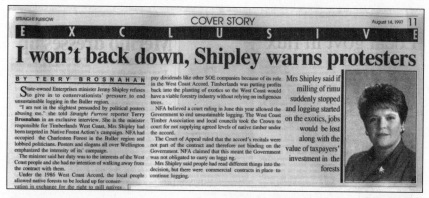

Jenny Shipley argued privately to other ministers that appearing to listen to green groups would send a bad signal to business.

few forests. A month later she deposed Bolger as Prime Minister. His conservation plans had been stalled and blocked for seven months since the first meeting, until he had lost the power to carry them out.

On 12 December, within days of announcing her Cabinet, Shipley made time for another ministerial meeting on Timberlands. Despite all the demands of her new office, she had become personally caught up in Timberlands' fight to the extent that it was a priority to use her new power to thwart the 'greenies'. Her attitude at the meeting, according to the report, was 'very rational'. She insisted that the objective for public native forests should be a 'level playing field', with public forests treated no differently from private forests. She specifically instructed that the opportunity for public input into the beech logging scheme plans be removed from the Cabinet papers,[4] and that no decisions be announced before Christmas (in order, she told the meeting, to 'stop the greenies going up the trees' over summer). She also said she wanted no Cabinet debate on the issue. She said there should be extra meetings in the two weeks before Christmas for the informal group of ministers to finalise a policy so that Cabinet would only need to rubber stamp it. It would be another whole year before Shipley's government announced its backing for Timberlands' beech scheme, but the decision had been made long before.

In normal circumstances, Jenny Shipley would be able to deny that she got so personally caught up in the Timberlands issue; the many months of ministerial wrangling were completely secret from the public. She might also claim that, as Minister of

JENNY SHIPLEY for Prime Minister

and minister responsible for rainforest restructuring

Jenny Shipley, as SOE Minister, is responsible for a state-owned logging company that is doing the worst logging of NZ rainforest in the country today. The company, Timberlands West Coast Ltd, is pushing ahead agressively with the destruction of important kiwi habitat in Charleston Forest, ignoring public opinion and misrepresenting the facts to try to hang on to this lucrative logging. Timberlands is unpopular even on the West Coast for its arrogant dealings with the locals. Why is Mrs Shipley backing it?

The environmentalists quickly realised that their main opponent was the State Owned Enterprises Minister. Although she refused to interfere in 'state-owned enterprise' business for conservation purposes, she took an enthusiastic interest in the company's anti-conservation campaign.

State Owned Enterprises, she was legally restrained from getting involved in the detail of Timberlands' operations, including its PR operations. Certainly she and her successor as SOE minister used this excuse repeatedly to decline to answer parliamentary questions about Timberlands' activities. But the Timberlands Papers leave no doubt that she was the main politician backing Timberlands at a political level and was also well aware of and assisting the state-owned company's PR campaign.

Throughout the Timberlands Papers there are examples of Jenny Shipley's staff helping Timberlands in the day-to-day execution of its PR strategies. They would obtain copies of NFA's latest posters or publications and send them straight to Shandwick to pass on to Timberlands.[5] They got Timberlands to draft ministerial answers to letters from the public on the logging issue[6] and acted as a conduit through which pro-Timberlands materials were circulated to other MPs. Shipley chimed in regularly to support Timberlands when it was in the news. As the company was systematically attacking each supporter and action of the environment groups, Shandwick or Timberlands would often make a point of sending a copy of their latest threatening letter or dismissive response to their minister.[7] She was well aware of Shandwick's campaigning on behalf of the company and presumably approved her staff's assistance – including passing on ministerial confidences – to the PR consultants. She appeared willing to let the state company do whatever it liked, provided its goals and anti-environmentalist prejudices matched her own.

Jenny Shipley's role in the PR campaign did not stop when she ceased to be SOE minister. Timberlands' teleconference minutes on 21 November 1997 noted that 'Cath Ingram will be going with J Shipley'. Soon Ingram was serving as a contact point for Timberlands and Shandwick in the new Prime Minister's office.[8] More surprisingly, the Timberlands Papers suggest that Jenny Shipley was taking a personal interest in the individual, sordid details of the anti-environmental campaign. For instance, only weeks before she became Prime Minister, Shandwick noted in an internal strategy paper that Shipley knew about and supported Timberlands' removal of environmental graffiti around Wellington city. 'The current erasure campaign has the support of the Minister of SOEs,' they wrote proudly. Soon, she went beyond just supporting.

Even in her first few days as Prime Minister, in early November 1997, Shipley made time to play a part in the anti-environmental campaign. On one of her frequent trips between Parliament and the airport she noticed new Native Forest Action graffiti on a concrete retaining wall and passed a message to her secretary to inform Timberlands about it. The next Friday's Timberlands teleconference minutes recorded: 'Our Minister / Prime Minister was travelling to airport and advised her secretary that there was more graffiti in Wellington'.[9]

Shipley knew about Timberlands' 'erasure campaign' and was clearly passing on the news in the expectation of action. The company responded promptly. A week later the teleconference minutes recorded: 'Graffiti noted en route to Wellington Airport has been taken care of'.[10] It is strange behaviour for a minister to suggest that a state company spend its money for this purpose. More important, it seems undignified and petty for a prime minister to be trying to silence her critics in this way.

The first conclusion we are forced to take from the Timberlands story is that, at the level of the National government, the PR campaign was a success. Despite public opinion being on the side of rainforest conservation and, for a time, the Prime Minister of the country backing an end to the logging, the concerted efforts of Timberlands and its PR companies (combined with Jenny Shipley's sympathy for their cause) won over key National and ACT politicians. The few million dollars of public money Timberlands spent on the PR campaign was small compared with the profits that could be reaped from ongoing subsidised rainforest logging.

If Jenny Shipley's government could win the 1999 election, the beech forests would inevitably be opened up to logging and the long-term cutting rights to the public rainforests would be privatised. All the disputed forests would be logged thanks, in a large part, to the PR tactics dreamt up by Timberlands, Shandwick and Head Consultants.

Luckily for the forests, by 1999 National was an unpopular government and the public campaign to have the forests preserved had convinced the Opposition parties. Although, as this book went to print, Labour had not announced its policy, we predict that the forests will not be logged.[11] So the second conclusion is positive. Despite the moni-

We will need to advise them of any delay	RM
Our Minister / Prime Minister was travelling to airport and advised her secretary that there was more graffitti in Wellington	RD
NFA / RF&B	
Still attempting to obtain original copies of material	ALL

PR teleconference minutes show that, in her first days as Prime Minister, Jenny Shipley made time to play a part in the anti-environmental campaign.

226

toring, the legal threats, the disparaging and harassment of environmentalists and the manipulation of news media and political allies, the rainforest conservationists kept their campaign going and they brought a majority of the public with them.

But it should not have to be that hard. It should not require dozens of largely unpaid environmental activists working year after year, 10,000 people writing submissions to the government and many more signing petitions and writing letters to politicians to balance the pressure of a small vested interest with a big PR budget. Many issues, whether small or crucial to the nation, do not have all those people able to give their time to try to ensure a democratic outcome.

Then there is the big picture. If a small company, 'heavily subsidised, barely profitable'[12] and opposed by a majority of the public, can hijack government policy to the degree that Timberlands managed, what are big companies and other vested interests doing? What influence are PR companies having on the general elections that decide who runs the country, and on economic and social policies? The tactics used by Timberlands are certainly not restricted to rainforest logging. Even in wars there are legions of PR staff, dehumanising the ordinary people being killed on the opposing side and controlling what audiences see and hear at home. The first casualty is the truth. As John Ralston Saul said of PR people, 'the purpose of these several hundred thousand communications experts is to prevent communications or any generalized grasp of reality'.[13]

The main difference between the Timberlands campaign and all the other PR campaigns being played out nationally and internationally is that usually the public never sees the puppeteers' hands. That does not mean that people do not feel that their reality is being manipulated: that politicians are not telling the whole story, that many stories which make it into the news are serving someone's agenda, that everyone is 'spinning' the truth and, sometimes, simply that they are being lied to.

Ministerial briefing document to be updated in consultation with CR.	AP
Delaying the presentation to Opposition parties has been discussed with W Young. Probably take place in the new year. RM has advised them of the delay.	
Graffiti noted en route to Wellington Airport has been taken care of.	
Attempting to get original copy of NFA/F&B 13 page booklet	ALL
Approach to be made to Minister's Office	RM
SG following up with an Akld media contact about this	SG

The minutes a week later show that Shipley's message was acted on promptly. The following week Timberlands began work on funding a mural to permanently cover this wall.

But what can they do about it? The cynicism exhibited by people in politics can breed in the public a reciprocal cynicism towards politics.

At present, the public can usually see the dark side of what PR companies are up to only if an insider takes it upon him or herself to spill the beans. But enough cases have leaked out to show that the Timberlands campaign was not unique. In the controversial area of genetic engineering, for instance, Green MP Jeanette Fitzsimons was leaked a copy of a 35-page PR strategy in April 1999 prepared by the Wellington PR firm Communications Trumps for a company involved in genetic engineering of salmon (pro-genetic engineering PR statements prefer the term 'genetically modified').[14] The client, New Zealand King Salmon, was experimenting with salmon that were genetically engineered to grow much faster than normal fish.

The paper is reminiscent of all the Shandwick plans: 'identifying allies' ('once the issue becomes public, those allies can support you'), offering to set up meetings with senior public servants, 'crisis management plans', a 'crisis planning session' ('this tactic has proved of great value to a wide range of organisations') and so on. The main environmental opponents are identified and the strategy talks of 'covering off' all the possible PR problems. For instance, it discussed devising 'messages' that would provide a 'comfort zone' on 'what would happen if the [transgenic salmon] got into the wild and could grow on'. That is important, they wrote, 'even though we know they can't get into the wild'. Only two pages earlier the paper had discussed various examples of salmon escaping from fish farms, concluding lamely that 'Our guess is that they won't provide much of a threat in small numbers'.[15]

Cath Ingram just called. NFA has just released a new run of posters + pamphlets which have been sent to all politicians – she asks you to ving her if you havent copits on. 471 9182.

Jenny Shipley's staff, before and after she became Prime Minister, had regular contact with Timberlands over its PR campaign and provided assistance.

Once again, the main strategy for controversial subjects was secrecy. Communications Trumps advised King Salmon that 'Issues such as deformities, lumps on heads etc should not be mentioned at any point to anyone outside' and that physical security to stop people getting into the research facility was important. 'Also important is how we can continue to keep wraps on the project, when it is probably discoverable under the Official Information Act,' they wrote. The priority in the 'communications' strategy was to avoid communication.

The reaction from Communications Trumps to the leaking of its PR strategy was also familiar. Through its lawyers Southall and Associates, legal action was threatened against Jeanette Fitzsimons and Kim Hill, who had discussed the leaks on her radio programme. Both women were asked to issue apologies and retractions; they both refused to so. Kim Hill commented: 'The two things that strike me about this year is the unbelievable incidence of headlice and the unbelievable incidence of threatened litigation. I don't know what that means. Are they connected?'[16]

Communications Trumps was especially sensitive about the revelations because it had a number of other irons in the genetic engineering fire. It had a contract with AgResearch, a Crown research institute

Genetically modified salmon: once again, the main strategy for controversial subjects was secrecy. PR company Communications Trumps advised King Salmon that 'Issues such as deformities, lumps on heads etc should not be mentioned at any point to anyone outside'. Photo: Marlborough Express

engaged in genetic engineering, and a contract to manage a pro-genetic engineering publicity trust called Genepool. The latter was a classic industry front group, in the tradition of the corporate-funded United States organisations that offer independent scientific comment on such issues as why smoking is safe. In late 1998 Genepool had arranged a national roadshow, supplying information on genetically modified food to food industry representatives, in which the New Zealand business manager of the genetic engineering giant Monsanto had shared the platform with various pro-genetic engineering scientists.[17]

What happens when a PR company is caught out advising its clients to act in debatable ways? The response of the PR industry in the salmon case does not inspire confidence. When the immediate past president of the Public Relations Institute (PRINZ), Gordon Chesterman, made a public statement after the leaking, he did not question Communications Trumps' actions but instead criticised Jeanette Fitzsimons for publicising the case. His concern was that 'electioneering by Ms Fitzsimons' had put the 'credibility of the public relations industry into question'. He said, 'The damage has already been done and from the PRINZ point of view this is not an ethical issue'.[18]

PRINZ argues that its members represent those in the PR profession who are prepared to meet the highest standards. Tony Cronin, the chair of the PRINZ Ethics Committee, agrees that, in terms of credibility, the PR industry probably does not have much to lose: 'I would think we are probably at about the same level as second hand car salesmen … I think very often we are seen as not really contributing a lot that is useful to the common weal.'[19] Cronin was not satisfied with the way the King Salmon issue was handled but, in the absence of a formal complaint to the ethics committee, 'the issue rather went away and was left hanging, once again possibly to the detriment of the image of the industry. We looked like a bunch of cowboys.'

It was a controversy, Cronin said, that was 'made far more difficult by the fact that it was the President of the [Public Relations] Institute's consultancy that was involved. It would be better for all parties concerned to have dealt with that out in the open and in the public.' The PR consultant managing Genepool, Norrie Simmons, was a director of Communications Trumps and was also the president of PRINZ.

The PR industry wants us to believe it can regulate itself. The PRINZ Code of Professional Practice, to which members are required to ensure 'strict adherence', obliges members to 'adhere to the highest standards of honesty, accuracy and good taste and not knowingly disseminate false or misleading information'. They should 'act primarily in the public interest and neither act nor induce others to act in a way which might affect unfavourably the practice of public relations, the community or the Institute'. Also members should not 'engage in any practice, which has the purpose of corrupting the integrity of channels of public communication'. The Timberlands Papers come to mind.

Breaches of the code can be investigated by the ethics committee and punished by disciplinary measures ranging from a reprimand for minor offences and fines for more serious breaches, through to expulsion from PRINZ. The punishments sound serious but there is a fundamental weakness. 'Even should you find a practitioner contravening the code, you can't stop them practicing public relations,' Cronin says. Even if a member were expelled from PRINZ, they could still do public relations work.

In the absence of a complaint, the ethics committee has nothing to investigate and few complaints are made. Between 1986 and 1999 there were just five complaints: including three in 1996, one of them lodged by Cronin himself, and another the one by Native Forest Action in 1997, which the ethics committee brushed aside for lack of proof. Proof is the problem in the secretive world of PR. The PRINZ Code of Professional Conduct actually enshrines the secrecy, requiring members to 'protect the confidences of present, former and/or prospective clients or employers'. Two of PRINZ's annual awards for excellence in PR in 1998 went to Communications Trumps consultants for work where both the title of the project and the name of the client were withheld for reasons of confidentiality.

The trap of self-regulation is that it relies on courageous individuals inside the industry willing to take a stand against behaviour that may be considered the norm by their colleagues. Most whistleblowers' careers suffer for their stand. It is a problem that Tony Cronin is all too familiar with. In 1996 he got involved in the case of a PRINZ member, Michelle Boag, whose client Fay Richwhite was appearing before the 'Winebox' Commission of Inquiry to give evidence concerning an alleged Cook Island tax avoidance scam in which the company had been involved. Fay Richwhite commissioned Boag to video the proceedings, presumably so that they could pore over it later to work out their tactics. She obtained permission to film, however, on the understanding that hers was an independent film crew. The real journalists who were covering the hearings day after day became suspicious and, when Boag's real agenda was discovered, controversy erupted.

231

According to Cronin, many within PRINZ were concerned but no one was prepared to lodge a formal complaint. Finally Cronin lodged a complaint himself in order to trigger an investigation, which he then ruled himself out of investigating. 'It was not a career enhancing move from my point of view however,' he said. 'There were various people who felt that I had overreacted.'

Cronin said that his letter of complaint 'had barely arrived on a desk when I had phone calls from three clients saying that was the end of the work that I was going to get from them'. Why was he punished for doing what others were too afraid to do? 'I have always assumed that they wanted to be able to tell their business colleagues and club mates that they had leaned on me, that I had been intransigent but they had taught me a lesson by taking away their business,' he said.

Despite Cronin taking a stand, the PRINZ ethics process proved ineffectual anyway. Boag simply resigned from the institute and the ethics committee had no power to investigate and impose a punishment.

Following the controversy over King Salmon, the PRINZ national executive considered ways that investigations might be initiated without relying on a complaint from an individual. One option considered was that, where an issue had 'public profile', the national executive might refer it to the ethics committee for consideration. According to Cronin, the national executive might say 'there is an issue here to be dealt with then get the ethics committee to rub its grey heads together to determine what action may or may not be taken'. To which one might reply, too little, too late. As long as a company could keep its actions secret and avoid 'public profile' in the first place, it would have nothing to fear.

Self-regulation of the public relations industry ethics through an industry association is doomed to be ineffective for imposing any more than the most minimal ethical standards. What incentive is there for the consultancies who belong to the public relations institute to clip their own wings? Even where the profession's officials like Cronin are serious about seeking to uphold standards, the system does not work.

Does this mean it is impossible to control the damage created by public relations activities? Not at all. Immediate changes can be introduced to impose more ethical standards. For instance, as has happened in the banking industry and is mooted in the legal profession, there should be a public relations ombudsman. This person could have statutory powers to investigate and rule on unethical behaviour, following a public debate about the implications of public relations in the political system and about what standards should be required. The ombudsman would have full access to confidential information. If lawyers, doctors or bus drivers can lose the right to practise their profession when they fail to meet decent standards, why not PR people, whose actions can damage the functioning of a democratic society?

Just as professional lobbyists in Washington are required by law to declare who they are working for, so PR people should have to declare regularly for which clients and on what issues they are working. PR companies would protest that this would compromise their consultant-client relationship, which is true, but the benefit to society would far outweigh the disadvantage to them. All government agencies should be required to disclose what their PR budget is, which PR companies they use and on what specific projects they are working. Increased public awareness of the PR industry and the possibility being investigated by an independent ombudsman would help to control the excesses.

But it would not be enough: the dominance of PR in politics and society cannot be dealt with just by passing a law. The growth of professional public relations in recent decades has been part of a dangerous trend, leading to a major redistribution of power within nominally democratic societies: more for the powerful, less for the public. Both the alienated many and the advantaged few can feel this shift of power, but there is little serious discussion of what is happening. Countries like New Zealand and Australia tend to take democracy for granted, lulled by the idea that a three-yearly election somehow implies democratic government. PR spin fills the growing gap between expectation and reality.

Our governments have always been ready to send soldiers to the far side of the world in the name of democracy. Now that fight needs to be fought at home. Although an ombudsman and statutory disclosure of clients would help a little in curbing abuses by the PR industry, the most important changes needed are those designed to protect the democratic system from being too easily influenced by pay-politics. The first step is to revitalise discussion of democracy, that overused word that is not talked about enough. And part of this is understanding the activities of the PR industry so that democratic groups can reclaim public space for debate.

The next step is to improve government processes, so that it is harder for PR networks to set up informal government processes that replace the democratic ones. Secrecy is the basis of modern government. Timberlands and Shandwick could not have manufactured their anti-environmental campaign without secrecy. Jenny Shipley would not have backed their campaign if the machinations had been visible. If select committees had been able to access all the papers – which otherwise came out only by leaking – and the public could have checked up on ministerial and public service processes under freedom of information law, many of the PR games could never have been played. More than anything else, a shift to open government would profoundly change the way politics is conducted.

Countries like New Zealand and Australia do have official information acts and select committees, but loopholes such as commercial confidentiality and protection of 'free and frank discussion' between ministers and public servants have kept the balance firmly on the side of secrecy. Secrecy is so ingrained that governments could not imagine operating without it.

The next step is improving public service processes. Public sector 'reform' during the post-1984 New Right years removed various protections that had evolved to avoid compromise of the public service by political pressures. The 1988 State Sector Act, in particular, introduced corporate structures and undermined the independence of government departments. The apolitical public service was replaced by one where chief executives follow directions from their minister. We saw some of the results in Chapter 11, where public servants came to act as political activists for their minister's political agenda and informal processes allowed people like Shandwick's Rob McGregor to compromise the neutrality of the public servants. These are stories repeated throughout the public service, underpinned always by secrecy. Strengthening the democratic basis of the public service is an important defence against corporate interests being able to use their PR budgets to buy influence in government decision-making.

State-owned companies such as Timberlands are an extreme case of the general problems in government. The idea of corporatising government activities (leaving aside the social services that often got lost in the process) was that state company managers could get on with running profitable businesses. But these managers were given control of public resources with little political oversight or accountability back to the public. The convenient plea of commercial confidentiality allows a level of secrecy in public business that is unnecessary and unhealthy. A public organisation like Timberlands should not have been able to get away with spending public money to manipulate the public and influence the government that controls it – but poor democratic structures allowed it to hide and bluff its way through.

The other key area where the democratic infrastructure can be

strengthened is the news media. The public depends on journalists to publicise the things that the powerful would rather keep quiet and to offer a
view of reality free of, or at least explaining and balancing, the PR spins of
the various interests involved. It is a unique and important role in society.

As Australian journalist David McKnight wrote, good PR relies on
bad journalism, and currently there is plenty of it. Increasingly, the prof-
itability of media outlets is driven by strategies to attract advertising and
by accounting decisions. Cross-promotions, editorial coverage for advertising deals and the growth of specialist advertising supplements have
proliferated. News staff have been cut back in both private and com-
mercialised public news organisations. Fewer journalists are expected
to produce the same amount of content, or more, and quality inevitably
suffers. Few organisations allocate the resources that would allow journalists to spend more than a few hours on a story.

Cost cutting has also led to experienced reporters being replaced
by a constant stream of inexperienced graduates who are cheaper to employ. Television news apes American channels with short, no-depth coverage, and in 1999 New Zealand's public television organisation was looking
at phasing out locally made current affairs programmes altogether because
they were considered too costly to produce. This was the environment in
which Shandwick and Timberlands were operating; and in which Coast
Action Network could 'launch' itself three times in a row and be taken
seriously by reporters who came fresh to the issue on each occasion.

A critical element missing from most journalism courses is any
detailed analysis of the PR industry and how it works. Without any real
knowledge of the PR industry, journalism graduates enter the workforce
oblivious of its machinations. Worse still, they remain largely oblivious.
There are many specialist journalists who report on everything from
cricket to the balance of payments, but there is not one specialist writer
focusing on the PR industry. In the absence of any regular coverage, the
industry can remain invisible.

Since good media coverage is not reliably provided by market forces
through private news organisations, at least part of the answer lies in good,
non-commercial public broadcasting. Our countries put literally billions
of dollars into military forces supposedly to protect our way of life. Hundreds of millions of dollars go to police forces in an attempt to keep our
communities safe. Billions more go to social security systems to support
those citizens for whom the market economy will not provide. The maintenance of an open and democratic society also requires generous resources, in this case to provide high-quality, publicly funded news organi-

sations that can also set a standard for private news organisations.

Journalists can help personally in another way too, by looking hard at their own cynicism. Under-resourced and pressed for time, journalists can become resigned to reporting misleading statements by people in positions of authority. 'Balanced reporting' can then come to mean little more than presenting two or three more or less misleading statements. That is not what the public expects: ordinary people rely on journalists also to seek the truth.

The allocation of resources for independently studying and increasing public awareness of important social issues is also a priority. In Scandanavian countries, for instance, there are all sorts of publicly funded research and policy institutes engaged in studying social trends and problems and in developing ideas for solutions. One Stockholm institute engaged solely in the study of work has about 100 researchers and academics, while another on constitutional design and reform of government has about 24 full-time staff. This is the kind of public interest infrastructure that creates much stronger democracies. In the specific area of PR, New Zealand and Australia would benefit greatly from the establishment of local equivalents of John Stauber and Sheldon Rampton's United States-based Center for Media and Democracy, investigating and writing about the activities of the PR industry.

A combination of these steps, controlling and counter-balancing the influence of public relations politics, has the potential to revitalise democratic society. But it should be said that, even though the PR industry may steer the new corporate activism we witness at the turn of the century, it is little more than a tool for defending and extending this business-based power. To focus overwhelmingly on the activities of the PR industry would be to concentrate on the monkey rather than the organ grinder.

Corporate activism has grown to a point where it does not even seem strange to us that the main voices in many public policy 'debates' are business and industry groups or 'market' commentators: spokespeople for only one narrow dimension of what is important for a healthy and prosperous society. Whether it is on social policy, taxation, sale of public utilities or even the electoral system, groups such as the Employers Federation and the Business Roundtable and 'commentators' from various self-interested financial institutions (banks, merchant banks and share-brokers) will usually have far more say than any groups representing the public interest.

Yet there is no reason why the groups of people and interests that make up the business sector should have special dominance in the political system any more than, for instance, those making up the education sector. If our armed forces were claiming and exercising that political dominance, with generals commenting on every issue and holding sway over government, it would be clearer that this is not how democratic societies are supposed to function. Purchasing the services of the PR industry is one of the main reasons that the new corporate activism is able to have its impact.

Countries urgently need to face up to fundamental issues surrounding corporate power and its current dominance. How should corporations be tamed so that real democracy can flourish? Many corporations pay large amounts of money to industry associations to argue for reduced public welfare, education and services spending and lower corporate taxation. Why should they be allowed to spend shareholders' funds on political donations or massive lobbying campaigns? Why are corporations allowed to claim money spent on legal actions against individuals as a tax deduction while the defendants cannot? The legitimacy of this corporate activism in a democratic society needs to be questioned. There need to be regulations aimed at controlling the extremes of the corporate activism and a rediscovery and strengthening of the institutions and processes of democracy to cope with this activism.

There is only one way that changes like this occur, and that is by people in all sectors of society caring enough to do something about it: journalists taking their social role seriously, public servants defending the public interest, businesspeople showing leadership in ethics and, generally, the public discussing and objecting and acting in spite of the alienating effects of PR-dominated politics. Out of this emerge the new leaders and the political will that create change. All countries have seen this potential proven over and over, even though in New Zealand, during the New Right years, it began to feel as though the political system itself had been privatised.

The PR industry is not monolithic. There are people in it who hold to high standards and use their skills for genuine public benefit. There is no doubt that effective communications skills are essential for handling everything from natural disasters to promoting preventative health. These people, in the words of the PRINZ Code of Professional Conduct, 'act primarily in the public interest and neither act nor induce others to act in a way that might unfavourably affect... the community'. All the big PR firms emphasise the work they do for good causes, but public interest use of PR skills is overshadowed by private interest work. Put bluntly, there is more money to be made helping private interests act in ways that often unfavourably affect the society in which we all live. Much of the emphasis of their 'issues management' is preventing public discussion; instead of helping the functioning of democracy, they are undermining it.

The people who work in public relations have a role to play in changing this. They can take a lead in much more rigorous debate about the issues and ethics of their trade. They are well placed, and have the experience in strategic thinking, to consider how they can protect society from the less scrupulous of their colleagues and their clients.

Why do people go into PR? Nearly everyone gives the same answer. A journalist can earn tens of thousands of dollars more each year by 'selling out' and moving across to PR. Some people are attracted by the power too, where their wheeling and dealing can influence major events and even make and break governments.

Paul Jackman, a former Radio New Zealand reporter turned corporate affairs manager of the Reserve Bank, discussed the choice facing journalists in an article written for the New Zealand Journalists Training Organisation newsletter, *Noted*. While saying he had a clear conscience about his job, he made the following plea to his former colleagues in journalism (whom, he said, PR people refer to as 'chooks'). 'I worry that too often good journalists change sides without having thought through the implications,' he wrote. 'Even if your employer's editorial line is loathsome, you can still attempt a basic integrity by at least being truthful in everything you write. You can be that, as a service to the public. I can make no such claim.'[20]

We would go further. As long as supposedly respectable PR companies continue to act, in Tony Cronin's phrase, like 'a bunch of cowboys', there should be strong peer pressure among journalists and in other professions discouraging people from taking their skills and knowledge into PR jobs. At times it is not so different from a police officer accepting a gratifying rise in salary for taking his or her skills and knowledge to a new job in the 'recreational pharmaceutical industry' (as their PR communications strategy might put it), helping the new employer avoid the unwelcome attentions of the old.

At present, the PR 'industry' in New Zealand earns a considerable part of its $1.5 billion each year in the unhealthy business of secrets and lies. Policies can be found to control the worst of this, but the ultimate cure lies in strengthening the infrastructure and processes of an open and democratic society.

Until changes are achieved, the only effective way of controlling unethical PR activities is through unwelcome publicity. Given that people who whistleblow openly are usually punished for their trouble, part of the answer is for thoughtful people in and around public relations to pluck up courage and quietly pass stories on to the public. The safe and effective 'leaking' of information has become increasingly important in enabling informed public debate. It is the logical and necessary democratic response when governments and companies become unhealthily secretive. (See guide to leaking in Appendix A.) That is how the hundreds of pages of strategy plans that make up the Timberlands Papers reached the light of day and also how the single paper that revealed the King Salmon secret came to public attention. There are many other questionable activities in need of publicity.

The last words, in case anyone still feels that the title of this book is unfair, should go to Timberlands chief executive Dave Hilliard (who, after all, was advised by Shandwick to stick to a consistent strategy of 'always having the last word').[21]

> *We don't call it public relations. It's others who call our expenditure public relations. Communications and marketing is what we call it....*
>
> *Klaus [Sorensen at Shandwick] has been accused in the media quite wrongly and quite libelously of all sorts of things, which is quite inappropriate. All he does is some passing of information for us, that's all he does. He's been accused of writing strategies, bringing things from the States, all those sorts of things, but Native Forest Action give themselves more credit than they're due, because we don't bother with those sorts of things. It's actually quite laughable to think that we sit here worrying about them or developing strategies the same as North America or whatever; I wouldn't even know what they're doing there....*
>
> *We don't produce public relations documents anyway.... We don't have a written strategy or document of how to get NFA; I mean, no such thing exists.*

A BRIEF GUIDE TO LEAKING

PUBLIC INFORMATION is the number one requirement of a healthy democracy. Although we live in a so-called information age, governments and private companies have become increasingly adept at restricting and controlling public access to all sorts of important information. For a while there was movement towards greater freedom of information; in New Zealand this peaked in the early 1980s. During the New Right years since 1984, however, secrecy in government and private businesses has grown to become a dominant feature of government processes.

Because secrecy is now so entrenched, corporations and governments can do things they would not dream of doing if they thought the public might find out. As a result, the back rooms of many government

Timberlands' headquarters in Greymouth. The file rooms of many government and private organisations contain information at least as dodgy as the Timberlands Papers – information which the public should know about but which the organisations concerned keep secret to protect their reputations or interests. Leaking involves individuals deciding to make principled (but unauthorised) releases of information in the public interest.

240

and private organisations will contain information just as dodgy as the Timberlands Papers. If the filing cabinets of the country were more open to journalists, MPs and the public, it would make a profound and positive difference to the conduct of politics and business. Until the culture of government and business is improved, unauthorised leaking of information by public-spirited individuals is vital for defending democratic society.

Whenever institutions have become unreasonably secretive, principled people have reacted by making sure that information reaches the public anyway. These people play a vital role: exposing dishonest or improper behaviour, alerting the public to questionable policies, actions and plans and ensuring accountability by people in positions of authority who would prefer to avoid scrutiny. Leaking information helps to give the public a role in issues that affect their lives.

Some of the people who leak information choose to do so openly and courageously, as whistleblowers. Unfortunately, this commonly results in the persecution of such people to the point where they are forced to leave their jobs. There is some weak whistleblower legislation on the books in New Zealand and other countries, but it is of limited use in protecting whistleblowers from victimisation. Whistleblowing therefore often means that people must make a decision between public interest and personal career. In most instances, therefore, we recommend careful leaking in ways that cannot be traced so that the public interest is served and personal careers are protected.

This famous leak occurred just before the 1984 election, revealing a secret deal between the Muldoon government and France.

Leaking information in the public interest may be one of the most important and rewarding political acts of your life. There is a long and honourable international tradition of people leaking material that proved vital in exposing corruption, harmful social and environmental plans and political dishonesty. Do not underestimate the power of leaking. Plans are often kept secret so that the public is prevented from influencing decisions that could stop some undesirable development, law or action. Publicity of secret activities and plans can sometimes be enough to end such initiatives. All it takes is a principled person (or two) inside an institution; the Watergate leaks brought down a corrupt president.

How does a person leak information safely?

Some people get caught leaking information and suffer the same consequences as whistleblowers. By far the majority of people leak information safely. Some simple planning makes all the difference. The key issues in leaking safely are choosing someone sensible and trustworthy to give the information to, thinking through what can be leaked without being traced, passing on the information safely and thinking through the ethical issues involved.

Who is it safe to leak to?

This is the most important decision. If you choose the right person, they will make it their first priority to look after you and help you sort out what is safe and what would be reckless. Do not risk your job by going to someone who could put getting a good story ahead of looking after the source (you) or who might just act carelessly.

We recommend picking a journalist, writer or public interest researcher who, based on what you have heard or seen, you respect. Alternatively, you can go straight to an MP or lobby group that you think will use the information well. If you are uncertain where to go, you can approach John Stauber, Center for Media and Democracy, 3318 Gregory Street, Madison, WI 5371, United States; or the authors Nicky Hager, PO Box 16088, Wellington, New Zealand, or Bob Burton, PO Box 157, O'Connor, ACT 2602, Australia; and we will suggest who we think is most suitable.

Some leaks are simply done anonymously. The journalist opens a letter and finds the photocopied papers. The disadvantage of this approach is that it means the journalist cannot ask you questions to authenticate the documents and fill out the story. (A lot of 'leaking' to journalists is actually 'planting', where the government or organisation concerned arranges a selective leak to serve its purposes. So journalists need to be cautious about the authenticity of and motive behind a leak.) The journalist also cannot work out how best to protect an anonymous source. We have, however, had extremely useful anonymous leaks, so this can be a perfectly good option.

The best first step, after deciding to leak information, is usually to identify the trustworthy person and arrange a discreet meeting. Phone them (not from work) and ask to meet for a coffee or even turn up on their doorstep. Never leak information by e-mail as it can easily be, and often is, monitored by the host organisation. Logs of past messages can also be easily retrieved. Even records of web pages that are accessed from your computer can be collected from the server.

You must ensure that the person you choose will be responsible about not giving away their sources. We believe it is reasonable to ask a journalist to agree not to publicise anything without checking it with you first. You can also insist that they do not pass on your identity to anyone else (even their employers).

If someone bulldozes you, saying that they would need to talk about you to others, or if they seem concerned only about getting the story, find someone else. It is not their job at risk. There are good, responsible journalists so there is no need to put your trust in someone with whom you feel uncomfortable. Often a relationship of trust between a journalist and someone inside an organisation can last for years.

WHAT IS BEST TO LEAK?

Leaking does not need to involve top secret papers. Often a useful relationship can develop where you help a journalist write good stories by being able to check out their facts and ideas with someone inside the system. The information involved need not be classified – even with unclassified information it can be hard for journalists to get past the organisation's PR staff if the story might be critical. At other times, big secrets may be involved.

Sometimes you will not want to leak documents at all. That is fine. Often just tipping off a journalist about what is going on is enough to flush out an important story. But if a journalist has nothing solid, it is common for the government, organisation or company concerned simply to deny the story. 'That is ridiculous, we have no plans to…' is an easy reply, even for something they know will become public later. Any specific details you can pass on make it harder to get away with a denial: dates of meetings, details of plans, exact figures and so on. Nicky Hager's book on secret intelligence systems, for example, was based almost entirely on interviews. It did not seem worth the risk of acquiring lots of documents. The level of detail provided in the interviews allowed the subsequent exposé to be credible in spite of the absence of documentary evidence.

Sometimes just suggesting some questions that should be asked and who should be quizzed about a topic is sufficiently useful information. If you are wary of leaking documents, simply suggesting what file should be sought from government agencies under the Official Information Act can be useful.

Leaking documents makes it easiest for a journalist to convince the news editors that the story is real and should be run. With documents, the big issue is choosing ones that are difficult to trace. If a particular report or memo could only have come from you and your immediate workmates, that creates a lot of pressure. The best papers are ones that have been circulated more widely, for instance around various government departments or to all Cabinet ministers or companies. This is where going to an experienced and trustworthy journalist is most useful, since you can talk through the best way to get the story out safely.

Sometimes information can safely be leaked out over time; sometimes the best thing is a big release, as with the Timberlands Papers, and then keeping your head down for a while. Another option is quietly to take papers home while you are in a job and pass them on only after you have left that position or organisation. There are many people who, as soon as they have some distance from a previous job, wish they had squirrelled away papers on the things that troubled them.

Often the most important leaks have come from people who did not even know they were sitting on a big story. If you are uncomfortable with what is going on where you work and want to do something about it, we recommend making contact with a journalist or someone in a public interest group. After talking, it may emerge that you can play an important role. It may be that you do not realise what papers and information around you are most politically significant. You may be able to add the crucial bit of confirmation or detail to allow publicity of a story they already know about. Or you may work in a non-controversial part of an organisation and not realise that you can help with issues of high public interest elsewhere in the organisation. Any serious journalist or researcher will welcome receiving a copy even of something as seemingly routine as an internal telephone directory or an index to the files. These can be useful for someone outside the organisation in understanding how things work, what goes on, where to look for information and who should be accountable.

Alternatively, you may be able to help the journalist over time with non-secret but hard-to-access information and insider insights. If there is a chance you will one day leak something, still choose the journalist or researcher with care and make contact discreetly, or you may not feel safe about passing on information later.

PASSING ON THE INFORMATION SAFELY

As secrecy has grown, so too have systems within organisations to try to keep the secrets in. But even in the most security obsessed organisation, common sense will help you to leak information safely.

Obviously you should not meet a journalist in the café next to your work or in their newsroom. Once you trust them, meeting at your or their home may be simplest, or in an out-of-the-way café. The wide availability of photocopiers makes it easier to copy papers. Usually it is not a good idea to leak original papers – go for 'sharing' rather than 'stealing' (unless you have copies of papers that no one in the organisation knows you have). The best option may be to take some papers away from work during lunch or overnight and copy them at a library or copy shop. Because of scratches on the glass, photocopiers sometimes leave little marks that could allow the leaked document to be traced back to your office photocopier. If you do photocopy at work, remember to take out the original when you finish. (This is by far the most frequent slip made by nervous people copying at the office!)

You may want to take identifying marks off documents, such as fax marks or e-mail details at the top or bottom of pages and handwritten notes and underlining. Often, though, this information can be important for verifying the authenticity of the document or revealing the date it was sent or received. It is best to remove this information only when essential or after it has been viewed.

If the document is a numbered copy, remove the numbers from *every* page. The simplest thing may be to copy the papers quickly first, then later take off all the marks and photocopy them again. Be aware that fingerprints can be detected on paper. If in doubt, allow the journalist (and maybe their editor) to view the documents, write down what they want to use and maybe photograph a page as an illustration – but on the understanding that they then give the papers back to you without taking copies. If you are the source, you have a right to control how the information is used.

Never give away your only copy of any document. No matter how important a document may be, sometimes material gets lost. Always try to keep a back-up copy in a safe location. Sometimes it may be worth ensuring that copies are distributed widely.

Speaking from experience, if you take these precautions then, when the information comes out in the news, it is very hard for the source ever to be traced. We have been involved in many leaks, large and small, and the people who provided the information have always remained anonymous. Of course you should be very careful and, at the time of the publicity, mentally prepared so that you do not give away your role. But there is no need to feel paranoid. Information leaks happen quite often. The organisations concerned may go through the motions of a 'witch hunt' to prove to their superiors they are serious about security, but then things settle down again. Remember all the famous leakers in history who have helped their countries and got away with it.

THE ETHICS OF LEAKING

When people leak information, they are deciding to put public interest and moral considerations above their obligations to maintain secrecy. It is important that they and the journalists think through the ethical issues involved.

There is plenty of information which, although it could create a news splash and help sell that day's newspapers, it is not ethical to leak. This includes information that intrudes on individuals' privacy. Even famous or notorious people have a right not to have their personal affairs publicised by the people in positions of trust around them. This involves telling the difference between the attraction of gossip and serving the public interest.

Except in special circumstances, the only staff in an organisation it is reasonable to identify are those at senior levels who should be accountable for the decisions or actions in question. There is a strong obligation to check that information is correct and up-to-date. Also, both the person considering leaking and the journalist, researcher or political person receiving it, need to be clear about the motive for the leak. Issues of public interest and justice should be the guide, not vindictiveness towards a difficult employer.

Various ethical issues will arise in particular circumstances. The main point is that those who take responsibility for leaking information also need to consider the ethical issues at stake. Often, after some thought and discussion, it is a straightforward decision. The current government and business culture of secrecy and the lack of respect for democratic processes mean that there are very many areas where leaking is justified and urgently needed. The individuals who choose to leak in these circumstances deserve, albeit anonymously, our respect and thanks.

Leakers come in all shapes and sizes, from the highest to the lowest levels of organisations and from both the public and private sectors. You, too, may have a role to play.

PR AND CRISIS MANAGEMENT – HOW TIMBERLANDS MAY DEAL WITH THIS BOOK

ONE OF THE SPECIALIST areas in the PR trade is called crisis management. When a chemical plant blows up, an oil tanker runs aground or a plane crashes, the PR strategists attempt to ensure that a 'crisis management team' is quickly in place, adapting and implementing its prepared 'crisis management plan'. Crisis management has been developed on the basis of a careful analysis of case studies to determine patterns of news media coverage and the interaction of media and decision-makers in society. The aim, of course, is to spin news coverage to the company's advantage and to minimise bad publicity arising from the crisis.

Shandwick recommended 'issues management and crisis preparedness planning' for Timberlands in a paper written in June 1997. Crisis preparedness, the PR advisers wrote, 'ensures that the company is as prepared as possible for any unforeseen crisis that may develop and has the skills and experience to react promptly and efficiently'. It listed the most likely issues and crises as being government curtailment of unsustainable logging, limitation of native forest logging, privatisation, accident or death of employees or members of the public, timber end users targeted, biosecurity issues, tangata whenua land claims, sabotage of equipment and protest occupation of the forests.[1]

Shandwick recommended that the Timberlands senior management team take part in a three- to four-hour Crisis Preparedness/Issues Management Workshop. The agenda for this workshop, which was scheduled for 13 August 1997, included 'identifying the issues currently (or potentially) facing the company' and prioritising them 'in terms of potential impact and risk'. It went on to discuss 'who needs to be influenced and who is part of the problem' and then looked at the strategies: 'selecting/confirming the preferred strategy to pre-empt, manage or minimise the issue/damage.'[2] The actual workshop was put off over the following weeks and it is not certain if it ever happened.

The Timberlands Papers did not include a crisis preparedness plan. To illustrate the thinking behind such plans, and drawing on real examples from the PR world, we have prepared a crisis management strategy for dealing with the leak of the Timberlands Papers and the publication of this book. The following is what a crisis strategy might look like in this case.

A   A CRISIS MANAGEMENT STRATEGY – INTRODUCTION

1. On the morning the book is published, the first step would be immediately to assemble the crisis management team including the Timberlands senior managers, the PR advisers from Shandwick and Head and possibly the company lawyer. The meeting would be by teleconference from the Timberlands boardroom, as with the weekly PR meetings. The first task would be evaluation of all available information related to the crisis.

2. Generally, the next step would be the issuing of a 'holding statement' to provide a brief initial comment to the news media until such time as they could provide a more detailed response. If the crisis had been anticipated, there might be a press statement already drafted in the 'holding statements file', containing carefully vetted typical statements to avoid loss of time. It would say, perhaps, that the company and its lawyers had not yet seen or were studying the book and would comment in due course. They would also seek legal advice at this early stage as any emergency decisions made without lawyers on hand could harm the company.

3. Crisis management teaches that the best strategies are to counter-attack, to portray yourself as the victim and to attempt to arrange other, seemingly independent, spokespeople to speak up in your defence and attack your critics. Issues to be dealt with would include not wanting to confirm the accuracy of the material in the book, attempting to minimise news media interest and reassuring political allies in an attempt to stop them distancing themselves from the company. The aim would be to have all the players speak with one voice and stick to a common message. Particularly important would be the management of the crisis for the first 24 hours, which is considered crucial in setting the themes that will frame the story.

B   POSSIBLE PUBLIC RELATIONS STRATEGIES:

1. Counter-attack

- Seek an injunction to prevent distribution of the book and/or issue warnings of legal action to news media organisations to attempt to stop or limit news publicity about the book.

- Issue a statement saying the claims in the book are scurrilous and defamatory and that you have referred them to your lawyer. This gives the appearance of taking the high moral ground even if the book is neither scurrilous nor defamatory.

- Claim that the leaked documents are fake, out of date or misrepresented (people who do not read the book or news coverage closely might believe you).

- Attack the motives of the authors. This avoids having to reply to the issues raised by the book and attempts to shift the spotlight to the authors. Claim that they have 'extreme' views and that they are known to support the environmentalists. Even if the leaked documents speak for themselves, hinting at bias by the authors serves as a diversion from bad publicity for the company.

- Ridicule the book. Dismiss it as conspiracy theories. Play up to journalist scepticism. This provides something to say in interviews without needing to address the criticisms.

2. Paint yourself as the victim

- Claim that a disgruntled staff member 'stole' the documents and that the police have been contacted. This paints you as the victim and your critics as criminal. The drawback is that it also implies the documents are authentic and thus confirms the allegations against the company.

- Say that the motive for the book was to damage the company's commercial viability and public standing. Explain that the company has worked sincerely to devise sustainable forest management systems and that attacks like this damage all that hard work. It also threatens all the West Coast jobs and community sponsorship provided by the company. Again, while not actually relevant, this can deflect from damaging revelations by reiterating practised PR statements about the company's virtues.

3. Use allies and mobilise third-party supporters, as the PR strategies intended, to become 'spokespeople' for Timberlands where implementation of Timberlands' plans appears threatened.

- Contact existing third party supporters. Urge that they jump to the defence of the company and attack the authors, as this would have more public credibility than the company doing it for itself. Suggest what they could say in defence of the company. (The dilemma of this tactic is that seeking public support from allies during the crisis risks straining the relationships with them. The need for support must be balanced against letting the allies keep their heads down and re-establishing contact when the controversy has passed.)
- Possible media angles: Coast Action Network could dismiss and condemn the book, saying that it was yet another attempt by people with extreme views to close down sustainable forestry on the West Coast and put local people out of jobs. Government ministers could attack the credibility of the authors and hint that they were linked to opposition political parties. Allies mentioned in the book could say it is scurrilous and defamatory and that they have referred it to their lawyers.
- Encourage a close ally to threaten or initiate legal action against the book in an attempt to discourage or moderate media coverage.
- Contact sympathetic journalists to give prominence to the company's responses.
- Mobilise letters to the editor from supporters and staff along the lines suggested above.

Overall, the aim of the crisis management strategy would be to avoid having to discuss the revelations about the company's PR campaign, to deflect attention onto diversions (such as attacking the authors) and to attempt to minimise the volume and duration of publicity for the book.

Needless to say, the crisis management plans, all contact with allies and any other actions resulting from the plans would have to be kept strictly secret. Even better, given the nature of the crisis: do not write anything down.

APPENDIX C

A HAPPY ENDING –
TIMBERLANDS' SCHEMES UNRAVEL

The anti-environmental campaign described in *Secrets and Lies* might have made a depressing story, where the secret tactics and constant lies succeeded in defeating the genuine community groups. However, despite illuminating some of the dark side of politics, the lessons from the New Zealand rainforest conflict are mostly positive and hopeful.

As this United States edition went to print, it appears that all the valuable forests on the West Coast will be put into reserves and the local communities will transfer entirely to plantation forestry. The environmental campaign has worked. The PR companies, particularly Shandwick, are embroiled in a major Public Relations Institute ethics investigation into the Timberlands campaign that has become an ethics test case for the whole PR industry.

The experience of the Timberlands-Shandwick campaign has been useful for the environmental movement in other ways too. The best defence against the kinds of PR tactics used in this campaign is to know about them. SLAPPs, front groups, systematic attacking of critics: if groups can recognise the tactics and cry foul when they are used, it helps to reduce their power. Recognising the tactics is also the first step to exposing them.

Perhaps the most powerful lesson coming from this case study is that when companies and governments resort to unethical tactics, they are wielding a double-edged sword. The dirtier the tactics, the more damage it does to the companies concerned if they are exposed.

Timberlands' reward for using these tactics is that it is seriously discredited. After the release of *Secrets and Lies*, Timberlands went into hiding, avoiding media interviews outside the West Coast. Its future existence looks doubtful. There may also be a government inquiry into the Timberlands campaign, revealing the hundreds of pages of documents that have yet to see the light of day.

We hope that this example will encourage others to seek inside information when they suspect unethical PR tactics are being used and that our 'Brief Guide to Leaking' may help people working inside PR campaigns to decide to release information to the public.

Secrets and Lies was first published, in New Zealand, in August 1999. It had been written, printed and distributed in complete secrecy because of the risk of legal interference. On the launch day was lead news, followed by days of political controversy over the Prime Minister's role in the PR campaign.

The reactions from Timberlands, Shandwick and the Government were predictably evasive. They refused to comment on any of the activities revealed. Instead we were dismissed as extremists and conspiracy theorists. Shandwick claimed that the papers had been stolen from their offices four weeks before the book came out (as if books can be written in that time) and Coast Action Network spokespeople angrily condemned the book as being anti-West Coast (while most other previous allies ducked for cover). Large numbers of letters to the editor appeared defending Timberlands in the West Coast newspapers.

Indeed, a week after publication a columnist in a weekly business newspaper joked that Timberlands and its supporters had followed our mock crisis management plan in every way except for the legal threats. The following week we received the first two legal threats (which were classic SLAPPs that we checked with our lawyer and then ignored).

Shandwick attempted to put on a brave face and denied it had done anything improper: 'We've never done anything to thwart NFA,' Shandwick's Klaus Sorensen said. In his only interview since the release of the book, he said: 'I don't think there's anything that Timberlands or Shandwick need be ashamed of, I don't think anyone's done anything illegal.'

The Prime Minister Jenny Shipley changed her story three times over the period of a week after the book's launch, looking increasingly exasperated at the bad publicity. By the week's end, and with the national elections only three months away, journalists were declaring that the revelations were another nail in her government's coffin.

The most important reaction, though, came from the opposition Labour Party. Pro-Timberlands pressure from the West Coast Labour MP had resulted in the party stalling for months over its policy on the logging. But in the wake of the publicity about Timberlands' dirty tactics – and especially its targeting of the Labour Party – the party leader personally pushed through a new policy. Under a Labour Government, all the logging of the West Coast rainforests would end.

Others reacted too. The Body Shop owners were so incensed at the tactics used against them that they made large donations to the environmental groups opposing the logging and used their buildings and shop windows around the country as prominent anti-Timberlands billboards. And as the news of manipulation sunk in on the West Coast, cracks began to appear in Coast Action Network, including leading members disagreeing publicly about how to react to the Labour Party's development proposals.

News coverage of Prime Minister Jenny Shipley's election campaign launch was dominated by native forest protests and the rest of her campaign was dogged by conservation protests. On November 27, 1999, her government was ditched from office and a Labour-led coalition government was elected. The Timberlands public relations campaign had failed. One of the first acts of the new government was to cancel a planning hearing for Timberlands' beech scheme, saying the scheme would not proceed. A week later the new Prime Minister, Helen Clark, began talks about ending the rest of the logging.

Nicky Hager and Bob Burton
December 1999

APPENDIX D

WHO'S WHO IN THE BOOK

Timberlands West Coast Limited (based in Greymouth)
 Dave Hilliard: chief executive
 Kit Richards: general manager strategic planning
 John Birchfield: general manager operations
 Anne Pearson: corporate communications manager
  until February 1998
 Paula de Roeper: corporate communications manager
  from April 1998
 Warren Young: chairperson, board of directors
 Ian James: Okarito-based contractor who designed
  logging plans
 Barry Nicolle: pest control contractor
 John Funnell, helicopter logging contractor: Heli Harvest
  general manager
 Pitt & Moore: Nelson Timberlands' lawyers

Shandwick New Zealand Ltd (based in Wellington)
 Klaus Sorensen: chief executive
 Rob McGregor: consultant
 Maree Procter and Lee Harris Royal: staff members

Head Consultants Ltd (based in Christchurch)
 Warren Head: principal
 Shelley Grell: staff member

Morris Communications Group (based in Wellington)
 Gerard Morris: principal

National Government politicians
 Jenny Shipley: Minister of State Owned Enterprises
  (SOEs) to 1998, then Prime Minister

David Carter: Associate Minister for Food, Fibre, Biosecurity
  and Border Control
John Luxton: Minister for Food, Fibre, Biosecurity and
  Border Control
Lockwood Smith: Minister of Forestry
Nick Smith: Minister of Conservation
Tony Ryall: Minister of SOEs (from 1998)

Labour MPs

Helen Clark: leader of the Opposition
Damien O'Connor: West Coast MP
Jill Pettis: conservation spokesperson
Jim Sutton: forestry spokesperson

Green MP

Jeanette Fitzsimons: co-leader
Rod Donald: co-leader

Forest and Bird

Kevin Smith: conservation director
Eugenie Sage: Canterbury/West Coast field worker

Native Forest Action

Dean Baigent-Mercer: spokesperson
Jenny Coleman: Charleston tree sitter
Annette Cotter: spokesperson

Maruia Society / Ecologic Foundation

Guy Salmon: executive director

World Wide Fund for Nature

Simon Towle: conservation officer

Coast Action Network spokespeople

Therese Gibbens
Barry Nicolle
Cotrina Reynolds

Academics supportive of Timberlands

John Craig: Centre for Marine and Environmental Sciences,
  Auckland University

Henrik Moller: Otago University and Ecosystems
Consultants Ltd
David Norton: Canterbury University School of Forestry

Public servants and government officials
Matthew Hooton: Minister of Forestry Lockwood Smith's
press secretary
Cath Ingram: Jenny Shipley's executive secretary
Mike Jebson: Ministry of Agriculture and Forestry
sustainable resource use policy group
Alec McLean: Minister of SOEs Tony Ryall's private
secretary
Angus Napier: Crown Company Monitoring Advisory
Unit (CCMAU)
Simon Taylor: Minister of SOEs Tony Ryall's press
secretary
Mary-Ann Thompson: Treasury official in the office of
the Treasurer, Winston Peters

Parliamentary Commissioners for the Environment (PCE)
Helen Hughes, until 1996
Morgan Williams, January 1997-

Public Relations Institute of New Zealand (PRINZ)
Tony Cronin: chair PRINZ Ethics Committee

APPENDIX E

WHAT MINISTERS TOLD PARLIAMENT

QUESTION FOR WRITTEN ANSWER DUE ON 15.7.99

QUESTION NO. 5627

JILL PETTIS to the Minister for Food, Fibre, Biosecurity and Border Control:

Has his staff in his office contributed in any way to the public relations efforts of Timberlands West Coast Ltd in relation to that company's proposed beech forest logging scheme; if so, what has been the nature and extent of this contribution?

ANSWER

Hon David CARTER (Associate Minister for Food, Fibre, Biosecurity and Border Control) replied:

No.

APPROVED/~~NOT APPROVED~~

David Carter

QUESTION FOR WRITTEN ANSWER DUE 15 JULY 1999

005619.   Jill Pettis to the Prime Minister:

Have the staff in the Prime Minister's office been involved in any way in relations between Timberlands West Coast Ltd and the Government; if so, what has been the nature of this involvement?

Rt Hon Jenny Shipley, Prime Minister, replied:

No.

QUESTION FOR WRITTEN ANSWER DUE 15 JULY 1999

005620.   Jill Pettis to the Prime Minister:

Have the staff in the Prime Minister's office contributed in any way to the public relations efforts of Timberlands West Coast Ltd; if so, what has been the nature and extent of this contribution?

Rt Hon Jenny Shipley, Prime Minister, replied:

No.

QUESTION FOR WRITTEN ANSWER

Notice given 7 July 1999

Reply due 15 July 1999

No. 5621 JILL PETTIS to the Minister for State Owned Enterprises:

Have the staff in his office contributed in any way to the public relations efforts of Timberlands West Coast Ltd in relation to that company's proposed beech forest logging scheme; if so, what has been the nature and extent of this contribution?

ANSWER

HON TONY RYALL (Minister for State Owned Enterprises) replied:

In the ordinary course of business, my staff have met with people with a range of interests, including representatives of Timberlands West Coast Ltd., to receive information and to discuss a number of issues regarding sustainable management of the Crown's West Coast indigenous production forests.

However, my staff have not contributed to the public relations efforts of Timberlands West Coast Ltd.

QUESTION FOR WRITTEN ANSWER

Notice given 7 July 1999

Reply due 15 July 1999

No. 5623 JILL PETTIS to the Minister for State Owned Enterprises:

Has he or any of the staff in his office ever been consulted by Timberlands West Coast over its public relations strategies; if so, what were the strategies he or his staff were consulted over and what was the nature of his input into them?

ANSWER

HON TONY RYALL (Minister for State Owned Enterprises) replied:

In the ordinary course of business, my staff and I have met with representatives of Timberlands West Coast Ltd.

However, public relations strategies of Timberlands West Coast Ltd. are operational matters that are the responsibility of the Board of the company. Neither my staff, nor I have had input to any such strategies.

REFERENCE FROM PAGE 50:

> ## "FOREST AND BIRD:
>
> ### An endangered species?"
>
> ### Discussion Paper

1.1 EXECUTIVE SUMMARY

The results of this study point to the need for a concerted campaign with the objective of undermining the position of the Royal New Zealand Forest and Bird Protection Society. Forest and Bird have progressed to a position that is in direct opposition to any discussion of sustainable resource use in this country. An over-view of Forest and Bird has illuminated areas where the Society is vulnerable. Analysis has indicated that a broad range of measures are the most suitable to effectively attack this organisation. The need for co-ordination is stressed, as is the necessity for initiating further research into strategies that will produce the desired objectives. A range of consultation with various interest groups that have been affected by Forest and Bird, and the prepartion of a damaging media campaign are also recommended.

1.2 INTRODUCTION

This paper is a response to a disturbing trend in New Zealand at this time. Environmental lobby groups are gaining ascendancy in environmental policy formulation and have refined their skills for manipulating the media. The traditional "green" tactics of physical protest , political lobbying and fuelling public outrage are now expanding. Direct interference in the internal affairs of corporates engaged in natural resource development is now a reality.

The New Zealand Forest and Bird Society (Forest and Bird) have adopted this strategy in their opposition to the P.T.G. West Coast operations. The use of minority shareholders as a disruptive element within the company is symptomatic of a new-found arrogance for conservation lobby groups.

An analysis of Forest and Bird has been undertaken in an attempt to conceive a co-ordinated response to this action. The internal structure of Forest and Bird is examined - its constitution, policy formulation and membership composition. A series of responses are then proposed. These range from interim measures to a concerted long-term campaign aimed at discrediting Forest and Bird and dismantling its support base.

The summary and conclusions indicate the need for astute management of any campaign, including the immediate need for further exploration of the proposed measures.

BIFS Consultants

262

Recommended Reading

John Stauber and Sheldon Rampton, *Toxic Sludge is Good for You: Lies, Damn Lies and the Public Relations Industry,* Common Courage Press, Monroe, Maine, 1995. This has a wealth of examples of tactics and strategies used in corporate PR campaigns against community groups in the United States.

Sharon Beder, *Global Spin: the corporate assault on environmentalism,* Scribe Publications, Melbourne, 1997. Beder's book synthesises into one volume the core elements of corporate activism against environmental groups. It also analyses of the role of advertising and corporate influence on the education system.

Center for Media and Democracy, *PR Watch: Public Interest Reporting on the Public Relations Industry.* This quarterly 12-page newsletter on the PR industry is a 'must read'. A subscription can be obtained from the Center for Media and Democracy, 3318 Gregory Street, Madison, WI 5371, United States: NGOs $US60, journalists and limited income $US35. Back copies are on the Web at http://www.prwatch.org.

David Helvarg, *The War Against the Greens,* Sierra Club Books, San Francisco, 1994. The most comprehensive account of the emergence of the anti-environment movement in the United States, including the activities of corporate-funded front groups and the harassment of environmental activists.

Mark Hollingsworth, *The Ultimate Spin Doctor: The Life and Fast Times of Tim Bell,* Coronet Books, 1997. The personal profile of former Saatchi and Saatchi ad man, Sir Tim Bell, who is considered the most powerful of the British PR practitioners.

David Michie, *The Invisible Persuaders: how Britain's spin doctors manipulate the media,* Bantam Press, Hodder & Stoughton, London, 1998. Mitchie's book focuses on the activities of the PR industry in Britain and the largely ignored world of financial and celebrity PR.

Joyce Nelson, *The Sultans of Sleaze: public relations and the media,* Common Courage Press, Monroe, Maine, 1989 (now out of print). A book about the creation and control of mainstream news through a combination of opinion polling and PR.

Andrew Rowell, *Green Backlash: global subversion of the environmental movement,* Routledge, London and New York, 1996. An excellent global overview of corporate activism and PR campaigns against environmentalism. A must read.

Susan Trento, *The Power House: Robert Keith Gray and the selling of access and influence in Washington,* St Martin's Press, New York, 1992. This book details some of the Washington DC campaigns involving Robert Gray, the then chairman of Hill and Knowlton, one of the major global PR and lobbying firms.

WEBSITES

Native Forest Action: www.nfa.org.nz
Forest and Bird: www.forest-bird.org.nz
Timberlands West Coast Limited: www.timberlands.co.nz
Public Relations Institute of New Zealand: www.prinz.org.nz

Clearinghouse for Environmental Advocacy and Research (CLEAR): For research on the anti-environment movement in the United States, the best single source is a searchable database on the CLEAR website at http://www.ewg.org.

Focus on the Corporation is a weekly column on corporate power written by Russell Mokhiber and Robert Weissman. It is distributed to individuals via a listserve corp-focus@essential.org.

Notes

Introduction

1 David Hilliard, letter to the editor, *Wanganui Chronicle*, 18 May 1999.

Chapter 1: The Privatisation of Politics

1 Amanda Little, 'A green corporate image – more than a logo', unpublished paper, Green Marketing Conference, Hotel Intercontinental, Sydney, 25-26 June 1990, pp. 12-13.

2 International Public Relations, 'Programme Outline: Timberlands West Coast', 16 May 1991.

3 Shandwick, Timberlands West Coast Communications Strategy, 12 June 1997, draft.

4 John Stauber and Sheldon Rampton, *Toxic Sludge is Good for You: Lies, Damn Lies and the Public Relations Industry*, Common Courage Press, Monroe, Maine, 1995.

5 *Ibid.*

6 Global Climate Information Project, press release, 9 September 1997.

7 From Ozone Action Fact Sheet, http://www.ozone.org/ shandwick.html, 16 October 1998.

8 Cameron Duodo, 'Shell admits importing guns for Nigerian police', *Observer*, 28 January 1996.

9 Daphne Luchtenberg, Shandwick New York office, fax to Shandwick New Zealand, 29 July 1997.

10 International Public Relations Ltd, Discussion Paper: A Public Relations Programme for Timberlands West Coast Ltd, 13 February 1991.

11 Klaus Sorensen, who joined the company in April 1997, was formerly business editor of the *National Business Review* and deputy finance editor of the *Dominion* before he entered PR in 1984. Before joining Shandwick he had his own company, Klaus Sorensen Communications, where he had already established an interest in environmental public relations.

12 Rob McGregor, who came to Shandwick from Ogilvie & Mather's public relations company, was described in an internal Shandwick document as 'one of New Zealand's leading and most experienced public relations practitioners' with expertise including 'crisis preparedness and issues management, government relations, and public information campaigns'.

13 Shandwick New Zealand Ltd is located on Level 5, 2 Woodward Street, Wellington.

14 Head Consultants is located at 62 Cashel Street, Christchurch.

15 *Press*, 11 December 1998.

16 *Ibid.*
17 Shandwick website, <www.shandwick.com>
18 'Holderbank Pitch – Environmental Expertise', Rob McGregor, Shandwick, 3 November 1997.
19 Klaus Sorensen, letter to the editor, *Wanganui Chronicle*, 4 May 1999.
20 Dave Hilliard, letter to the editor, *Wanganui Chronicle*, 18 May 1999.
21 Tony Cronin, pers. comm., 16 June 1999.
22 David McKnight, 'The growing threat from the public relations industry to journalism', unpublished, 1994.

CHAPTER 2: 'NEUTRALISING' THE OPPOSITION

1 Timberlands West Coast Corporate Communications Strategy, 1994.
2 Shandwick , Issues Management and Crisis Preparedness Planning Paper, 17 June 1997.
3 Rob McGregor, Shandwick, fax to Timberlands, 16 February 1998.
4 'Pest worker denies ecology group's "plant" accusation', *Press*, 11 December 1998.
5 *Ibid.*
6 Nicolle's name was on a Timberlands notice in the Maruia forest, dated 14 February 1999.
7 Barry Nicolle, pers. comm., at the 'Invest in the West' expo, 28 April 1999.
8 For instance, Maree Procter, fax to London Shandwick, 25 July 1997.
9 Weekly PR telephone conference minutes, 9 April 1998.
10 Weekly PR telephone conference minutes, 17 April 1998.
11 Weekly PR telephone conference minutes, 1 May 1998.
12 Weekly PR telephone conference minutes, 8 May 1998.
13 Weekly PR telephone conference minutes, 14 May 1998.
14 'Current Status: Monitoring NFA Auckland. To Action: Ongoing. Responsibility: LHR [Lee Harris Royal, Shandwick]', Timberlands West Coast – Communications Update, 31 August 1998.
15 Weekly PR telephone conference minutes, 25 July 1997.
16 Weekly PR telephone conference minutes, 16 January 1998.
17 *Ibid.*
18 Weekly PR telephone conference minutes, 10 October 1997.
19 Weekly PR telephone conference minutes, 17 October 1997.
20 Weekly PR telephone conference minutes, 14 November 1997.
21 Weekly PR telephone conference minutes, 28 November 1997.
22 Weekly PR telephone conference minutes, 12 December 1997.
23 Weekly PR telephone conference minutes, 9 April 1998.
24 Weekly PR telephone conference minutes, 8 August 1997.
25 Weekly PR telephone conference minutes, 12 September 1997.
26 Weekly PR telephone conference minutes, 19 September 1997.
27 Weekly PR telephone conference minutes, 26 September 1997.
28 Weekly PR telephone conference minutes, 5 December 1997.
29 Weekly PR telephone conference minutes, 12 December 1997.
30 Weekly PR telephone conference minutes, 23 January 1998.
31 Rob McGregor, fax to Dave Hilliard, 12 August 1997.
32 Shandwick, Timberlands West Coast communications strategy, 12 June 1997.
33 Dave Hilliard, letter to government ministers, 21 July 1997 (drafted by Shandwick).

34 From the 'Background for the Minister of Forestry's Office', faxed to Timberlands from Shandwick, 18 May 1998.

35 Dave Hilliard, letter to the editor of the *Otago Daily Times*, written by Shandwick, faxed to Timberlands 13 November 1997.

36 Timberlands' role in creating and directing the group is discussed in Chapter 9.

37 'Battle-lines drawn on beech', *Greymouth Evening Star*, 15 December 1998.

38 'Native Forest Action Motives Challenged', *Greymouth Evening Star*, 26 May 1998.

39 Shandwick, Key Messages For Proactive Responses to Letters to Editors, 18 July 1997.

40 Timberlands, letter to the editor of *Salient*, 14 October 1997.

41 Shandwick, contact report of meeting with Paula de Roeper, 28 August 1998.

42 Paula de Roeper, 'Public relations strategy – Where to from here?', December 1998.

43 Gerald Lynch, e-mail to the Rainforest Information Centre, 10 November 1998.

44 George Pring and Penelope Canaan, 'Strategic Lawsuits Against Public Participation (SLAPPs): An Introduction for Bench, Bar and Bystanders', *Bridgeport Law Review*, Vol. 12, No. 4, Summer 1992, pp. 937-961. See also Pring and Canaan, 'Strategic Lawsuits Against Public Participation', *Social Problems*, Vol. 35, No. 5, December 1988, pp. 506-519.

45 Gordon vs Marrone No. 185 44/90, Supreme Court, Westchester County, New York (13 April 1992, cited in Pring and Canaan (1992), *ibid.*, p. 944.

46 Jane Pearson, Pitt and Moore, fax to Timberlands, 18 April 1997.

47 *Ibid.*

48 Jane Pearson, Pitt and Moore, 10 March 1997.

49 'Tree sitters may face compo bill', *Greymouth Evening Star*, 10 March 1997.

50 Jane Pearson, Pitt and Moore, 18 March 1997.

51 'Protesters May Face Further Action', Timberlands media release, 19 March 1997.

52 Jane Pearson, Pitt and Moore, 16 May 1997.

53 Jeanette Fitzsimons, letter to John Funnell, Heli Harvest Ltd, 6 March 1997.

54 John Funnell, letter to Jenny Shipley, 7 March 1997.

55 John Funnell, letter to Jeanette Fitzsimons, 21 March 1997.

56 'Helicopter logger threatens legal move', *Greymouth Evening Star*, 26 March 1997.

57 *Focus on Politics*, Radio New Zealand, 21 November 1998.

58 Timberlands West Coast Ltd, Tax Invoice, 23 March 1999; and Jacqui Low, letter to Native Forest Action, 10 June 1999.

59 Weekly PR telephone conference minutes, 31 October 1997.

60 Weekly PR telephone conference minutes, 27 Febuary 1998.

61 See Chapter 6.

62 Weekly PR telephone conference minutes, 3 October 1997.

63 Weekly PR telephone conference minutes, 10 October 1997.

64 Klaus Sorensen, Shandwick, 'An analysis of the recent financial performance of Forest and Bird Society', 28 October 1997.

65 Weekly PR telephone conference minutes, 27 February 1998.

66 'Forest and Bird: An endangered species?', prepared by BIFS Consultants, October 1995, p.10.

67 Rob McGregor, Shandwick, fax to Timberlands, 16 July 1997.

68 Weekly PR telephone conference minutes, 25 July 1997.

69 Maree Procter, 'for Rob McGregor, Director Government and Corporate Relations', fax to overseas Shandwick offices, 25 July 1997.

70 Neil Huband, fax to Shandwick New Zealand, 29 July 1997.

71 Daphne Luchtenberg, fax to Shandwick New Zealand, 29 July 1997.

72 Weekly PR telephone conference minutes, 3 October 1997.

73 Weekly PR telephone conference minutes, 10 October 1997.

74 Weekly PR telephone conference minutes, 17 October 1997.

75 'Body Shop backs tree huggers', *Independent*, 17 October 1997.

76 Lee Harris Royal, fax to Timberlands, 29 September 1998.

77 'Timberlands has its say', *Salient*, 13 July 1999.

78 Dave Hilliard, answers to supplementary questions from the Primary Production Committee, 8 December 1998.

CHAPTER 3:
GOLIATH STRIKES BACK

1 'Timberlands has its say', *Salient*, 13 July 1999.

2 'Bellamy invited to inspect forests', *Greymouth Evening Star*, 3 April 1997.

3 John Birchfield, memo to the Civil Aviation Authority, 23 April 1997.

4 Jenny Coleman, statement to the Civil Aviation Authority, 18 April 1997.

5 Kit Richards, interviewed by Becky Rose, April 1997.

6 Damian Payne, preliminary report on complaint by Native Forest Action Group Incorporated, 26 April 1997.

7 Timberlands' staff diary of the operation, 16 April 1997.

8 Hansard, 23 April 1997.

9 Rob McGregor, Shandwick New Zealand Ltd, fax to Timberlands, 8 July 1997, stamped 'CONFIDENTIAL'.

10 'Minister calls for calm over West Coast Accord', Jenny Shipley news release, 18 April 1997.

11 Ted Hawker, 'Complaint by Native Forest Action Group, 97/ENI/118', 29 July 1997.

12 Dave Hilliard, letter to Toby Manhire, 14 October 1997.

13 'Accusations fly as bomb inquiry continues', *Westport News*, 29 April 1997.

14 Interview with TV One, 28 April 1997.

15 'Bomb taped to helicopter', *Westport News*, 29 April 1997.

16 'Accusations fly as bomb inquiry continues', *Westport News*, 29 April 1997.

17 'Put safety first, Minister urges', *Greymouth Evening Star*, 29 April 1997.

18 Peter Christian, 'Explosive found taped to helicopter', *Press*, 29 April 1997.

19 John Funnell, interview by Larry Williams, ZB City Edition, 5.45 p.m., 29 April 1997.

20 *Ibid*.

21 John Funnell, YA Morning Show 7.25 a.m., 30 April 1997.

22 Jenny Shipley, Hansard, 29 April 1997.

23 The most notorious incident was two days before the 1993 Federal election when a hoax 'bomb', without detonators, was discovered on a railway line near the Wiltshire Junction log yard with a banner

stating 'Save the Tarkine: Earth First'. Strangely the 'Earth First' on the banner lacked the usual trademark exclamation mark that transforms the name into a slogan. The log yard, in the North West of Tasmania, adjoined the Tarkine, Australia's largest temperate rainforest wilderness threatened by clearfelling for woodchips and plantations.

The media worked itself into a frenzy with headlines such as 'Railway bomb: Environment group linked'. The Premier issued a media release stating it was the work of conservationists while the Forest Industry Association of Tasmania stated that it could well have been the work of radical environment group Earth First!

The Tasmanian Greens Senate candidate, damaged by the blanket media coverage of the 'eco-terrorism' claims, missed out on a seat by 1 percent. Months later, long after the ballots were counted, police cleared conservationists of any involvement. In the years that followed, the timber industry funded front group, the Forest Protection Society, sought to mobilise police, including at a joint media conference, denouncing environmentalists publicly as 'eco-terrorists' involved in damaging logging equipment.

It had sufficient effect for Inspector Haldane from the Bairnsdale office of Victoria Police to write a memo to his own officers warning against being aligned with one group in the debate over the forests. Haldane wrote: 'In recent months members of the Forest Protection Society have attempted to align themselves with police personnel in the logging versus anti-logging debate. Members are advised that the Forest Protection Society is an industry funded pro-logging group with a vested and one-sided interest in the continuance of native forest timber harvesting. Members having dealings with the FPS should do so in this knowledge and be careful not to compromise the impartial position of the force.'

Days later, Haldane, acting on information that he received, warned officers against assuming that incidents of damage to machinery in controversial forest areas had been done by environmentalists. 'Information has been received that with the fluctuating politics of the woodchipping debate, instances of damage to logging equipment might become more prevalent,' he wrote. 'This relates in particular to damage being done by pro-logging interests in an attempt to discredit the anti-woodchipping and conservation movements. Any member attending an incident of this type should notify the relevant CIB and ensure that all investigation options are explored – DO NOT assume that any act of damage to logging equipment or logging infrastructure is done by conservationists or members of anti-logging groups'.

24 Native Forest Action, 'Native Forest Action says West Coast Police highly unprofessional: Timberlands continues campaign of bully tactics', media release, 29 April 1997.

25 New Zealand Police, 'Forest Action Group assured police have open mind', media release, 1 May 1997.

26 Christine Cessford and New Zealand Press Association, 'Firm backs off bomb claim', *Evening Post*, 30 April 1997.

27 'Accusations fly as bomb inquiry continues', *Westport News*, 29 April 1997.

28 *Ibid.*

29 Radio New Zealand, *Checkpoint*, 29 April 1997.

30 Nick Sinclair, Department of Labour, letter to Nicky Hager, 28 April 1999; New Zealand Police, letter to Nicky Hager, 15 April 1999.

31 Jenny Shipley, Hansard, 29 April 1997.

32 'Accusations fly as bomb inquiry continues', *Westport News*, 29 April 1997.

33 *Ibid.*

34 David Helvarg, *The War Against the Greens: the 'wise use' movement, the New Right and anti-environmental violence*, Sierra Club Books, San Francisco, 1994, p. 408.

35 Annette Cotter, pers. comm..

36 Shandwick, report for Timberlands West Coast, 10 June 1997.

37 Shandwick, contact report of meeting with Timberlands and Head Consultants, 1 July 1997.

38 Weekly PR telephone conference minutes, 9 April 1998.

39 Weekly PR telephone conference minutes, 14 August 1998.

Chapter 4: Countering Freedom of Speech

1 'Timberlands has its say', *Salient*, 13 July 1999.

2 Shandwick, draft letter, 10 June 1997.

3 Shandwick, fax to Timberlands, 12 June 1997.

4 Shandwick, fax to Timberlands, 21 August 1997.

5 *Ibid*.

6 Weekly PR telephone conference minutes, 25 July 1997, action Klaus Sorensen.

7 Weekly PR telephone conference minutes, 1 August 1997, 'DH signature to Shandwick for signing'.

8 Tony Sage, 'No such thing as "sustainable logging" in our native forests', *New Zealand Herald*, 23 January 1998.

9 Dave Hilliard, fax to Rob McGregor of Shandwick, 23 January 1998.

10 Klaus Sorensen, 'Conspiracy theories refuted by facts', letter to the editor, *Independent*, 16 June 1999.

11 Weekly PR telephone conference minutes, 12 September 1997.

12 Weekly PR telephone conference minutes, 19 September 1997.

13 *Greymouth Evening Star*, 22 November 1997.

14 'Religious "Green" Letter', Robin Kingston and John Williams, *Greymouth Evening Star*, 24 November 1997.

15 Lee Harris Royal, Shandwick, letter to Kit Richards, undated.

16 Shandwick (signed by Kit Richards), letter to Professor Holborow, 22 December 1997.

17 Weekly PR telephone conference minutes, 12 December 1997.

18 Weekly PR telephone conference minutes, 16 January 1998.

19 Cath Wallace, letter to Professor Neil Quigley, 15 January 1998.

20 David Round, Soapbox, *Marlborough Express*, 9 July 1997.

21 Shandwick, fax to Timberlands, 29 July 1997.

22 Weekly PR telephone conference minutes, 1 August 1997.

23 Shandwick, Timberlands Communications Strategy, 12 June 1997, draft.

24 Shandwick, contact report of meeting of Timberlands and two PR firms, 1 July 1997.

25 Shandwick, standard letters, 18 July 1997.

26 Fax from Rob McGregor, Shandwick, 24 June 1997. The Timberlands Papers contain dozens of entries like the following: 'draft letter for approval replying to Annette Cotter, *Westport News*' (25 July 1997); 'request to draft response to Dave Kelly in the *Press*' (28 August 1997); 'reply to Dr Michael Morris for *Evening Post*' (14 October 1997); 'letter for approval replying to Peter Clayworth, in *ODT*' (13 November 1997); 'draft reply to "the prolific Dean Baigent-Mercer"'.

27 Shandwick, contact report of meeting with Paula de Roeper, 28 August 1998.

28 See Chapter 9.

29 Weekly PR telephone conference minutes, 3 October 1997.

30 Weekly PR telephone conference minutes, 15 May 1998.

31 Fax from Shandwick to Timberlands. Also, 'Draft letter to *Otago Daily Times* in preparation for any reaction to the NFA setting up a branch in Dunedin', action Rob McGregor Shandwick, weekly PR telephone conference minutes, 3 July 1998.

32 Shandwick, draft letter signed by Dave Hilliard, 3 July 1998.

33 Fax from Rob McGregor, Shandwick, to Anne Pearson, 22 October 1997.

34 Letter from Rob McGregor, Shandwick, 10 June 1997.

35 Weekly PR telephone conference minutes, 12 September 1997.

36 Shandwick paper, 15 September 1997.

37 Weekly PR telephone conference minutes, 26 September 1997.

38 Weekly PR telephone conference minutes, 3 October 1997.

39 Fax from Shandwick, 3 October 1997.

40 Weekly PR telephone conference minutes, 14 November 1997.

41 Weekly PR telephone conference minutes, 31 October 1997.

42 PRINZ, 27 November 1997.

43 'Bruce McLean, Asset Programming, WCC', 6 January 1998.

44 'Forest group and loggers wage poster war', *Evening Post*, 15 September 1997.

45 Anne Pearson, 4 December 1997.

46 Weekly PR telephone conference minutes, 28 November 1997.

47 Weekly PR telephone conference minutes, 12 December 1997.

48 PRINZ website, 1998 Case Studies, Morris Communications Group, 'I Feel Lucky Exhibition' media programme.

49 'WCC Mural to be painted by School of Design. Resene paints to donate materials. Budget of $2,500', action KS/RM Shandwick, weekly PR telephone conference minutes, 29 May 1998.

50 Neal Palmer, WCC letter to Timberlands, 3 June 1998.

CHAPTER 5:
GREENWASHING

1 Paula de Roeper, letter to the editor, *Press*, 2 October 1998.

2 Timberlands West Coast Beech Scheme Communications Strategy, 1994.

3 *Ibid.*

4 Shandwick, Beech Scheme Communications Strategy, 24 October 1997.

5 Weekly PR telephone conference minutes, 30 January 1998.

6 Beech Management Communications Strategy – Tasks, 2 February 1998.

7 Weekly PR telephone conference minutes, 29 May 1998.

8 Shandwick, 'Timberlands West Coast Issues Analysis, Wellington Graffiti Campaign', 15 September 1997.

9   'Misleading Comments About West Coast Beech Logging – here are the facts', Timberlands press release, 10 September 1998.

10 Shandwick, fax to Timberlands, 16 October 1997.

11 Shandwick, Timberlands West Coast Ltd – Communications Strategy, draft, 12 June 1997.

12 Paula de Roeper, Timberlands PR manager, 2 October 1998.

13 Timberlands letter (written by Shandwick), 21 August 1997.

14 *Independent*, 22 October 1997.

15 Dave Hilliard, letter to the editor, *Evening Post*, 14 October 1997.

16 Fax from Paula de Roeper to Shandwick, 'Beech strategy: commencement of public consultation', 14 May 1998.

17 The World Business Council for Sustainable Development website, www.wbcsd.ch

18 Dave Hilliard, letter to the editor, *Press*, 14 May 1999.

19 Andrew P. Nichols, 'Timberlands' standards', letter to the editor, *Press*, 19 May 1999.

20 'Evaluation of model evidence for sustainability in Timberlands West Coast beech plans', Landcare Research Contract Report LC 9899/032, 1998.

21 Timberlands, 'Debate over Growth Modelling for Sustainable Management of Beech Forests', December 1998.

22 Timberlands, 'Debate over Growth Modelling for Sustainable Management of Beech Forests', March 1999.

23 Klaus Sorensen, *Timberlands West Coast Ltd School Resource Kit,* 30 June 1997.

24 *Ibid.*

25 *Ibid.*

26 *Timberlands West Coast Ltd School Resource Kit, Guide Notes for Teachers,* undated.

27 Shandwick briefing on *Timberlands School Resource Kit,* 17 June 1998.

28 'Timberlands claims research only hope for wildlife', *West Coast Times*, 7 January 1999.

29 Backgrounder for the Minister of Forestry's Office, faxed to Timberlands from Shandwick, 18 May 1998.

30 Timberlands, answer to supplementary questions from the Primary Production Committee, 8 December 1998. During that year $3,600 was also spent on wasp research, no stoat or wasp control was conducted, no bird research was conducted and $41,400 was spent on possum control (including in pine forests).

31 See chapter 7.

32 Shandwick, Timberlands West Coast – Sustainable Beech Management Project Communications Strategy, 24 October 1997.

CHAPTER 6:
CONTROLLING THE MEDIA

1   Rob McGregor, fax to Timberlands, 3 December 1997.

2   Paula de Roeper, 'Public relations strategy – Where to from here?', December 1998.

3   Timberlands West Coast Corporate Communications Strategy, 1994.

4   Weekly PR telephone conference minutes, 5 September 1997.

5   Paula de Roeper, 'Public relations strategy – Where to from here?', December 1998.

6   'Government plans assault on peppercorn rimu lease', Pattrick Smellie, *Sunday Star-Times*, 27 December 1998.

7   'Chopping through the politics of trees', Pattrick Smellie, *Sunday Star-*

Times, 27 December 1998.

8   *Ibid.*

9   Contact report of meeting at Shandwick with Paula de Roeper, Timberlands, 28 August 1998.

10   Weekly PR telephone conference minutes, 14 August 1998.

11   Weekly PR telephone conference minutes, 4 September 1998.

12   Peter Christian, 'Visiting forestry experts laud TWC's management systems', *Press*, 23 November 1998.

13   Weekly PR telephone conference minutes, 26 June 1998.

14   Weekly PR telephone conference minutes, 3 July 1998.

15   Paula de Roeper, 'Public relations strategy – Where to from here?', December 1998.

16   'Timberlands takes watchdog role', *Westport News*, 27 April 1999.

17   Rob McGregor, fax to Timberlands, 12 June 1997.

18   Rob McGregor, fax to Timberlands, 5 September 1997.

19   Weekly PR telephone conference minutes, 5 September 1997.

20   Weekly PR telephone conference minutes, 12 September 1997.

21   Derek Grzelewski, 'Paparoa, The Turbulent Coast', *New Zealand Geographic*, October-December 1998.

22   *Kim Hill*, National Radio, 3 March 1998.

23   Shandwick, fax, 5 March 1998.

24   Weekly PR telephone conference minutes, 13 March 1998.

25   Weekly PR telephone conference minutes, 20 March 1998.

26   Weekly PR telephone conference minutes, 9 April 1998.

27   Klaus Sorensen, fax to Timberlands, 25 March 1998.

28   Shandwick, letter to TVNZ, 10 September 1998.

29   Shandwick, letter from David Hilliard to Jacinta Sutton of TV3, 10 September 1998.

30   Weekly PR telephone conference minutes, 18 July 1997.

31   Dave Hilliard, letter to Paul Gittens, 5 August 1997.

32   'Soap poster given chop after complaint', *Sunday Star-Times*, 27 July 1997.

33   Weekly PR telephone conference minutes, 16 January 1998.

34   Weekly PR telephone conference minutes, 23 January 1998.

35   Weekly PR telephone conference minutes, 20 March 1998.

36   Weekly PR telephone conference minutes, 9 April 1998.

37   Dave Hilliard, fax to Shandwick, 3 December 1997.

38   Rob McGregor, fax to Timberlands, 3 December 1997.

Chapter 7: Manufacturing Political Allies

1   'Timberlands has its say', *Salient*, 13 July 1999.

2   Timberlands West Coast Corporate Communications Strategy, 1994.

3   *Ibid*.

4   *Ibid*.

5   ANOP Research Services Ltd, Community attitudes to environmental issues, Department of Environment, Sport and Territories, Australia, 1993, p. 55.

6   Primary Production Committee, 1997-98 Financial Review of Timberlands West Coast Ltd, Supplementary Questions, 17 September 1998, No. 32.

7   Parliamentary Commissioner for the Environment, Beech Management Prescriptions Progress Report No. 2, p. 18.

8   Allan Sayer, letter to Shandwick, 7 May 1998.

9 Grant Carruthers, letter to Jim Bolger, 4 August 1997.

10 Native Forest Action, 'Forest campaigners hire market research company to investigate logging poll', press release, 6 August 1997.

11 UMR Insight poll, 28-31 August 1997, commissioned by Native Forest Action.

12 *Westport News*, 21 August 1997.

13 *Ibid.*

14 Timberlands, political briefing, 21 July 1997.

15 Timberlands report of meeting, 1 July 1997.

16 Weekly PR telephone conference minutes, 14 November 1997.

17 Weekly PR telephone conference minutes, 9 April 1998.

18 Weekly PR telephone conference minutes, 1 May 1998.

19 Dave Hilliard, letter to the editor, *Otago Daily Times*, faxed 13 November 1997, written by Rob McGregor, Shandwick.

20 Timberlands West Coast Corporate Communications Strategy, 1994.

21 *Ibid.*

22 Timberlands West Coast Beech Scheme Communications Strategy, 1994.

23 Weekly PR telephone conference minutes, 7 November 1997.

24 Weekly PR telephone conference minutes, 14 November 1997.

25 Timberlands, Briefing Paper for Ministers of Finance and SOEs on Timberlands West Coast Ltd, 8 January 1997.

26 Weekly PR telephone conference minutes, 22 May 1998.

27 Timberlands, *Sustaining Our Natural Beech Forests*, video, undated.

28 Timberlands West Coast Corporate Communications Strategy, 1994.

29 Weekly PR telephone conference minutes, 16 January 1998.

30 David Norton, various audits of the Okarito and Saltwater Sustainable Management Plans.

31 Shandwick, contact report of meeting with Paula de Roeper, Timberlands, 28 August 1998.

32 Maruia Society national executive minutes, item 6.1, 1989.

33 Maruia Society, 'Confidential national executive minute', unpublished, 31 October 1992.

34 Maruia Society, President's Annual Report to members 1994-95, p. 11.

35 These consultancies involved Maruia interviewing other environment groups about their plans in relation to these industries.

36 'Maruia Society to vote on name change', *Press*, 3 June 1999.

37 The New Zealand Landfill Association is made up of about 10 local authorities that operate landfills (rubbish dumps) and the four large private rubbish companies in New Zealand, including the environmentally notorious multi-national Waste Management NZ Ltd. The managing director of Waste Management NZ Ltd approached Guy Salmon to act as a consultant to the association (according to Landfill Association chair, Denny Jack, in conversation with Michael Szabo, 10 June 1999).
    In July 1998 Salmon wrote a campaign proposal for the association. The campaign's primary objective was to achieve agreement on standards for landfills, in the form of a highly publicised 'accord' between environmental groups and the association. It also aimed to 'establish a positive public image and reputation for landfilling as part of society's overall waste management strategy.' (Guy Salmon, 'Maruia Society/Landfill Association Pro-

posed Campaign', July 1998.) In stage one, which lasted about a year, Maruia personnel investigated the 'attitudes and perspectives of key players' and the willingness of other environmental groups to participate in the accord process.

The major environmental groups involved in waste issues refused to take part. Greenpeace responded that it did not support the voluntary controls the Landfill Association had in mind because they appeared to be an attempt to head off the development of more stringent compulsory controls by government. (A similar tactic had been mooted by the New Zealand Chemical Industry Council, aiming to get the industry's very loose voluntary standards adopted into law as the national environmental standards for hazardous waste.) Greenpeace pointed out that the National Government had been supporting a voluntary approach by industry to waste reduction since 1990 and that since then the quantity of waste produced nationally had increased every year.

Salmon argued that the campaign would be 'most credible and effective' if 'it is publicly led by the Maruia Society', with the Society providing its 'environmental reputation and its skill at campaigning and lobbying.' He also proposed that it be 'broadly focused on waste minimisation and waste management, with the need for landfill standards set within that context' – in other words, that the industry's political objective not be emphasised. (Guy Salmon, 'Maruia Society/ Landfill Association Proposed Campaign', July 1998.)

38 Guy Salmon, 'Maruia welcomes beech forest recommendations',

press release, 14 December 1995.

39 *Nelson Mail*, 17 February 1997.

40 'Secret logging lobbying denied', *Evening Post*, 19 August 1997.

41 Guy Salmon, fax to Lockwood Smith, Minister of Forestry, 13 August 1997.

42 Timberlands West Coast Corporate Communications Strategy, 1994.

43 Timberlands, Briefing Paper for Ministers of Finance and SOEs on Timberlands West Coast Ltd, 8 January 1997.

44 David Round, quoted in 'Green groups at loggerheads', *Sunday Star-Times*, 23 November 1997.

CHAPTER 8:
EXPLOITING THE ALLIES

1 Maruia Society news release, 10 September 1998.

2 'Two environmental groups praise beech logging plan', *Press*, 11 September 1997.

3 All three extracts from Timberlands West Coast Corporate Communications Strategy, 1994.

4 Maruia Society news release, 10 September 1998.

5 'Two environmental groups praise beech logging plan', *Press*, 11 September 1997.

6 *Ibid.*

7 Dame Cath Tizard, 'WWF-NZ states its position on Timberlands', media statement, 13 October 1998.

8 Henrik Moller, 'This time Timberlands is right', *Press*, 19 September 1998.

9 Henrik Moller, letter to Jill Pettis, 19 August 1998.

10 *Greymouth Evening Star*, 30 September 1998.

11 David Norton, letter to Jill Pettis, 22 September 1998.

12 David Carter, 'Green Party misleading public on forestry management

– again!', press release, 6 October 1998.

13 John Craig, letter and article sent to Jill Pettis, 19 November 1998.

14 Shandwick, Beech Scheme Communications Strategy, 24 October 1997.

15 Beech Management Communications Strategy – Tasks, 2 February 1998.

16 Ministry of Agriculture and Forestry, 'An Analysis of Public Comments on the Sustainable Management Plans for the Beech/Podocarp Beech Production Forests of North Westland', December 1998; Timberlands, Overview Plan for Sustainable Beech Management (bibliography), 1998.

17 Guy Salmon, 'Defender of the forest up the wrong tree', *Independent*, 15 August 1997.

18 Fax from Maruia Society, header: '12August 1997 Tuesday 18.11 p.m.'.

19 Weekly PR telephone conference minutes, 15 August 1997.

20 Rob McGregor, fax to Dave Hilliard, 13 August 1997.

21 Weekly PR telephone conference minutes, 15 August 1997.

22 John Morton, 'Why logging of our indigenous forests has to cease', *New Zealand Herald*, 2 April 1997.

23 Guy Salmon, 'Native forests can be preserved, and logged too', *New Zealand Herald*, 7 May 1997.

24 Guy Salmon, 'Should we fight them on the beeches?', *Maruia Pacific*, November 1998.

25 Guy Salmon, 'Helen Clark's stance on beech creates some hard choices', *Maruia Pacific*, March 1999.

26 Crown Law Office briefing, 17 June 1997.

27 Weekly PR telephone conference minutes, 12 December 1997.

28 Weekly PR telephone conference minutes, 30 January 1998.

29 Ross Philipson, Treasury, 'Aide memoire for your meeting with Guy Salmon of the Maruia Society on Wednesday, 18 March 1998 at 3 p.m.', 17 March 1998.

30 Rob McGregor, fax to Dave Hilliard, 2 October 1997, marked 'CONFIDENTIAL'.

31 Kit Richards, letter to WWF chairperson, 15 December 1988.

32 Weekly PR telephone conference minutes, 25 July 1997.

33 Jim Sutton, memorandum, 23 February 1999.

34 Graeme Speden, 'Loggers' PR targets Labour', *Independent*, 28 April 1999.

35 Notes from the 3 March 1999 meeting at the Parliamentary Commissioner for the Environment's office.

36 Morgan Williams, letter to Tony Ryall and David Carter, 17 March 1999.

37 Kit Richards, 'A Suggested Solution to Independent Audit of the Crown's Indigenous Production Forests', undated.

38 Morgan Williams, *op. cit.*

CHAPTER 9:
USING WEST COAST LOCALS

1 'Timberlands has its say', *Salient*, 13 July 1999.

2 Jim O'Regan, *Assignment*, 25 September 1997.

3 MRL Research Group, Perception and Attitude Research for Timberlands West Coast Ltd, August 1996.

4 Shandwick, Timberlands Communications Strategy, 12 June 1997, draft.

5 Timberlands West Coast Beech Scheme Communications Strategy, 1994, p. 18.

6 Mark Megalli and Andy Friedman, Masks of Deception: Corporate

Front Groups in America, *Essential Information*, 1991, p. 4.

7 *Alburqueque Journal*, 11 December 1991.

8 'Green campaign just cover says "hit man"', *New Zealand Herald*, 19 March 1986; Phil Stewart, 'Warning on "environmentalism", *Press*, 4 April 1986.

9 Shandwick, Timberlands communications strategy, 12 June 1997, draft.

10 Shandwick contact report of meeting of Timberlands, Shandwick and Head, 1 July 1997.

11 'Coast action group challenges greens', *Westport News*, 16 July 1997.

12 Rob McGregor, letter to Jacqui Low, Timberlands, 4 November 1997.

13 Paula de Roeper, fax to Rob McGregor, 14 July 1998.

14 Rob McGregor, fax to Paula de Roeper, 14 July 1998.

15 'Paula de Roeper to discuss with Dave Hilliard', action de Roeper / Warren Head, PR telephone conference minutes, 14 August 1998.

16 Timberlands, 'Beech Strategy – Commencement of Public Consultation', prepared 14 May 1998.

17 Paula de Roeper, Timberlands PR manager, 14 May 1998.

18 'Timberlands has its say', *Salient*, 13 July 1999.

19 Timberlands West Coast Sponsorship Policy 1994.

20 Timberlands West Coast Corporate Communications Strategy, 1994.

21 Dave Hilliard, replies to supplementary questions, Primary Production Committee, 1997-98 Financial Review of Timberlands West Coast Ltd, 8 December 1998.

22 West Coast Principals Association letter, 13 October 1998.

23 Dave Hilliard, letter to presumed allies, 2 October 1998.

24 Shandwick, contact report of meeting between Timberlands, Shandwick and Head, 1 July 1997.

25 Shandwick, Timberlands West Coast Ltd – Communications Strategy, 12 June 1997, draft.

26 Dave Hilliard, replies to supplementary questions, Primary Production Committee, 1997-98 Financial Review of Timberlands West Coast Ltd, 8 December 1998.

27 Cath Wallace, letter to Professor Neil Quigley, 15 January 1998.

28 Jacquie Grant, speaking on Radio Pacific's *Jenny Anderson Show*, 11 September 1998.

29 Andy Green, letter to the editor, *Greymouth Evening Star*, June 1998.

30 Timberlands West Coast Sponsorship Policy 1994.

31 Shandwick, contact report of meeting with Paula de Roeper, 28 August 1998.

32 Timberlands West Coast Corporate Communications Strategy, 1994.

33 'Merit of badges divides councillors', *Greymouth Evening Star*, 13 April 1999.

34 Y. Davison, letter to the editor, *Greymouth Evening Star*, 19 April 1999.

35 Shandwick, Timberlands West Coast Communications Strategy, 12 June 1997, draft.

36 Radio Scenicland, 30 August 1998.

37 Radio Fifeshire, December 1998.

38 Timberlands PR strategy plan, Paula de Roeper, 8 December 1998.

Chapter 10:
Targeting Labour

1 'Labour delegates "ill-informed" over Coast logging', *Press*, 24 November 1998.

2 'Accusations fly as bomb inquiry continues', *Westport News*, 29 April 1997.

3 'Honour forest accord', *Press*, 17 December 1998.

4 'Action Network dismisses NFA regional plan', *Greymouth Evening Star*, 19 January 1999.

5 Paula de Roeper, 'Public relations strategy – Where to from here?', December 1998.

6 *Ibid.*

7 'CAN plans strategy', *Greymouth Evening Star*, 24 February 1999.

8 'One Tree Hill protest makes it two-tree hill', *Evening Post*, 23 December 1998.

9 'Unified Coast needed', *The Coaster*, 20 January 1999.

10 'Action Network dismisses NFA regional plan', *Greymouth Evening Star*, 19 January 1999.

11 'Power to the people on the Coast', *Press*, 30 April 1999.

12 Confidential source.

13 'Protesters choose bail, NFA seeks donations', *Westport News*, 3 February 1999.

14 'Network unimpressed by Green party vision', *Greymouth Evening Star*, 25 March 1999.

15 'Alliance plans for logging anger Coasters', *Press*, 24 April 1999.

16 'Action Network dismisses NFA regional plan', *Greymouth Evening Star*, 19 January 1999.

17 Graeme Speden, 'Loggers' PR targets Labour', *Independent*, 28 April 1999.

18 *Ibid.*

19 'West Coast goes to Wellington', *Westport News*, 19 April 1999.

20 Graeme Speden, 'Loggers' PR targets Labour', *Independent*, 28 April 1999. Barry Nicolle gave a briefing to Labour's Primary Industries and Rural Affairs Caucus Committee at 8 a.m., 29 April 1999.

21 'Coast Action Network', advertisement, *Greymouth Evening Star*, 27 April 1999.

22 Guy Salmon, Coast Action Network public meeting, Greymouth, 27 April 1999.

23 'Minister dismissive of NFA sale plan', *Greymouth Evening Star*, 18 January 1999.

24 'Timberlands outlines employment possibilities', *Greymouth Evening Star*, 7 October 1998.

25 'Parties at odds over beech scheme', *Greymouth Evening Star*, 7 October 1998.

26 'Tasmanian Firm Eyes Coast Beech', *Westport News*, 12 January 1999.

27 'Japanese forest bid denied', *Press*, 15 January 1999.

28 Groome Forestry Consulting Ltd, fax to Tony Ryall, 11 November 1998. When Timberlands had earlier tried to interest Carter Holt Harvey (CHH) in a joint venture, Shandwick had prepared a PR plan titled '"Project Downstream" Issues Paper'. It noted, under 'issues arising' that 'cynics will see [the CHH entry] as dollar driven; another example of NFA contention re big business exploiting the environment.' On the positive side, though, Shandwick noted that it would 'divert attention away from Timberlands.' (Shandwick, '"Project Downstream" Issues Paper', 23 September 1997.)

29 'The value of the West Coast Accord to New Zealand Furniture Manufacturers, a submission to all Labour MPs', prepared by the Furniture Association of New Zealand, 25 May 1999.

30 'Furniture Manufacturers Call on Labour to Honour the West Coast Accord,' Furniture Association of

New Zealand press release, 27 May 1999.

31 Memorandum to Labour Caucus, subject: Forestry Visit, 26 May 1999.

32 Radio Scenicland, 7 May 1999.

33 'Big package on logging', *Press*, 14 July 1999.

34 'O'Connor faces tough test over government forestry bill', *Westport News*, 14 July 1999.

35 'TWC condemns suggestions of beech chipping', *Greymouth Evening Star*, 14 July 1999.

36 Tony Ryall, 'O'Connor shafts West Coast', press release, 14 July 1999.

37 The Minister who had announced the review of the Forests Act in October 1997, Lockwood Smith, had assured Parliament that the government would not lift the ban that stopped Timberlands exporting beech chips (Lockwood Smith, reply to Question for Written Answer No. 15141 from Jeanette Fitzsimons, 11 November 1997). But the Timberlands Papers now show the reason for the change. In October 1997 Timberlands thought it had a domestic market for woodchips. It was secretly negotiating with the timber company Carter Holt Harvey (CHH) to see if it would buy large quantities of beech chips. (c.f. Shandwick, '"Project Downstream" Issues Paper', 23 September 1997). Later that year, however, after meetings with Forest and Bird where it was revealed what Timberlands was planning, CHH backed out of the proposal, not wishing to buy a fight with environmental groups. Thus the need for an export market for beech chips.

38 'Buller council considers "legal options" for logging', *Westport News*, 26 May 1999.

39 Grant Carruthers, letter to Jim Bolger, 4 August 1997.

40 By 1997, most of the West Coast native timber industry had already wound down, precisely as it was intended to under the West Coast Accord.

Chapter 11: Singing From One Song-Sheet

1 'Timberlands has its say', *Salient*, 13 July 1999.

2 State Services Commission, *Public Service Code of Conduct*, September 1998.

3 Timberlands West Coast Beech Scheme Communications Strategy, 1994.

4 Timberlands Corporate Communications Strategy Plan, 1994.

5 Rob McGregor, fax to Timberlands, 16 July 1997.

6 Rob McGregor, file note: 'Conversation with Cath Ingram, SOE Secretary, Minister of SOE's Office, 9.30 a.m., Thursday, 19 June 1997'.

7 'Shipley refuses to meet native forest protesters', *Press*, 14 February 1997.

8 For example: 'Arrange through Cath Ingram to distribute [a pro-Timberlands] "Independent" response', action Rob McGregor, weekly PR telephone conference minutes, 15 August 1997. 'NFA: A new series of posters is appearing in Wellington. To be sent once received from Minister's office – Klaus Sorensen', weekly PR telephone conference minutes, 10 October, 1997. 'Attempting to get original copy of NFA/F&B 13 page booklet. Approach to be made to Minister's Office – RM' [i.e. actioned Shandwick], weekly PR telephone

conference minutes, 14 November 1997. 'Political: KS and RM met with Minister's staff... Shandwick to contact C Ingram', weekly PR telephone conference minutes, 4 February 1998. 'RM has made contact with C Ingram', weekly PR telephone conference minutes, 12 February 1998. 'RM is to talk with Peter Wood and Cath Ingram re Timberlands. Will also try to make contact with Minister's office', minutes, 27 March 1998. 'RM discussing with P Wood and C Ingram re communication into parliament', minutes, 9 April 1998. Some of Timberlands' allies were in contact with Jenny Shipley via Ms Ingram too. For instance, the day after the platform-smashing operation in Charleston Forest, the manager of the helicopter company, Heli Harvest Ltd, wrote a three-page letter to Ingram – opening on a first name basis, 'Dear Cath' – presenting his version of the day's events. He wrote: 'I thought it might be of assistance to the Minister to have the following facts available.'

9   Shandwick note, undated.

10 Rob McGregor, Shandwick, fax to Dave Hilliard, 2 October 1997, marked 'CONFIDENTIAL'.

11 Rob McGregor, Shandwick file note: 'Conversation with Dr Mary Ann Thompson, Senior Policy Advisor, Treasurer's Office, 10.30 a.m., Thursday 19 June 1997'.

12 Rob McGregor, Shandwick file note: 'Conversation with Dr Mary Ann Thompson, Senior Policy Advisor, Treasurer's Office, 4.45 p.m., Monday 23 June 1997'.

13 In other notes the SOE minister's staff said all ministers except Nick Smith wanted the beech scheme to go ahead; Nick Smith doubted the economics of it; Birch was pushing for end to Buller overcut in 2000 for political reasons.

14 Timberlands West Coast Corporate Communications Strategy, 1994.

15 Weekly PR telephone conference minutes, 12 December 1997.

16 Weekly PR telephone conference minutes, 16 January 1998.

17 Weekly PR telephone conference minutes, 23 January 1998.

18 Weekly PR telephone conference minutes, 30 January 1998.

19 Weekly PR telephone conference minutes, 4 February 1998.

20 Weekly PR telephone conference minutes, 12 February 1998.

21 Weekly PR telephone conference minutes, 3 July 1998.

22 Shandwick, Beech Scheme Communications Strategy, 24 October 1997.

23 Fax from Rob McGregor, Shandwick, 4 June 1998.

24 Rob McGregor, fax to Timberlands, 18 May 1998.

25 Weekly PR telephone conference minutes, 1 May 1998.

26 Weekly PR telephone conference minutes, 15 May 1998.

27 Weekly PR telephone conference minutes, 10 June 1998.

28 Weekly PR telephone conference minutes, 26 June 1998.

29 For instance, 'We are to be joined for lunch by Simon Taylor, who said he was about to contact you. He has been following the clippings with interest and is concerned to read that NFA look as if they are gearing up for a big summer offensive', Shandwick fax to Paula de Roeper (about her visiting Wellington), 24 August 1998. 'Have spoken to Simon Taylor – there are questions in the House today [about leaking of the beech scheme plans] but I guess you know that. He believes, as a

result of his contact with the Press Gallery, that unless the PQs generate anything new, the first round of this war is substantially over', letter from Shandwick to Timberlands, 10 September 1998.

30 The itinerary for an earlier meeting, shortly after she began the job, was: 'Paula de Roeper Visit, Wednesday 29 April 1998: Introduction to Shandwick Team. Coffee. Background on Timberlands / Shandwick relationship. Introduction to the Minister's Office – 11.00am at the Beehive: Alec McLean, Senior Private Secretary, Simon Taylor, Press Secretary, Patricia Husband, SOE Secretary. Review of Current Projects: Education Kit; Political Intelligence; Beech and other announcements, reserve news releases; Letters to Editors; Annual Report. Communications Strategy Review 1998.' (Shandwick, 29 April 1998.)

31 Weekly PR telephone conference minutes, 13 March 1998.

32 Rob Dalley, Timberlands, fax to Shandwick, 12 September 1997.

33 Ministry of Agriculture and Forestry, MAF Policy Discussion Paper 8, October 1998.

34 Ministry of Agriculture and Forestry, 'An Analysis of Public Comments on the Sustainable Management Plans for the Beech/Podocarp Production Forests of North Westland, Report to Ministers', December 1998.

35 Ministry of Agriculture and Forestry, '"Substantive" Comments on the Sustainable Management Plans for the Beech and Beech/Podocarp Production Forests of North Westland', January 1999.

36 Peter Russell, Native Forest Action, pers. comm., on his 28 June 1999 conversation with MAF.

37 Paula de Roeper, letter to Shandwick, 8 December 1998.

38 Paula de Roeper, 'Public Relations Strategy – Where to from here?', 8 December 1998.

39 David Carter, 'Conditional green light for sustainable beech on West Coast', press release, 23 December 1998.

40 Timberlands Corporate Communications Strategy Plan, 1994.

41 Timberlands, letter to ministers, 21 July 1997.

42 Political Party Policy Summary, Shandwick New Zealand Ltd, September 1997.

43 Rob McGregor, fax to Timberlands, 5 November 1997.

44 'We should talk to Owen Jennings re our concerns with the continuous PQs coming from Pete Hodgson', action Klaus Sorensen, weekly PR telephone conference minutes, 25 July 1997; 'Kit Richards – K Shirley [ACT] believes the agreement to overcut rimu should not be changed', weekly PR telephone conference minutes, 9 April 1998.

CHAPTER 12:
SECRETS AND LIES

1 Klaus Sorensen, 'Conspiracy theories refuted by facts', letter to the editor, *Independent*, 16 June 1999. Ian Robertson, of Robertson-Hill and Knowlton, told the Public Affairs in Minerals and Energy Conference that 'any PR person who is speaking to an audience of greater than two should resign' (Ian Robertson, 'Community relations – government approvals are not everything', Proceedings of Public Affairs in Minerals and Energy Conference, 19 March 1996).

2   'Timberlands has its say', *Salient*, 13 July 1999.

3   Jenny Shipley, reply to Parliamentary Question for Written Answer Number 005619, by Jill Pettis, 16 July 1999.

4   She later had to back down on her objection to public consultation.

5   For instance, 'NFA: A new series of posters is appearing in Wellington. To be sent once received from Minister's office – Klaus Sorensen', weekly PR telephone conference minutes, 10 October 1997; 'Attempting to get original copy of NFA/F&B 13 page booklet. Approach to be made to Minister's Office – Rob McGregor', weekly PR telephone conference minutes, 14 November 1997; 'Cath Ingram just called. NFA has just released a new run of posters and pamphlets which have been sent to all politicians – she asks you to ring her if you haven't got copies on 4719182.'

6   For instance, Timberlands was asked by CCMAU to provide 'points of reply by way of response to a series of letters to the minister from various F&B branches and members' (Rob Dalley, Timberlands, fax to Shandwick, 12 September 1997).

7   For instance, after Shandwick drafted letters challenging two school principals over a student conservation rally, Rob McGregor sent a 12 June 1997 fax to Timberlands saying 'could you please send me copies of the letters when you have sent them and I'll fax a copy to Cath Ingram in the Minister's [Jenny Shipley's] office'.

8   For instance: 'RM has made contact with C Ingram', weekly PR telephone conference minutes, 12 February 1998; 'RM is to talk with Peter Wood and Cath Ingram re TWC. Will also try to make contact with Minister's office', weekly PR telephone conference minutes, 27 March 1998; and 'RM discussing with P Wood and C Ingram re communication into parliament', weekly PR telephone conference minutes, 9 April 1998.

9   Weekly PR telephone conference minutes, 7 November 1997.

10 Weekly PR telephone conference minutes, 14 November 1997.

11 The Green Party and Alliance Party had already pledged to protect the Timberlands-controlled rainforests.

12 'Government plans assault on peppercorn rimu lease', Pattrick Smellie, *Sunday Star-Times*, 27 December 1998.

13 John Ralston Saul, *The Doubter's Companion*, Penguin, Toronto, 1995.

14 The Communications Trumps website listed 22 government and private clients in March 1999, including New Zealand Employers Federation (including the 'Let's not go back' campaign aimed at retention of the Employment Contracts Act after the 1996 election), the Ministry of Defence, Navy and Army, Transit New Zealand, EDS (NZ) Ltd and 'overturning and or changing legislative and regulatory proposals of behalf of a number of influential Wellington clients including IHC, Heinz-Watties, Watercare Services and Talleys Fisheries'.

15 Communications Trumps, PR paper prepared for New Zealand King Salmon, undated.

16 Kim Hill, quoted in the *Listener*, 1-7 May 1999.

17 Three weeks after the leaking of the King Salmon strategy paper, it was announced that Communications

Trumps had lost its contract to manage Genepool. Director Norrie Simmons said the loss of the contract was unrelated to the salmon controversy. (Graeme Speden, 'Genepool bids no trumps, *Independent*, 28 April 1999.)

18 Michele Simpson, 'Greens attack makes public relations firm see red', *National Business Review*, 9 April 1999.

19 Tony Cronin, interview with Bob Burton, Tuesday 15 June 1999.

20 Paul Jackman, 'Here, chook, chook, chook!', *Noted*, April 1999.

21 'Timberlands has its say', *Salient*, 13 July 1999.

APPENDIX B:
HOW TIMBERLANDS MAY DEAL WITH THIS BOOK

1 Shandwick, 'Timberlands West Coast Issues Management and Crisis Preparedness Planning', 17 June 1997.

2 Shandwick, 'Timberlands West Coast Crisis Preparedness/Issues Management Workshop, Wednesday 13 August 1997'.

INDEX AND GLOSSARY